Television on Demand

Curatorial Culture and the Transformation of TV

MJ Robinson

Bloomsbury Academic
An imprint of Bloomsbury Publishing Inc

B L O O M S B U R Y
NEW YORK • LONDON • OXFORD • NEW DELHI • SYDNEY

Bloomsbury Academic
An imprint of Bloomsbury Publishing Inc

1385 Broadway	50 Bedford Square
New York	London
NY 10018	WC1B 3DP
USA	UK

www.bloomsbury.com

BLOOMSBURY and the Diana logo are trademarks of Bloomsbury Publishing Plc

First published 2017

© MJ Robinson, 2017

All rights reserved. No part of this publication may be reproduced or transmitted in any form or by any means, electronic or mechanical, including photocopying, recording, or any information storage or retrieval system, without prior permission in writing from the publishers.

No responsibility for loss caused to any individual or organization acting on or refraining from action as a result of the material in this publication can be accepted by Bloomsbury or the author.

Library of Congress Cataloguing-in-Publication Data
A catalog record for this book is available from the Library of Congress.

ISBN: HB: 978-1-4411-9398-8
PB: 978-1-4411-4809-4
ePub: 978-1-4411-1133-3
ePDF: 978-1-4411-7358-4

Typeset by Newgen Knowledge Works Pvt Ltd., Chennai, India

For my father, Bob Robinson, and to the memory of my mother, Jean Robinson.

Contents

Acknowledgments		viii
List of Abbreviations		x
1	Rites and Rituals of Transformation and the Television Industry/ies	1
2	From Surf to Search to Seek … Curatorial Culture and the Transformation of Viewer Agency	17
3	Who's Watching? When? Why? Where? The Limits and Liminality of Audience Quantification	57
4	The Industry: Ritual, Tricksters, Response, and Reification	77
5	Containment, Common Carriage, and Net Neutrality—Regulating the Long Tail of OTT Television	131
6	Curatorial Culture Goes International	151
7	The Curatorial Future	169
Glossary		187
Notes		209
Bibliography		231
Index		241

Acknowledgments

Thanks first to my friends, mentors, and past colleagues. I list them in alphabetical order as most, if not all, fall into one or more of the categories: Kay Alden, Linda Bannister, Heather Barry, Adrienne Baxter Bell, Sue Behrens, Lisa Bocchini, Diane Calhoun-French, Cheryl Casey, S. Mary Ann Cashin, Mary Cassata, Brian Cogan, Giovanna Chesler, Sue Collins, Michael Colvin, Ray D'Angelo, S. Karen Donohue, Rob Dutiel, David Feldman, Sam Ford, S. Suzanne Franck, Suzanne Frentz, Richard Greenwald, Thomas Grochowski, Ted Hamm, Antoinette Hertel, Mary Herold, Michael Hanophy, Barbara Irwin, Ann Jablon, Eileen Jahn, Staci Jenkins, S. Eileen Kelly, Anastacia Kurylo, Gail Lamberta, Gigi Lamens, Katie Langan, Dawn Lee, Alessandra Leri, David Linton, Ted Magder, Kathleen Magistro, Alyssa Marko, Peter Mascuch, Anna McCarthy, S. Loretta McGrann, Terry Moran, Susan Murray, Susan Nakley, Christine Nystrom, Sophie Painchaud, Cheryl Paradis, Renee Payne, Judy Phagan, Bill Phillips, Freddy Plate, Amy Poland, Elizabeth Pollicino Murphy, Susan Pollock, Neil Postman, Linda Ryan, Peter Schaefer, Rachel Schwartz, Matthew Simonette, Laura Tropp, Wendy Turgeon, Benedick Turner, Siva Vaidhyanathan, Aurora Wallace, Andy Warshaw, Marion Wrenn, Gail Wronsky, Bilge Yesil, and Debra Zaech.

Jane Jones of Up In Consulting provided invaluable feedback throughout the drafting process and was an excellent sounding board, astute reader, and writing coach.

Progress on this book was partially supported by a Dean's Research Grant from St. Joseph's College, New York, where I was honored to serve as associate chair of the Journalism and New Media Studies Department. I am particularly grateful to Christopher Frost, senior vice president for Academic Affairs of St. Joseph's College for his generosity.

I am proud to be a current member of the faculty of the Department of Television and Radio at Brooklyn College, City University of New York. For their warm welcome in Fall 2015 and their good humor and support, I thank my departmental colleagues: Mobina Hashmi, John Jannone, Miguel Macias,

Stuart MacLelland, Jason Moore, Irina Patkanian, Brian Dunphy, George Rodman, Irene Sosa, and Frederick Wasser.

Many thanks also to Dean Maria Conelli of the School of Visual, Media, and Performing Arts at Brooklyn College/CUNY.

Very special thanks to my friend, colleague, officemate, and trenchmate John Anderson, assistant professor and director of Journalism and Media Studies at Brooklyn College for his support and valuable feedback. Jenny Dixon, associate professor and chair of the Communication Arts Department at Marymount Manhattan College deserves special mention for her sanity-saving encouragement while she also finished a book in the summer of 2016. Lastly, tremendous gratitude to Katherine Fry, professor and chair of the Department of Television and Radio, Brooklyn College whose generous accommodation of my new faculty release time in fall 2016 made the completion of this book possible.

My Bloomsbury editor Katie Gallof merits her own paragraph in grateful acknowledgment of her stalwart belief in this endeavor as well as her patience through a much longer composition period than either of us anticipated when we first met and discussed this project ... many linear television seasons ago.

Abbreviations

API	application programming interface
AVOD	advertiser-supported video on demand
CF	collaborative filtering
CPM	cost per thousand
DIY	do it yourself
DMA	designated market area
DRM	digital rights management
DSL	digital subscriber line
DTT	digital terrestrial television
DVD	digital video disc
DVR	digital video recorder
EPG	electronic program guide
EST	electronic sell through
EULA	end user license agreement
FCC	Federal Communications Commission (US)
FOMO	fear of missing out
FORETP	fear of revealing embarrassing taste preferences
GATT	General Agreement on Tariffs and Trade
GRP	gross ratings point
HDMI	high-definition multimedia interface
HUT	households using television
IP	internet protocol
IPG	interactive program guide
IPTV	internet protocol television
ISP	internet service provider
LCD	liquid crystal display
LED	light emitting diode
LPM	local people meter
MIPCOM	International Market of Communications Programmes
MIPTV	Marché International des Programmes de Télévision
MSO	multiple system operator

MVPD	multichannel video programming distributor
NAB	National Association of Broadcasters (US)
NAPTE	National Association of Television Programming Executives
NTI	Nielsen Television Index
O&O	owned and operated
OTA	over the air
OTB	on the box
OTT	over the top
OVD	online video distributor
PSB	public service broadcasting
RCA	Radio Corporation of America
RCD	remote control devices
ROI	return on investment
RSS	really simple syndication
SEO	search engine optimization
SVOD	subscription video on demand
TOS	terms of service
UHF	ultra high frequency
VCR	video cassette recorder
VHF	very high frequency
VHS	video home system
VOD	video on demand

1

Rites and Rituals of Transformation and the Television Industry/ies

It is Wednesday night and I am going to watch television. For the first third of my life, I would turn on the box in the corner of the room and then either "surf" a collection of about seven channels with my remote control or tune in to a specific show at a specific time on a specific day, knowing from the newspaper listings or the *TV Guide* magazine that from September until May, a new episode would be broadcast each week. For the second third of my life, I would review the program guide channel on my basic cable system. This was a perpetual scroll of the viewing options on about fifty channels. Admittedly, this channel sometimes wound up being my favorite "show" since I would often watch the entire scroll through more than once (wishing it would move faster, but being powerless to speed it up). I did this to ensure that I was not missing anything "better" on another channel, driven by what we now know as FOMO (fear of missing out). This was followed by a period of almost Talmudic review of the interactive program guide (also provided by my cable company). While keeping me within their channel offerings (and of course my tier of service), this allowed me to plan an entire evening if not a week's worth of entertainment. It ensured that I kept current with "my" shows and allowed me to prioritize my "favorite" channels. At the same time, it left open the possibility of a serendipitous discovery of something on a channel I rarely watched, but whose offerings I could review as I moved up and down through the listings.

Now, however, television viewing requires considerably more mental and physical engagement and energy. Network? Cable? Network or cable live or on digital video recorder (DVR) or video on demand (VOD)? VOD through my cable company? Free or pay VOD through my cable box? Per episode subscription video on demand (SVOD)? Or *Sons of Anarchy* (an original F/X cable series) on Netflix? *Modern Family* (a current ABC network series) on Hulu? *Orange Is the New Black* (a current Netflix series) on Netflix? iTunes season pass to the last season of *Mad Men* (AMC) which I can start now but continue watching tomorrow on my iPad during my commute? Past seasons of *The Good Wife* (a current CBS show) on the CBS All Access app so that I can finally get caught up and begin watching the new episodes from the current season on CBS that are clogging my DVR? *Transparent* (an original Amazon Studios series that all my friends have been after me to watch so that I will stop shushing them and chanting "spoiler alert" when they want to talk about it at brunch) on Amazon Instant Video which is included in the Amazon Prime membership I purchased to get free shipping on books and digital video disc (DVD) box sets of old TV shows? Just watching "what is on" to have some company requires choices to be made: the back catalog of *Law & Order Special Victims Unit* on a TNT marathon or Hulu, *The Big Bang Theory* in off-network syndication on MyNetwork9 or TBS or *The IT Crowd* (a British sitcom from the mid-2000s never distributed to US broadcast or cable networks, but available on Netflix)?

On this night, I check the two PBS stations I receive—WNET/13 and WLIW/21—not because I know their schedules, but because my time may be limited due to a possible late dinner engagement. I turn to the PBS "brand" as one I trust for the delivery of content I reliably enjoy. Later, upon returning from dinner with a colleague, I view televisual content it had not even occurred to me to check out earlier: the second of a three-part Australian documentary on the golden age of dirigible airships, posted by a YouTuber who I know only by his or her YouTube channel name, but who has uploaded all three of the documentaries in their entirety. In so doing this amateur programmer is sharing this content with the international viewing community of YouTube and probably violating a variety of intellectual property/copyright laws in the process (although they've been on YouTube since 2014). I found the documentaries because YouTube recommended them to me, guessing (correctly) that based on my previous searches and viewing that I am fascinated by dirigibles, partial to content about the history of technology and also a bit of a steampunk.

All of this viewing takes place on my living room television, and I control and access this content through a simple stick remote that looks very much like the one I used when I began to channel surf so many years ago.

This anecdote describes both the banality and the complexity of the viewer/user's (sometimes, called the "viewser") experience of television in the current moment. And yet, it is not merely the viewer whose practices have been transformed—there is more "television" being produced by more "entities" than ever before—no longer do legacy production companies have the monopoly on television production nor do broadcast and cable networks control the venues through which viewers view. National advertisers promoting those products, companies, and services that had previously bankrolled television production no longer provide the majority of funding to create television. Finally, Nielsen, the quantifier that began, quite literally, by assessing the sales patterns of soup in the 1930s, now finds itself figuratively "going nuts" as it attempts to capture myriad ways and locations in which television is consumed and to create reliable and monetizeable "ratings products" for an industry in flux. Its efforts to stay relevant are further complicated by the existence of subscription-only venues (Netflix, Amazon Instant Video) that have no need for "ratings products" as well as hybrid endeavors (Hulu) that stream content from broadcast and cable "brands" in the same window as the broadcast or cable premieres and also carry advertising from the same companies that make network ad buys. Complicating this further, broadcast and cable television networks, free and pay-per-view "on demand" content, subscription "television" networks and internet streaming services such as Netflix, Hulu, Amazon Instant Video, Vudu, and YouTube are all delivered to the home by cable and/or satellite operators who are also the United States' largest providers of internet services.

In March 2012, political economist and media scholar Janet Wasko hosted a four-day conference at the University of Oregon devoted to answering the question: "What is television?" The 150 participants, industry executives, producers, writers, archivists, and academics proffered about 150 answers. The different definitions of "television," of course, reflect not only the different academic perspectives and stakeholding positions, but also the multifarious and mutable aspects of "television" as a technology, an industry, a cultural form, and a federally regulated mass medium. Horace Newcomb, arguably one of the founders of the academic field of television studies, has used the term "prismatic" when discussing the medium—as a way of acknowledging that perceptions of it change depending on the perspective through which one approaches it.[1]

In short, the television industry has never faced such tectonic shifts. The changes in production, distribution, and reception cut across all televisual industry practices, companies, technologies, narrative structures, and usages and affect the very definition of "television" in an era when the production and consumption of "television shows" may never have been greater. We are in a crucial moment of change for arguably the most influential mass medium and culture industry of the twentieth century. While it remains to be seen what will be the most influential of the twenty-first (although at this point "the web" would seem to be the obvious leader), television's "marriage" with web technology and streaming distribution ensures that it will remain an influential, popular, and ubiquitous media form. What is not clear is how the technological, industrial, cultural, and economic attributes of television will change—as television moves from mass medium to niche media. TV has become, irretrievably, an "on demand" media form. As such, it demands new ways of thinking and considerations of the transformations it has and continues to experience. As TV gets bigger (more series, more creators, more channels, more streaming options) it is simultaneously becoming more niche. It is massive, but no longer mass.

This book investigates transformations in viewer behavior and program discovery; audience quantification; program development; regulation and the international market for televisual content that combine, collaborate, and collude to redefine and re-create "television" in the twenty-first century. Like the wavelengths of light revealed by a prism, these five facets can be examined individually. They must also be considered in relation to each other and in combination for their effects on the transformation of the medium as a whole. The challenge this poses to the theorist should not be underestimated. None of these areas has completed its transformation. All are in flux and change on an almost daily basis—sometimes imperceptibly (the announcement of a new series on Hulu, a YouTube "influencer" landing a network development deal), sometimes with great fanfare (the first Emmy win by an internet streaming entertainment company, net neutrality rulings by the FCC). A great deal of current scholarship and commentary is descriptive or proscriptive, but in terms of analysis it can be slippery and it is hard to push beyond conclusions such as "we shall see." Articulating a perspective and analysis that will not be obsolete by the time of publication is a constant challenge.

It is for this reason that one of the foci of this book examines ways of talking about these transformations, using metaphor and comparison to hive out intricate shifts in perception and understanding of traditional practices, drawing upon other frameworks (such as the fine art industry and museological practices) to illuminate the players, structures, and processes of the transitions. In her contribution to *Reality TV: Remaking Television Culture*, Susan Murray and Laurie Ouellette's anthology of scholarship on the then-new genre cycle, Murray quotes anthropologist Margaret Mead speaking in 1972 to *TV Guide Magazine* about the PBS show *An American Family*: "I do not think that *An American Family* should be called a documentary. I think we need a new name for it, a name that would contrast it not only with fiction, but with what we have been exposed to up until now on TV."[2] Murray discusses how discourse around shows and genre distinctions affects decisions about programming, distribution, and marketing as well as audience reception and engagement. What we call things creates meanings that affect how they are perceived and chosen, or, placed in an environment from which they could be chosen.

The way that we call or name things is a function of meaning creation which George Lakoff and Mark Johnson argue is ultimately and inextricably metaphorical. In *Metaphors We Live By*, Lakoff and Johnson free the study of metaphor and meaning from the boundaries of epistemological philosophy and structural linguistics, arguing that "metaphor is a matter of central concern, perhaps the key to giving an adequate account of understanding."[3] What Lakoff and Johnson discovered is that "metaphor is pervasive in everyday life, not just in language but in thought and action. Our ordinary conceptual system, in terms of which we both think and act, is fundamentally metaphorical in nature."[4]

As a result, we often engage in the communication of meaning via metaphor without really investigating the totality of what we have communicated, so metaphors can also mask hidden meanings, perceptions, or concepts since "a metaphorical concept can keep us from focusing on other aspects of the concept."[5] An example of this would be the metaphor of "binge watching" which borrows its conceptual framework from the discourse of food pathologies (bulimia). One would note that the metaphorical connection ends there since we do not talk about "purge watching" (which would be conceptually illogical since we perceive watching to be an act of bringing a text "into" our experience rather than "expelling" something from ourselves).

More to the point, Lakoff and Johnson's discovery that: "the concepts that govern our thought are not just matters of the intellect. They also govern our everyday functioning, down to the most mundane details. Our concepts structure what we perceive, how we get around in the world, and how we relate to other people. Our conceptual system thus plays a central role in defining our everyday realities."[6] How we use metaphor to express our experiences of the cultural texts, technologies, activities, processes, and procedures of our environment structures our understanding of our world and our experience of it. When we adopt new metaphors for activities (curation for the act of program selection—either by a viewer or a network), these metaphors bring with them hidden and unintended meanings as well as opportunities. This book interrogates the old and new metaphors that viewers, creators, critics, and regulators use to codify "television" and our experience of it.

The very term "television" has become a very particular type of metaphor—it is a synecdoche. Synecdoche is the use of any part of a larger concept or entity to refer to the whole or by naming a much larger conceptual existence of which the part is a contributing component.[7] In short, the part stands for the whole or an overarching whole stands for the/a part of that whole. The process by which synecdoche occurs is metonymy, which differs from metaphor: "metaphor is principally a way of conceiving one thing in terms of another, and its primary function is understanding," write Lakoff and Johnson.[8] "Metonymy, on the other hand, has primarily a referential function, that is, it allows us to use one entity to stand for another."[9] In this case, the consumer good—the "television set"—has come to stand for the cultural texts originally watched on it, the industry that produces these texts, the distribution methods through which one receives these texts, and the alternative cultural forms developed for distribution to the screens that occupy our homes. And yet the actual artifacts—while still referred to as televisions—would be much more accurately defined and described as "computer monitors." As a result our understanding of "television" tends toward the monolithic and presents the challenge of having to define (often through the invocation of other metaphors) which "activity," "sector," "experience," or "aspect" of television one is naming by use of the term.

The process, possibilities, and power of the liminal

The range of experiences that currently inhere, affect, and pertain to all of the facets of the televisual whole can be characterized as "rites of passage," a concept first codified in Arnold van Gennep's *The Rites of Passage*; a groundbreaking, yet underappreciated work of anthropology published in French (*Les rites de passage*) in 1909 but not translated into English until 1960. This term is used to name a variety of ritualistic transformations that are employed by societies in response to either expected cyclical changes (adolescence, death, a transfer of cultural power) or externally enforced or introduced interventions (extreme weather, the encountering of strangers in a previously familiar territory). These rites have very distinct phases, the middle one of which is highly fluid and transformative and is known as "the liminal." Television, its industrial practices, its texts, its technologies, and its viewers are, I would suggest, experiencing a prolonged "liminal" state.

The anthropological conception of "the liminal" is part of Van Gennep's original project—to make sense of the rituals and rites he observed in the ceremonies of preliterate and literate peoples by creating a taxonomy based on the characteristics and functions of events that ordered their societies. His schema resulted in the identification of three distinct but interrelated phases that are present in all rites of passage: separation, transition, and incorporation. Individuals passed through these states on their way from fetus to infant, child to adult, injury or illness to health, unattached to married, live to dead—in other words they marked, organized, and aided in all stages of the life cycle of the people within these societies and were relied upon to codify and structure society. These rites were, according to Van Gennep, crucial for the continued viability and existence of these societies since "rites of passage, with their symbolic representation of death and rebirth, illustrate in a more general way the principles of the regenerative renewal required by any society and by any human being."[10]

Van Gennep's taxonomy of the rites of passage is tripartite and sequential: there are rites of separation (preliminal rites), rites of transition (liminal rites), and rites of incorporation (postliminal rites).[11] Clearly all three rites are characterized by their relationship with "the liminal" as it is this stage in which the transformation occurs and, as Van Gennep notes: "in specific instances these three types are not always equally important or equally elaborated."[12] (That a society or an individual may experience an extended liminal stage is an argument that has been widely taken up by scholars such as Thommassen who argue that modernity itself is an extended state of liminality in which we find ourselves).[13] Following the publication of an English translation of *Les rites de passage* in 1960, Van Gennep was rediscovered by contemporary anthropologists, in particular, Victor Turner who drew extensively on Van Gennep's ideas in his discussion of ritual as "redressive mechanisms for the tensions produced in the secular order."[14] Van Gennep's influence on Turner can also be seen in the latter's creation of the term "social drama," the "liminoid" and his study of "literature, film, images and various forms of spectacle" which has continued to influence certain branches of the discipline of Performance Studies.[15]

What is important to note is that "liminality can also be applied to both single individuals and to larger groups (cohorts or villages), or whole societies, and arguably even entire civilizations."[16] For our inquiry here, it can be applied to the entirety of the parts that make up the whole of "television." This is not a negative state, far from it, as liminality describes a state of tremendous possibility and revolution, even as it carries within it considerable threat to established orders of hierarchy and control. However, it is this destruction and reordering of the traditional means and forms of control that make the liminal a rich and illuminating lens through which to view the transformations—television and traditional understandings of it are in considerable flux which creates levels of anxiety for all those who work, interact, view, or experience it. This, according to Van Gennep, is the liminal stage in which, "reality is experienced as contingent and uncertain, with lasting forms yet to be made."[17]

"The anxiety and doubt that characterizes liminality is ultimately overcome by shaping the subject, who through a series of tests is brought to reflect on his or her self, in the search of a new identity and role to take up on the return to his or her society."[18] As we invoke and experiment with ritual liminality, a way of understanding the interventions of content providing and distributing companies from the world of the internet emerges: "the playfulness of the period of liminality is at one and the same time unstructured and highly structuring: the most basic rules of behavior are questioned, doubt and skepticism as to the existence of the world are radicalized, but the problematizations, the formative experiences and the reformulations of being during the period of liminality proper will feed the individual (and his or her cohort) with a new structure and set of rules that, once established, will glide back to the level of the taken-for-granted."[19] We are in the stage in which the traditional orders and ordering principles of the media industries are no longer self-evident nor inevitable. New structures and new organizational principles and activities are being determined. As Amanda Lotz concludes in the second edition of her groundbreaking *The Television Will Be Revolutionized*: "The ways that new television technologies, uses, and programming both separate us and bring us together provide rich new topics for study and interrogation. Acknowledging the fluidity of the medium's use is crucial."[20] Liminality gives us a way to examine this fluidity in all of its complexity.

As "television" as an entity has no agency in and of itself, what we see instead is the "actors" within, around, and enmeshed in the medium who, whether they be persons (Jeff Bezos, Reed Hastings, Jeff Zucker, Tom Wheeler) or entities wrought by these individuals (Amazon Studios, Netflix, NBC, the FCC) have sought to "question most radically their own sensory apparatus, just as they challenge social order by setting themselves apart from any normally accepted social rules from their betwixt and between position; they become nameless, timeless and socially unstructured, existing in a floating state of being, even as they acquire throughout the liminal period the necessary knowledge and experience in order that their transformed beings may eventually re-enter society and take up their new roles."[21] The lessons of innovation and the pioneering of nonstandard practices by both outsiders and insiders offer learning opportunities for legacy broadcast networks, cable networks, cable providers, regulators, and the new entrants into the industry as they experience their rites of passage from and through their particular subject positions and facets of the larger series of interactions and technologies that comprise television in the twenty-first century.

Van Gennep offers us rich analytical possibilities and ways of investigation: "the liminal state, in its classical anthropological usage as referring to life-crisis ritual passages, for example from boyhood to manhood, is always clearly defined both temporally and spatially: there is a way into liminality and a way out of it."[22] Those in the society understand that they are experiencing the liminal state and that they will pass through it eventually. They also have guides (masters of ceremony) to direct the rituals and rites of passage and to guide them. These rites of passage are transformative but bounded.

Liminality takes a much different form when it occurs as part of a transformation or collapse of a society or larger entity:

"1. The future is *inherently* unknown (as opposed to the initiand whose personal liminality is still framed by the continued existence of his home society, awaiting his reintegration); and
2. There are no real masters of ceremony, since nobody has gone through the liminal period before."[23]

This is key and the embarkation point for this investigation—there has never been this sort of transformation of a mass medium before—one which cuts across every single technology, industrial activity, narrative element, usage, distribution venue, and audience experience equally. Transformations such as the introduction of color, the explosion of viewing options encouraged by cable, off-network original programming, and even the digital conversion of 2009 did not bring with them the all-encompassing disruptions we are currently experiencing. Instead it was the actions of viewers who first began to look to alternative viewing and leisure options that were, in those first moments of the rise of the VCR and home recording, videogames, YouTube, and social media, not called television but, which have now, each and in their own ways, become part of the whole that is the synecdoche: "TV." The production and distribution industries, screen makers, audience quantifiers, technology companies, and regulators are all currently experiencing liminal phases initiated by these viewer-users.

"Words are themselves condensed symbolic forms, derived from real human experiences," writes Bjorn Thomassen in his analysis of liminality and the modern.[24] He continues: "Sometimes things happen for which we have no proper words; and that is when we start looking for such words."[25] These things often happen during the liminal periods of rites of passages—the stage of not-still-what-we-were/not-yet-what-we-will-become as initiands strive to assess, explain, and make sense of their experiences and transformations. "A founding characteristic of liminality is indeed to replace the outside chaos with an order of the inside, having radicalized and brought to exhaustion doubt and skepticism through personal and collective reflexivity."[26] Thus, another illuminating lens through which we may examine contemporary television and televisual practices (descriptors multiply in the attempt to codify meaning) is that of "the curatorial" and "curatorial culture," which I argue are both wrought by the digital revolution and its effects on the production, distribution, and consumption of all output of the culture industries. In this view, the viewers, previously the passive consumers of produced content, have the opportunity to become users of technologies that allow, enable, and encourage the customization of viewing—the ripple effects of which begin the nichification of a mass medium.

The television industry/ies (for it is no longer possible to talk about television as a singular entity) are in a period of liminality that affects every industrial practice, fiduciary arrangement, distribution strategy, and production process—indeed the very concept of what is or is not "television" (or perhaps now, "televisual") is in flux. But, in liminality there inheres the power of transformation, the suspension of tradition, the obviation of structures, and rules that have previously controlled people, societies, cultures, and the activities that define and create them. Liminality disrupts and destroys while opening avenues to completely new concepts, possibilities, activities, structures, and subject positions.

This process appears to have no end date but that does not mean it cannot be analyzed and studied in particular through a closer examination of the transformations being experienced by each facet of the prism and the stakeholders who are experiencing the passages from

- mass medium to niche media;
- an environment that turns on the scarcity of viewing options to one that hinges on scarcity of viewing time;

- geographically fixed consumption medium to transitorily and space- and international border-shifted consumed media;
- mature oligopoly to immature start-up/conglomeration/reintegration;
- federally regulated broadcast medium to common carrier;
- gatekept professionalized creative industry to do it yourself (DIY)/pro-am creative commons;
- professionalized gatekept distributor to crowd sourced social virality.

Chapter outline

The chapters that follow each take one particular "facet" of television's prism as their main focus. They begin by tracing the major developments in the evolution of that facet prior to the influence of nichification—the overarching rite of passage that all facets are experiencing. A discussion of the current liminality and its characteristics follows as well as hypotheses about future possibilities and/or the impact of these facets upon each other and any larger industrial/cultural/regulatory practices.

Chapter 2 begins with a discussion of the evolution of viewer behavior and control, the first, and arguably the most widely influential televisual facet to undergo a transformation and the one that has ignited the others. This is the activity experienced by the majority of the viewing audience and through which they experience the other transformed elements of the television "medium formerly known as mass." An explosion of viewing options and venues has created unlimited choice for viewers—transforming television from a "push" medium to a "pull" medium. Yet this transformation also creates a new set of responsibilities and requirements for viewers. Viewers must now expend labor to find and arrange their own viewing schedules and either "curate" their television or rely upon computer algorithms and network aggregators to find content for them. This chapter also introduces and defines "curatorial culture"—a new era of media consumption that has affected all media forms—and a phenomenon that arose first and perhaps most observably in the consumption of journalism and music. However, its growing impact on television cannot be underestimated and it is, quite possibly, the activity at the heart of the twenty-first century long tail economy. The economic shift from scarcity of viewing access and options to scarcity of viewer time and attention is one of the engines of nichification—creating new challenges and metrics for audience quantification; making room for the development of shows that would otherwise never see production and posing new challenges to the regulation and very definition of mass media.

Curatorial culture further complicates the role of cultural intermediaries in the televisual world. If curation relies upon human expertise and agency, it makes sense that some will want to turn to trusted voices to outsource the curatorial activity. In a linear televisual environment, these would be television critics, a specialized type of journalist that emerged in the mid-twentieth century just as the lively arts began to merit the same critical attention as high arts. Today, the "yelpification" of feedback, the rise of the fifth estate, and the influence of social networking all have eroded the authority of traditional cultural intermediaries such as professional critics. What has happened to the "water cooler" moments that drew us together as a culture and a viewing nation? How relevant are social media platforms to the creation of shared viewing space or community? How do viewers "watch" and "use" television? As seen, television will not completely transform into an "on demand" medium, even as it nichifies and becomes a major site of curatorial activity. The transformation will be "yes and" rather than "either/or" and the ability to quantify viewers will remain an important metric for the industry even as it transforms.

The new techniques and challenges of audience quantification in an increasingly curatorial viewing environment are the topic of Chapter 3. While Nielsen has long been the gold standard of and held the monopoly on the "counting of eyeballs," it, too, is experiencing a rite of passage, one whose beginning might be dated to the creation of off-broadcast distribution systems such as cable and satellite and time-shifting technologies such as videocassette recorders (VCRs). Current and recent innovations in audience measurement and the rising importance of "engagement" rather than "viewership" are examined, particularly in relation to their role in monetizing televisual content and translating "audience" into revenue for program producers and distributors. The multiplicity of "off tube" venues for engagement (social media) create additional data points, but how are these quantified and can they be harnessed to demonstrate advertising effectiveness? What is a "hit" according to these new metrics? Can new "ratings products" create more granular measures of engagement without violating privacy laws or creating security risks? What do social media metrics or mentions really mean to the consumption of long-form linear content?

Chapter 4 looks at "the industry"—no longer a monolithic oligopoly of legacy broadcasting companies, and no longer able to rely upon its traditional fiduciary relationships and revenue streams. Since the development of the rerun in the 1950s, program development has relied upon a lucrative aftermarket of restricting "windows" to support its deficit financing of new series. Producers put up their own money to create shows that cost far more than the licensing fees networks are willing to pay to air them, all with the expectation that eventual syndication will make their money back several times over. This chapter examines myriad new financing schemes and structures, some of which have evolved from an increasingly international aftermarket, some of which have developed in response to a reduction in advertising revenue, and some of which are strategies that could only be viable after the development of online delivery systems. Today, programming may be financed by broadcast or cable networks, independently or in collaboration with production companies. Funding may come from presold advertising, sponsorship, or product placement, retransmission fees, season passes sold through a third party, streaming rights, overseas syndication, and/or monthly subscription fees paid by audiences who will never watch the series. "Showrunners" have become bankable brands, as have refugees from the film industry and YouTube "stars." Amazon Studios runs a "pilot" season for DIY aspirants. Streaming services such as Hulu, Amazon Instant Video, and Netflix now produce series that are indistinguishable from those produced and distributed through broadcast and cable networks and traditional syndication companies. Yahoo and AppleTV have recently announced new production wings that will create and distribute "television" via their platforms. Unscripted reality series, cheap to make and capable of attracting a large viewership and a lucrative, if unfortunate genre cycle of the early 2000s have been pushed to the hinterlands of the televisual menu in the new "platinum" age of complex storylines, high production values, and top-billed stars of the contemporary televisual offerings. A cornucopia of high-quality narratives has exploded in a carnival of televisual offerings with, quite literally, "something for everybody." But—is this model sustainable? How have new venues for program discovery and engagement challenged traditional programmers and gatekeepers of "the televisual" to reenvision their practices and priorities as "viewsers" create and curate their own viewing schedules? How has and will viewer behavior affect programming and scheduling decisions? What is a "saturation point" in a genre cycle of unlimited distribution venues and options? How is viability quantified and/or articulated in a curated world of on demand offerings?

Chapter 5 examines the role that the Federal Communications Commission (FCC) is playing in the transformation of television. Recent decisions have approved the increased ownership of both delivery systems (multisystem cable operators such as Comcast) and the producers of content that these systems deliver (NBCUniversal). While the obvious way for a consumer to avoid monopolistic control over access to televisual content may be to "cord cut" and rely solely on online distribution, this does not free the consumer from the subscription fees of the cable companies. The majority of consumers must rely upon cable companies for internet access. If the net neutrality rules the FCC passed in 2015 are not upheld (net neutrality requires that internet providers allow equal speed of access to all websites); internet service providers (ISPs) will be able to "throttle" websites at will. This would allow them to make streaming sites such as Netflix or Amazon Instant Video unusable or frustrating to use. Controlling upload and download speeds, especially of video content could hamstring and price out DIY producers such as YouTube or Vimeo "televisors." The FCC's regulation of broadcasting was predicated on the importance of preserving localism and a diversity of voices (ownership) in all designated market areas served by a spectrum that was technologically limited. Digital transmissions and web-based content providers have arguably created an endless possibility for the distribution of diverse voices. But—if the delivery systems are all in the same government-sanctioned corporate family, or legislatively defined as "free market luxury services" rather than a utility whose right of access is key to the functioning of society—who will ensure the level playing field the regulatory structure promises? Additionally, who will the increased movement to wireless distribution and consumption privilege or disadvantage? What happens if wired internet access and wireless internet access are regulated differently and/or subject to different conditions of operation?

The transformations that television is experiencing are not unique to the United States, which has always relied upon a robust international market for its programs as a major source of revenue. Internet protocol television (IPTV) has a strong presence in most, if not all industrialized and developing nations and the circulation of international programming is occurring on the largest scale in history. Chapter 6 examines the international market for televisual content, the major players, markets, and stakeholders and the challenges of trying to take streaming content across borders (or to limit its availability, since the web knows no geography).

Finally, the conclusion considers the state of transformation these facets are in at present and proposes likely or possible outcomes of the rites of passage. It considers the likely futures of these facets as practices and structures become codified or emerge as best practices. What is clear is that the rites of passages all of these facets are experiencing are a movement from a bounded and structured world of linear television delivered and consumed in environments based on scarcity and managed choice to a new, curatorial culture of boundless choices of content over multiple viewing sites. However, as these rites of passage are experienced by the stakeholders enmeshed in these facets, organizational structures will emerge and reemerge and revolution will be managed. At stake is not the continued existence or operation of the televisual medium—that is guaranteed—what has yet to be hived out are the definitions and understandings of television, traditionally conceived as a linear, scarcity-driven mass media as it becomes nichified, ubiquitous, and on demand. Like music, journalism, contemporary art, and social media, television is becoming "just" another activity in which citizen curators may choose to invest their time.

2

From Surf to Search to Seek … Curatorial Culture and the Transformation of Viewer Agency

The rite of passage being experienced by today's television viewer may be perceived as merely the expansion of viewing options. However, increased choice has been part of the evolutionary process of television since its inception—the opening of the ultrahigh frequency (UHF) broadcast band to licensees in the 1950s, the legislative establishment of Public Broadcasting Service (PBS) in 1967, the expansion of cable systems and creation of superstations and cable networks in the 1970s and 1980s—all created additional viewing options without causing drastic disruption to the traditional industrial practices of programmers. Like all mass media, television was a "push" technology,—programming was pushed to the viewer at a time determined and controlled by the media provider. The advertising time that was inserted into these shows was sold to advertisers and that ad money went back to the producers to fund the development and production of new shows. Even the multichannel transition of the mid-1980s to the mid-2000s did not markedly upset this traditional model.[1]

We are now in what Lotz refers to as the "post-network era," a new phase of viewing created by the convergence of digital production technologies, internet distribution and traditional television.[2] Over the past ten years the movement to digital distribution of entertainment content, increased availability of high-speed internet in the home, and multiplication of non-television "screens" upon which video can be viewed have transformed television into a "pull" technology: one that places the viewer in control of his or her consumption in a way that elides the traditional agreement between program provider and viewer in an advertiser-supported environment. It is not solely the explosion of viewing options that has created this—the multichannel transition has been increasing linear viewing options for years. What is different is the development of total viewer control coupled with a long tail of endless choice and a multiplication of viewing platforms. Viewers have become viewsers—viewer-users of television and its related technologies, especially those that are now also and easily consumed via the synecdochtal television "set" or through a convergence of technologies, including their mobile phones.[3] The transformation from push to pull culture requires more active engagement in media discovery and consumption by the viewer/user, a phenomenon for which the movement of journalism and music to digitized online distribution has already paved the way. In becoming more active and engaged in the planning of their media consumption, viewers move from surfing to searching to seeking, and ultimately, curating.

From choosing to curating . . .

In *The Television Will Be Revolutionized*, Amanda Lotz writes: "New technologies involve new rituals of use."[4] These new uses change viewer habits, most recently by making viewing more deliberate, and perhaps most importantly—asynchronous and mobile. Developments in technology have completely freed viewers from any attempts by content providers to schedule mass viewing and/or control "flow"—the strategic arrangement of linear programming that guides viewer eyeballs to quantifiable consumption moments.

Lotz describes the characteristics of this new world order of television as "the 5 Cs": choice, control, convenience, customization, and community.[5] These have huge implications for content producers and distributors and require new fiduciary models for production and distribution. Traditional producers of resource-heavy programs are now in competition with online amateur video which, due to the development of "smart television" now appears seamlessly as one of the viewing options of the standard, traditional viewer controlled via a familiar stick remote.

The increasingly active audience that is now able to customize and alter its consumption strategies is also being confronted with the largest possible choice of televisual content ever available. The cornucopia of choice made possible by new television producers such as Netflix, Amazon Studios, YouTube,

AppleTV, and always-connected always-on app viewing takes television out of the home and into the public sphere in a personal and personalized way. Further threatening the traditional business model of the industry is that digital natives (those born after 1980) have a completely different concept of what both "television" and "television watching" entail.[6] The customization of viewing schedules made possible by internet distribution would not be that threatening to the status quo if there were still network or content producer control over the availability of choices and the number of choices. What has happened simultaneously with the explosion of immediate and eternal syndication made possible via the internet is an explosion of viewing options:—professional, amateur, and pro-am, which can easily go "around" the traditional distribution channels and gatekeepers and directly to the audience which is watching them on a multiplicity of screens, not just the one on the box.

Many different types of software have been developed in an attempt to guide viewers and consumers to particular forms of video on the web and to steer viewers toward shows they may find interesting. These aggregators use algorithms that examine prior viewing choices as a way of predicting what a viewer will be interested in seeing. However, the actual choice of show is often much more complex. Therefore, to Lotz's list of five "C's," I would add a sixth: "curation." Viewers must grapple with a multiplicity of viewing options, venues, and increased interactivity—with shows and each other. This requires a substantial reenvisioning of their role in the traditional televisual transaction and the amount of responsibility they have for their viewing choices. Their "mission, should they choose to accept it" involves much more active engagement with the medium and transforms them from passive viewers of television to active users of it. The human action of not just choosing a particular text based on availability and accessibility, but actively *seeking* and selecting a particular text based on private or public taste preferences is curation.

Curationism

Since the late 2000s, "curation" has become *the* buzzword in media distribution and circulation as well as in advertising and social media marketing. It is impossible to avoid the term curation when assessing discussions of the distribution or consumption of content via the internet, and its usage exemplifies the type of semantic abuse that so often happens to terms that are decontextualized and bandied about in the consumer commons. In 2013, Jay-Z "curated" the music for the Macy's 4th of July fireworks show in New York Harbor. Curatesnacks.com offers snack bars called "curate," Maille offers "a beautifully curated collection of mustards" for sale on its website, readers of peacefuldumpling.com can learn "How to Curate an Ethical Wardrobe: Underwear," and myriad advice blogs proudly offer curated lists of everything from dog treats to diapers to other advice blogs. While these examples demonstrate the somewhat correct use of the term as synonymous for "selection," the concept and activity of curating is much more involved.

The term "curate" has Latin and medieval Italian roots and retains its original meaning of "belonging to or having a cure or charge" when it first appears in English in the late 1300s.[7] (This occurs in Chaucer's *Troilus & Criseyde* in 1374 where it refers to the action of curing or healing.) For the next 400 years, it continues to be used exclusively to refer to healing various ills, both physical and spiritual. Usage of this term to reference "the officer in charge of a museum, gallery of art, library, or the like; a keeper, custodian" dates from a 1667 reference to the "Curator of the Royal Society."[8] "Curatorial" is, of course, the adjective form of curate and "of or pertaining to a curator." Its appearance as a term traces to 1734 where it is used in reference to a curator's duties to organize the faculty in many European universities of the time, and develops predominantly in what could be considered an educational context for the next 100 years.[9] What is important is that regardless of the context, the concept of curating/curation has always carried with it two essential components of meaning: that the curator is "one who has a charge" and that this charge involves "guardianship" or "stewardship" as well as management. Curators are those with substantial knowledge of the holdings of an institution, an understanding of the nature and location of those holdings, and the ability to make those items accessible and contextually meaningful for those who wish to view them (and articulate the value one has found in them).

The recognition of "the curator" as a separate, professionalized entity within the art world is a relatively new phenomenon (post–Second World

War) and one that has and continues to be debated within the professional art world even as its usage outside that field is contested. Kate Fowle, currently the director-at-large of International Curators International and an oft-published voice in curatorial studies posits the current definition of curating as: "caring for the culture, above all by enabling its artistic or creative transformers to pursue their work. This facilitation is done, preferably, with empathy and insight, effectively and with some style."[10] This definition clearly deviates from the entrepreneurial one advanced by Steven Rosenbaum and other new media workers and theorists for whom curation is "being understood as aggregating 'manageable, inviting, online experience' from within the 'chaos of digital noise.'"[11] Yet both understand that they are in a time "when curating is everywhere being extended, encompassing every kind of organizing of any body of images or set of actions. The title of curator is assumed by anyone who has a more than minimal role in bringing about a situation in which something creative might be done, who manages the possibility of intervention, or even organizes opportunities for the consumption of created objects or orchestrated art-like occasions."[12] I would suggest that not only are these definitions of curation not mutually exclusive, but also that a comprehensive understanding of the present moment—the *curatorial culture* in which we now find ourselves, benefits greatly from a deep investigation of the traditional curating of the art world and its transformation into the digital realm of the web.

Searches run in Google's n-gram viewer for "curation," "curator," and "curatorial" show a marked increase in the appearance of all three terms in the texts indexed by Google books in the past thirty years. By 2011, this alternate usage had become so widely accepted that the online *Oxford English Dictionary* posted a draft of a new entry that acknowledged the neologic uses of "curate" and legitimized its use in new media contexts: "In extended use: to select the performers or performances to be included in (a festival, album, programme, etc.); (also) to select, organize, and present (content) on a website."[13] First among the support the online *OED* offers for this new use is an article from the *New York Times* in 1982 which states: "The Kitchen presented three different programs of 'New Performances from P. S. 122,' curated by and including Mr. Dennis." Other examples refer specifically to music or arts festivals until 2006 when the *New York Times Sports Magazine* uses it in a web context: "As you wade through the millions of words on ESPN.com, you wonder if anyone is curating what reaches the screen." The most recent example is from 2010 and refers to the expanded role of publishers in networked media industries: "Publishers will be … engaged in the business of generating, curating and aggregating content."[14] What this demonstrates is that the movement of the term "curation" from museum studies and the world of high art to the world of new media parallels the explosion of web-based content and digital distribution.

The problem is—the majority of ways in which this term is being used aren't actually curatorial—they are what I would characterize as "choosetorial." They refer to giving audiences the power to make "choices" from a pre-curated or gatekept selection of items. Or, in the most egregious of misusages, "curation" is used to describe "aggregation"—which is machine-based algorithmic choice masquerading as human input, agency, or discernment. Aggregation is the answer to a networked environment in which the possible choices of consumption have become, quite simply, "too big to know." The ensuing possibility of chaos and need to gain some sort of order, ranking, or coherent structuring of the options opens the door to a new type of monetized web-based endeavor. This has already happened to online journalism as evidenced by the popularity of *The Huffington Post*, *FARK*, and *The Daily Beast*. These sites rely upon automated aggregator programs that search keywords, headlines, and tags to collect related news articles that are then decontextualized from their original source and recontextualized on the aggregator's portal or website. This has an upside for the reader seeking content on particular topics as it allows viewers to more coherently and efficiently review their consumption options. At the same time, the ad revenue generated by this aggregated content goes to the owner of the aggregated site, not the original sources who paid for the creation of the content. News readers and really simple syndication (RSS) feeds allow for a type of primitive curation, more akin to subscription although they add a level of customization by collating material in which the user has expressed an interest.

Search engines such as Google provide aggregative services through the use of algorithms that assess how useful other searchers for these topics have found various sites as well as the purported "authority" of the sites to which these pages are linked. Among the dangers here are that search engine algorithms can conflate "most popular" with "most pertinent." They provide a modicum of both user control and its illusion since the curatorial impulse of the user must, of needs, intersect with the algorithmic organization of the content—which, unlike traditional museum holdings, is infinite and infinitely expanding with every passing minute. Further complicating this is that search engines are, of course, monetized and engage in deal-making that prioritizes certain sites, giving them higher placement in the results. While the word curation may seem to be a synonym for aggregation and is often used as such, in current parlance it is, perhaps more appropriate to think of as "intelligent aggregation."[15] And yet, it's so much more than that—it is the creation of context through the placement of selections next to each other.

As web-native content and web-delivered distribution venues have grown exponentially, there has been a greater need for human intelligence in the selection of content,—a need for human discernment to separate the wheat from the spam. As there already existed an activity that was defined by the actions of an expert—the art curator—it makes sense that this term would be first borrowed and then coopted to name this need for human intervention. The distinctions are key: aggregation is automated, it collects data based on metadata such as keywords not sentiment or content comprehension and it is unable to evaluate context and quality.[16] Curation relies upon expertise and connoisseurship,—an understanding of the criteria by which a collection is being assembled--because ultimately the role of the curator is to impart value through contextualization.

The key difference between aggregation and curation is human agency and *evaluation*. Curation is related to guardianship, guidance, custodianship and the careful assessment and evaluation of content prior to its selection and presentation to the world at large. Curatorial culture brings human expertise into the information economy of the world wide web, privileging tastemaking. Curators may start with aggregators, or aggregation to see what the algorithms or even other curatorial-minded webizens have found valuable or selective, but then they make it their own—by adding their own input to present their own choices and contextualize and organize what they have found. It is this new cyborgian mixture of democratized organic expertise and algorithmic aggregation that defines the new information economy.

Curatorial culture

In *Fans, Bloggers and Gamers*, Henry Jenkins theorized the activities of fans and bloggers. Driven by affinity for and an intense involvement with certain televisual texts, these viewers devoted considerable cognitive surplus and time to the creation and sharing of blog posts, unofficial websites, fan fiction, and other nonprofessional labor which created a participatory culture of viewership.[17] In hindsight it is easy to see that these were certainly the first viewers who began to engage "curatorially" with televisual texts. That these subcultures developed around established texts and could be easily quantified and analyzed by market researchers made them a positive site of engagement and an identifiable market for advertisers. At the same time, these engaged viewers were beholden to the programming schedules and availability of the texts they were so enraptured by —structures of scarcity kept programming and access firmly in the hands of content producers and distributors. Their choices, like those made by the many service and good providers claiming "curation" as a unique selling proposition were pre-curated for them by the industry. These sites of distribution, consumption, mediation, and interactivity of and with cultural texts have now become democratized, a transformation also chronicled by Jenkins in his book *Convergence Culture*.[18] Curatorial culture is related to and yet different from convergence or participatory culture and denotes the widespread ability of viewers to now select and contextualize their own viewing schedules without concern for provenance, genre, gatekeeping, licensing agreements, or network programming strategies. It is perhaps the next evolutionary stage which awaits us on the other side of the collision between old and new media.

Curatorial culture is what happens when "everyone" is doing the programming and choosing from among a seemingly endless supply of first-run, off-net, and cable syndicated, professional, prosumer, user-generated, and internet streamed choices. The audience becomes demassified, and best understood as "a collection of niche audiences."[19] These dispersed niche audiences are observable but are nearly impossible to quantify, let alone coherently define. Quantifiable audience is the coin of the realm for any content-producing industry. How do you find, count, quantify the media usage of and ultimately sell advertising to a viewer who DVR's *This Is Us* but doesn't watch it during the "live + 7" ratings period; has a season pass to *The Walking Dead* via iTunes; is a season behind on his or her vertical viewing of *Grey's Anatomy* through his or her Amazon watchlist, and is recording the current season for binge watching at Thanksgiving; regularly watches snippets of *Jersey Shore* and *Real Housewives* on YouTube at work; binge-watched the second season of *Orange Is the New Black* the day after the third season "dropped;" never misses PewDiePie's latest video on YouTube, grazes on *Law & Order: SVU* on Hulu from time to time; catches up with *The Sorrentinos* on his or her phone via the TV Guide Network app during the morning commute yet religiously watches Jimmy Fallon on *The Tonight Show* via digital rabbit ears? Participatory and convergent cultures turn consumers into creators and commentators. Curatorial culture turns them into television programmers. The relationship is much more like gallery owner or art dealer to artist—selecting, arranging, choosing, and contextualizing becomes a form of cultural production.

Preconditions of a curatorial culture

A consideration of recent technological, consumer, and industrial developments and activities reveal the preconditions necessary for a curatorial television culture. While clearly some of these are more important or must precede others, the order in which they appear here is not necessarily an indicator of importance, nor timing. Many of these have happened over a period of time or coterminously with each other, and they are a combination of technological, economical, and cultural innovations, evolutions, and transformations.

- Digitization of content: cultural texts need to be converted into compressed digital formats that are easily distributed through the internet (and easily copied, remixed, and shared across platforms).
- Video and audio content must be able to be distributed (and experienced) as an optimized "stream," not a buffering download.

- Ubiquity of high-speed mobile internet access and the devices through which video and audio content can be streamed to consumers regardless of location, providing "liveness" to their listening or viewing experience that was previously only available through traditional stationary, or home-based viewing venues.
- The development of internet-only media distributors that provide content that is competitive with traditional television. This content can be licensed from traditional mass media outlets, or new material created specifically for internet distribution.
- Traditional mass media content producers must embrace digital distribution through licensing deals with internet-only distributors, or the establishment of their own internet distribution outlets (thus creating an eternally available syndication library of existing shows and established franchises).
- A lowered barrier to entry into production (made possible by prosumer digital technologies) and distribution (enabled by platforms that stream nonprofessional video). Citizen/amateur involvement in the creation and distribution of content must increase and become an attainable possibility.
- Consumers must have their viewing experience reconfigured: nonbroadcast viewing must be naturalized so that viewers perceive no difference between the content they receive over the internet, and that which they have traditionally received through broadcast, cable, or satellite. Their experience of the content must be immediate, continuous, and uninterrupted. It must "mimic" the traditional viewing experience through use of a stick remote or similarly naturalized intermediary. It must also have a low "technological expertise threshold." This must happen in agreement if not collusion with existing technology producers so as to make the viewer/user experience of changing from on the box (OTB) to over the top (OTT) viewing seamless.
- Social networking sites (either general ones, such as Facebook, or more specific communities like those provided by comments feature of YouTube or the now defunct televisionwithoutpity.com) must emerge as places for discussing, sorting, suggesting, critiquing, and interacting with, in, and around televisual texts. These interactions take place in the new "virtual public sphere" in which all can potentially participate and in which hierarchies of authority are in flux and not beholden to linear or

legacy claims of elitism. This erodes, reifies, and reconfigures the role and characteristics of traditional cultural intermediaries such as professional television critics.
- These social networking sites also, and perhaps this is the biggest difference between choosing something to watch and curating viewing options from the long tail, operate as exhibition venues for the viewer/user/curator. They are public spaces in which the selection, arrangement, and commentary of the viewing choices are presented for observation and review by those outside of the viewers' lived circle of co-viewers, friends, and people with whom they have day-to-day interaction. Regardless of the individual viewer's presence or participation on these sites, the cultural ubiquity of these sites must make our media choices more public and our motivations for those choices more panoptic.

Metaphors of consumption: Theories of viewership

"Watching television" is itself a concept that requires an orientational metaphor—it is based in our spatial orientation to the activity—and such metaphorical orientations are not arbitrary. They have a basis in our physical and cultural experience.[20] Viewers in the earliest days of television "watching" were much more passive. Television was new and "spectacular"—viewers gathered around the television and "watched it" in the same way listeners gathered around radios to "listen" in the 1920s and 1930s. That the metaphor persists today is an indicator of both its strength and its firm roots in the lived experience of those who engage in the activity. Structural metaphors allow us "to use one highly structured and clearly delineated concept to structure another."[21] These metaphors "emerge naturally" because "what they highlight corresponds so closely to what we experience collectively and what they hide corresponds to so little. But not only are they grounded in our physical and cultural experience; they also influence our experience and our actions."[22] We can see this as program discovery and engagement moves through a series of terms—"surf," "search," and "seek"—each resonating with a different proportion of passive to active involvement and engagement.

Viewership has long been the subject of considerable social science research and remains quite simply, the elusive quarry of all television program producers and distributors. Throughout broadcast history, the most unpredictable variable in the television industry has been the audience itself. Why viewers like certain shows and not others, is rarely clear and "despite television's apparently steady success in absorbing people's attention, television audiences remain extremely difficult to define, attract and keep. The institutions have always and forever had to 'desperately seek the audience.'"[23] There are some "working theories" that media professionals tend to operate by in hiving out what they can know about audience behavior. The first is that "people will have consistent preferences for content of a type."[24] This means that particular genres may see periods of popularity for a particular time which yields genre cycles which are discussed in much greater detail in Chapter 4. The second is that "people's dislikes are more clearly related to program type than are their likes. In other words, what we like may be rather eclectic, but what we dislike is more readily categorized."[25] Finally, "linkage is often found between certain types of content and the demographic characteristics of the audience."[26] This can be observed most explicitly in the "narrowcasting" techniques of MTV and cable networks devoted to programming purposely created to attract a particular segment of the audience (which could then be sold to advertisers interested in that particular demographic).

Much audience and viewership research may seem to be an extrapolation of common sense and there has yet to be offered any intellectually or academically indubitable explanation or algorithm offered to demonstrate what will or will not be "a hit." In the early 1970s, NBC researcher Paul Klein suggested that "audience behavior is a two-stage process in which a decision to use the media precedes the selection of specific content."[27] Thus, viewers turned on the set out of habit, because it was after dinner, because they were home and lonely, because it was there and then chose what they would watch from the options that were available to them, a behavior that has also been called "ritualistic viewing." Ritualistic viewing is having the set "on," out of boredom, habit, or company and does not privilege content, the television programming is ambient and background to whatever else is going on in the room.[28] What viewers then wound up watching, according to Klein was the "least objectionable program" (LOP) from among the offerings available at that given time.[29] This least objectionable programming is what Lotz calls "linear content/plain old television" and it and the motivations for viewing it ("companionship, distraction, or entertainment") are still with us.[30] This passive viewing did not and does not require much from its audience.

Active viewers who turned on the television only when the show they wanted to see was on and turned it off when that show ends, were considerably less likely to exist in large numbers as an audience segment in the era of linear television. However, their activities were theorized as "instrumental viewing." Instrumental use is tied directly to the content and predicated on the watching of a particular show at a particular time.[31] Instrumental viewing is also the obvious precursor to on demand viewing and the transition from push to pull media that television is currently experiencing.

This transition is reversing the proportion of ritual to instrumental viewers and is driven by the increased production of appointment television—aka Lotz's "prized" televisual content. It is further supported by technological developments that expand and enable "the viewers' ability to watch 'whatever show you want, whenever you want, on whatever screen you want.'"[32] Therefore, as Lotz suggests, we are probably in an era where more than ever, the type of content will dictate not just the type of viewing that ensues but if viewing occurs at all. Some viewers may be paralyzed by "search fright"—in a world where any and all shows you would ever want to watch are available, choosing just one show can seem an insurmountable task.[33] Perhaps most important is the reversal of the traditional scarcities: scarcity of available programming has been replaced by the scarcity of viewer time. This reversal has not yet been fully accepted by the stakeholders of the traditional viewing transaction, even though its impact is clearly beginning to be felt.

Metaphors of control: The transformation of viewing

The evolution of viewer control has been mostly aided, abetted, and encouraged by technological innovations and program distribution strategies developed by the industry. What the traditional industry did not anticipate, perhaps, was the space it was creating for disruptors such as OTT producers and distributors to enter the market and begin catering to and targeting the audience that they had created and empowered. Once a viewer decides to watch television or watch a particular show, there is, of course the question of how that viewer watches and interacts with the screen. These interactions can lead to different viewing activities and privilege (and encourage) some forms of activity over others.

The first development that increased screen interactivity and gave viewers more control over their viewing experience was the remote control, which sold convenience, "the" selling point of all durable goods of the 1950s. What the remote did (and does) was to allow "viewer-dominated flow" created by the television user to replace the "programming centered" flow structured by the network.[34] It did this by facilitating a variety of viewer behaviors: grazing (changing the channel during the program); multiple program viewing (watching two programs at essentially the same time by flipping back and forth between them); and orientational searching (using the remote to flip through channels to "see what's on" upon sitting down to view).[35] The name that came to characterize these activities in common parlance was "surf"— the viewer maneuvering across a wave of programming which, like real waves, was beyond the viewer's control. The viewer could choose "how" to surf, but the options of where and at what time content was accessible were predetermined by the linear schedule which was, of course, controlled by the network programmers.

Remotes also encouraged and enabled a series of viewer behaviors that interfered with the original covenant of free advertiser-supported content in return for attention to advertisements. "Zapping" is a variation on grazing or channel surfing where the motivation to surf is sparked by the appearance of the commercial. Once viewers had the ability to record shows for playback later, zapping became "zipping," fast-forwarding through commercials completely.[36] "Muting" silences the commercial, but leaves its visuals displayed, so out of the three activities it is the least odious to broadcasters and their advertisers.

Scholarship on remote control devices (RCD) use boomed in the 1980s and 1990s and examined factors like channel repertoire and the motivations for television watching. The predominantly social-science researchers discovered that while cable subscribers had more channels available than non-subscribers, large channel repertoire* did not necessarily result in more diverse channel viewing.[37] (An important point to keep in mind when considering the unending choice of the long tail of OTT on-demand programming.) It also revealed that RCD research itself was methodologically challenged because the activity of remote control use while watching TV had become so "mundane" that research subjects found activity reporting difficult. In other words, use of a remote control had become such an integrated part of the television-watching experience that it was hard to isolate what one did with the remote while watching as a separate activity.†

As the cable and satellite systems expanded their channel inventories, they instituted noninteractive Program Guide channels to provide viewers with an inventory of their viewing options. The current offerings scrolled past the viewer who could input the number of the channel he or she wanted to watch on the remote control at any time, but could not control the speed of the crawl, nor otherwise interact with the screen. In practice, watching the crawl of options could become an evening's viewing in itself. By the time one reached the end of a 100 channel system, one may have forgotten the show one saw during the crawl that one wanted to watch, or one might sit for repeated cycles of the entire scroll so as to ensure there was not "something better" on another channel (possibly an early manifestation of FOMO). The introduction of interactive or electronic program guides (EPG) that viewers could navigate through and control gave viewers active curatorial power but, the ability to "favorite" channels and create sublists of viewing options also worked against the discovery of new viewing options, making extra-systemic promotional strategies, such as off-the-box advertising even more important for networks seeking to launch new shows and encourage the viewing of new seasons of

---

* Channel repertoire is the number of channels regularly or most commonly watched by a particular viewer. Research has discovered that despite an average channel inventory numbering in the hundreds (on most cable and satellite systems), the average number of channels in the average subscribers repertoire is about fifteen.

† This is important to consider given the quick integration of OTT (over the top) viewing options into the banal "stick remote." Internet viewing originally required a high level of technological expertise as one had to access the content through a computer connected to a DSL or home Ethernet connection and know not just how to connect the computer to the television, but how to ensure that the content "played" correctly on the screen. The ability to change from cable viewing to Netflix with the same ease as one used to flip from NBC to CBS is an important step in the expansion of viewer control as it puts OTT options on a level playing field with all other traditional viewing options available via "the box."

existing shows. However, the program distributor still maintained control over the range of choices since viewer choice in these cases is limited to the offerings in their tier of service.

Developments in television technology in the 1990s, such as picture-in-picture (PIP), expanded viewer-dominated flow behaviors to allow for concurrent viewing/sampling. The viewer could also use the PIP function to actively search for a show that he or she might rather watch by scrolling through the EPG as the picture in picture. Both of these activities accustomed viewers to second-screen experiences, making the eventual inclusion of mobile as a second (or even third) screen in the viewing transaction possibly inevitable. Eventually, of course, audience control extended to include what "had" been on as VCR, DVD, and now DVR technology made it possible for viewers to time shift

Cultural shifts in our conception of viewing

Jason Mittell writes about the simultaneous arrival of his first child and his first TiVo in the winter of 2001. What he chronicles in the ensuing pages is that his children are growing up with a completely different relationship to television than he and his wife did—they reject the "now-arbitrary notion that a particular program is only available to be watched at a given time."[38] "For children in a TiVo household," he writes, "all television is part of an ever-changing menu of programming to be accessed at our convenience, not a steady stream of broadcasting to be tapped into at someone else's convenience."[39] The larger cultural effect of this is "a cognitive shift in how the medium is conceived. For my generation, television equalled its scheduled flow, complete with ad breaks, programming blocks, and a knowledge that other kids were watching the same cartoons at the same time, ready to discuss around the water fountain at school the next day."[40] As a result, "DVR's reveal the arbitrariness of the television schedule and flow model, but that system still feels natural for those of us who have accepted it as the default for decades."[41]

In short, the DVR is a service "where recording and time-shifting functionality is complemented by superior navigation, consumer tracking, and the possibility to narrowcast individualized content."[42] It is a curatorial storage technology which requires viewers to pull televisual content to them—to make decisions about their interest in a program or series, scroll through EPGs to view options and otherwise interact with the content distributor's software. This interaction "seductively engages viewers, offering visual pleasures and crucially, a sense of individualized control over forces and quantities [of programming] that seem unmanageable."[43] It also takes place within a pre-curated ecosystem (the pay tier of channels to which the viewer-customer has subscribed) and one in which ad placement alongside and within EPGs is becoming increasingly popular. Because cable- or satellite service- provided DVRs are provided in conjunction with cable or satellite companies, the DVR is seen as a "bonus" to the distribution service, or the most convenient (and only) way to optimize the service (and an incentive for cable and satellite companies to make it very difficult for viewers to use a third party DVR, such as TiVo, on their systems). DVRs do not allow for the playing of content that is outside the DVR (or the DVR's manufacturers') ecosystem. Therefore, DVRs are one way to lock viewers into sanctioned viewing choices, as cable companies have done by providing their own non-TiVo DVRs into which they have integrated their cable tuners. So, while the provision of the DVR as part of a cable or satellite service creates a bond between the distributor and the viewer, it also creates another revenue stream for the service provider. The viewers/consumers benefit from this exchange: they enjoy the freedom of time shifting, ad skipping, and customization of their viewing schedules, but they act out this freedom within the constraints of the distributor and, thanks to the DVR backchannels, under the surveillance of the content provider.

DVDs—we learn to binge

DVD technology, commercially introduced to the home market in 1997 reinvigorated the home video market for films and also created a truly viable direct-to-consumer sell-through market for television.* The major innovation

---

* To be sure there was a television sell-through market produced in the VCR format; however it was a rather stagnant market outside of sales to rental stores. Traditional network seasons are/were 22–26 weeks long with shows that ran between 22 and 46 minutes. Given the two hour limit of VHS tapes, the number of tapes required to distribute an entire season of a show and the resulting shelf space required of the home viewer made the VHS technology both unattractive to and impractical for the

in the TV sell-through market was the box set. Fox's 2000 release of a box set for the first season of *The X Files* is widely pointed to as the watershed moment after which all television content owners sought to package the old and new content they owned into DVD box sets and marketed these directly to the viewing public for individual library creation and home viewing. Derek Kompare states that "the box set materializes all the significant discourses of early twenty-first century media change: high technology, corporate consolidation, user convenience, and commodity fetishism."[44] The addition of "special features" (what Jonathan Gray calls "paratexts") makes the box set "a multi-layered textual experience distinct from television and only obtainable via DVD."[45] DVD box set sales "extend[ed] the reach of the institution of television into home video to an unprecedented degree" culminating "the decades-long relationship between television and its viewers, completing the circle through the material purchase—rather than only the ephemeral viewing—of broadcast texts."[46] It also activates what cognitive psychologists call the "endowment effect"—"the fact that people value objects more when they think of them as their own."[47] Distinctly curatorial impulses and behaviors are activated and exemplified in the purchase of a DVD box set (or an entire series) and the exhibition of said series in one's home. The exhibition of one's viewing choices becomes a social act whose effect is similar to that of exhibiting a work of art that one owns: it is a marker of identity and taste. By 2004 television-on-DVD sales reached $2.3 billion, and like the film industry, television producers had integrated projected sell-through income as an important revenue stream in their business models.[48]

Kompare ultimately argues that DVD box sets make an intervention into the viewer-text relationship by conflating two previously contradictory modes of cultural production: publishing and flow. Publishing is the creation of cultural products for sale directly to consumers. Flow is based in the more complicated relationship between television content producers, television content

wholesaling, retailing, and home storage and viewing of television. (Kompare notes that a complete release of *The X Files* 202 episodes on VHS would take up over one hundred VHS cassettes and 10 feet of shelf space (342).) Add to this the ubiquity of older television shows in syndication on local broadcast affiliates and the ever-growing number of cable outlets, and there was also an "always or reasonably available" aspect to the viewing of older shows or an inclination to reexperience them in the original medium of appointment or time-shifted television that worked against television show ownership.

distributors, and advertisers. In this model, "producers sell programming to broadcasters, who then sell access to potential viewers—that is, time within programming on their widely distributed channels to advertisers."[49] The viewer's experience of texts in the flow model is "premised ... on the aggregate experience of television over time, rather than on individual texts."[50] While the individual episodes and series may end, the viewer's immersion in the televisual flow does not—it is the central experience of television.[51]

The widespread availability of television box sets created and encouraged the pattern of consumption we now identify as binge viewing (the viewing of multiple episodes of a show at one sitting). DVD box sets, whether purchased or rented, taught viewers how to "binge" on what were previously considered (and created to be) texts that were viewed sequentially, but over time. The unintended consequence of this practice has been to accustom pull viewers to a different consumption experience. This has had effects on the linear television industry. It was a death knell to traditionally scheduled network offerings that languished on viewer's DVRs while awaiting "binge day." New viewer-empowered viewing patterns were largely reported as the reason for the premature deaths of shows such as *666 Park Avenue* and *Last Resort*, and became part of the argument used by television producers to push for the increased use of the C7 rating to quantify a show's performance.[52] Binge viewing has also and perhaps most obviously guided the release patterns of OTT content producers and distributors such as Netflix "making available" all episodes of *House of Cards* or *Orange Is the New Black* on the same day. Cable networks that rely upon off-net syndication of popular shows have also catered to viewers inclined to this behavior as seen in TNT's *Law & Order* "binge-a-thons."

Time has demonstrated that DVD releases of popular shows do not negatively impact nor negate their syndication pricing. The release of one-season DVD sets is timed to promote the series's next or current season and has demonstrably aided certain shows in finding their audience and thus returning to broadcast after cancellation (*Family Guy*) or in finding alternative production and distribution venues (*Arrested Development* on Netflix). It has even demonstrated that shows lasting only one season due to poor ratings or overly expensive negative costs, are deemed valuable enough by enough of the population to justify a DVD release (*Pan Am, Swingtown*). What is yet to be seen is if the eternal syndication and accessibility made possible by the internet will erode the DVD market.

DVDs are also the pioneering space-shifting technology. Because of their size they are incredibly portable, as are their players, which were marketed as stand-alone portables, integrated into the "entertainment systems" of vehicles, and of course laptop computers. As computers began to integrate DVD drives and DVD burners into their hardware, two consumer behaviors developed: first, business travelers with DVD drives in their laptops began to use their computers as media consumption devices—to watch a DVD on a plane, to take their television viewing to different locales. This concept of space-shifting or "mobile privatization" as Raymond Williams would call it further transformed the concept of television watching by completely freeing it from the "electronic hearth" metaphors that adhered to it for the first sixty years of its existence and preconditioned the viewing audience for the mobile viewing explosion made possible by the popularity of tablets in the early 2010s.

As DVDs are also a digital technology the increased availability of computers with readable-writable DVD drives created a situation very similar to what happened to the music industry when the computer industry began to incorporate CD players into its hardware: consumers with a lot of storage and computing power began to be able to rip and copy DVDs. While the first stage of this was no doubt the sharing of purchased DVDs among friends, this eventually led to the posting of ripped content to bit torrent sites and YouTube aided by the growing availability of DSL and broadband technology for the home; all of which opened the door that Netflix, Hulu, and Amazon Instant Video would eventually stream through.

OTT: Viewing outside of the box

By 2009, nearly a quarter of American households were consuming some television online. Ninety percent of the web viewing took place in the home with new shows being watched by 43 percent of the web viewers and 35 percent watching shows that could be classified as "in syndication."[53] While these viewing patterns began with computer viewing of video content, primarily on

YouTube, the change in the "television set" itself normalized and naturalized internet viewing in the late 2000s and early 2010s.

As consumers begin to shop for new televisions, they found that their "boxes" had changed substantially for the first time in sixty-five years. New flat screen LED, LCD, or Plasma televisions were rectangular, required no bulky tubes, and did not require the real estate previously needed by their forbearers in the family living space (they could even be hung on walls, like pictures). They were also, increasingly, "smart" (capable of being directly connected to a broadband internet modem via Ethernet cable or wireless). By 2011, "virtually every major television manufacturer embraced the Web-connected set" at CES (the Consumer Electronics Show) and 20 percent of existing sets were already web-connected.[54] Sales of connected TVs were projected to reach 123 million by 2014 with saturation of the market occurring in 2018.[55] These televisions have the ability to deliver online content to the viewer—their connectivity essentially turns them into giant computer screens (or more likely, Netflix, Amazon Instant Video, YouTube, or Hulu viewers). This changes the viewer experience of online content since it makes the "switch" between traditional forms of television (channels and networks delivered through broadcast, cable, or satellite) and online video seamless—all is controlled via one, traditional, familiar, TV "stick" remote.

While web-enabled TVs are one viewing choice, the past ten years has also seen an explosion of internet connected "boxes" in the market. While some of these are extensions of existing content ecosystems (Apple TV), others, (Boxee, Roku, GoogleTV) are more open in the web-based content they allow their viewers to access. These boxes can be updated and changed out more often than the estimated six year average replacement schedule of televisions.[56] This has resulted in a fight for prominence in the connected TV "box" market that is still unwon. In general, all boxes, regardless of provenance do the same thing: stream internet video to the television. Roku, which began as simply an attempt to stream Netflix content to the television, now has over three hundred channels, Boxee embeds social media features to allow users to share and tweet directly from their viewing experience of the web and also has an integrated iPad app.[57] In perhaps the ultimate convergence of new and old, in 2011, Netflix "inked deals with 11 manufacturers to add a one-click button to remote controls for their Internet-connected devices to access Netflix's video-streaming service."[58] This made the branded "red button" with the company logo ubiquitous on remotes that control Roku, Boxee, Iomega internet streaming boxes, smart TVs from Sharp, Sony, and Toshiba, and internet-enabled Blu-ray disc players from Dynex (Best Buy), Haier, Memorex, Panasonic, Samsung, Sharp, Sony, and Toshiba.[59]

Google, in addition to providing its Android operating system to "smart TV" manufacturers and partnering with Sony to produce Blu-ray players that are also internet ready, (albeit with remotes containing "Netflix" buttons) provides through GoogleTV an interface that allows users to search for a show name or genre and click through its results to whatever web venue they want to view the content on.[60] GoogleTV is complemented and further enabled by Chromecast, a platform-agnostic Google product that plugs into the high-definition multimedia interface (HDMI) port on TVs and streams content from a computer or mobile device to the television via Wi-Fi. (While platform agnostic, Chromecast does come bundled with a month of free GooglePlay music at the moment, so as with AppleTV, attempts to lure users into a particular content ecosystem are standard operating procedure.)

Receiving content through an internet-connected smart TV or a set-top internet streaming box has come to be known as OTT delivery as opposed to OTA delivery. This creates a purely "pull" video environment in which the viewer must choose viewing experiences from a seemingly endless number of possibilities. However, OTT platforms come with content limitations. The four viewing experiences that are absent from over-the-top viewing environments are: "news, sports, reality TV (or any show that relies upon time-sensitive sequential viewing, such as *American Idol* or *The Amazing Race*) and lastly, premium content on subscription channels"[61] Viewers wishing to access the live OTA broadcast channels in their area need to either continue a cable and satellite subscription or invest in a digital antenna to receive the signals through the "ether." While the conglomeration, convergence, and synergy of the past twenty years may have emphasized the larger station group and the national television audience over the local market, the new developments in and saturation of internet viewing technology may, ironically, return cord cutters and early adopters of internet-based video viewing to reliance upon the local broadcast signals for the experience of "liveness" and immediacy that, at present, only broadcast is providing.* This has not been lost on producers and network executives whose strategies for maintaining the viability of traditional television service and flow are discussed in great detail in Chapter 4.

Cord cutting and cord shaving are two viewer behaviors that have emerged as a result of the increased availability and ease of access to OTT content. Both have MSOs and satellite distributors worried. Cord Cutters are: "a hard to pin-down percent of TV viewers who have entirely given up their traditional cable or satellite services and found alternative methods to satisfy their television viewing needs."[62] One interpretation is that cutting the cord is a reaction to and protest against the increasing costs of cable or satellite subscriptions. Another is: "It doesn't matter that there isn't an exact percentage of cord cutters. What matters is why people are doing it and how this opens a window that allows us to see how people are going to use television in the future."[63] Cord shavers are those who merely downgrade their cable subscription in favor of additional viewing options brought to them via the web. Both cord cutting and cord shaving rely on there being a critical mass of content that is attractive to viewers, priced less than cable, and easy to locate and view via the web—conditions created by the development of mobile viewing technologies and social programming guides.

Television goes "off the box"

When the Apple iPad launched on April 3, 2010, mobile viewing truly came into its own. Android tablet makers joined the market with their own devices and a flurry of similar apps appeared for the Android operating system. In 2011, the Kindle Fire brought mobile streaming capacity to the Amazon ecosystem and Amazon Prime provided access to video content in a way that combined the free streaming of Netflix with the electronic sell through (EST) either by the episode or by the season of iTunes. Six years after the iPad's launch, it is clear that tablets and the increased size of smart phones have had

---

* To be sure, live streaming without live broadcast is technologically possible. At present it is used primarily as an adjunct to broadcast. It does not defy logic, however, to expect that stand-alone live "streamcasts" may become much more common in the convergent future.

a substantial impact on the way that people consume all media, but particularly television.

The majority of tablet and mobile phone viewing apps, and all of the ones that offer "live" streaming content are part of the industry's "TV Everywhere" initiatives—which require that users sign in with their pay TV subscription credentials in order to use the apps. These apps integrate "social television" functions within them so they enable and encourage a variety of viewing behaviors, both old and new. Time- and space- shifting behaviors are already ingrained in the contemporary viewer's experience. The new viewing activity integrated into these platforms is that of "social television." For example, the HBO Go app entered the market on May 2011 and was downloaded 2.5 million times in the first six weeks. It is both a viewing and a social television app, with embedded Facebook "like" buttons and also the ability to tweet about content from within the app.[64] It has now been joined by HBO Now and CBS All Access which are viewing apps that do not require purchasers to be current subscribers to any cable or satellite service. These not only make the viewing experience mobile and platform agnostic; as discussed in Chapter 4, but they also completely reorganize the fiduciary relationships between viewers and program providers.

The different types of viewing as well as the variety of ways in which they are being assessed and analyzed by scholars most definitely indicates a liminal stage. We are in a period of flux when traditional rituals and new forms of behavior are coexisting. What is clear is that the transition is being driven largely by demographics. Millennials now outnumber baby boomers and their experience of television has been quite different—it has not been tied to the scarcity of the network era or the increasingly brand-driven efforts of the multichannel television age. It has also not been tied to location or traditional "television set" technology which creates media agnosticism and "new norms of use."[65] This agnosticism extends beyond the screen that the content is being watched on to what types of content are being perceived as "televisual." Ultimately, viewers care about finding and accessing the shows they want to see and the stories they want to follow. They are not interested in the fiduciary relationships between advertisers and networks, nor in production budgets and costs. They want their shows where, when, and how it makes the most sense for them to consume them. And this battle for control over the television schedule, the viewing device, and the viewing experience, (always contested spaces) has now, irretrievably, been won by the viewer.

But, of course, as viewing options expanded, so did the problem of program discovery, a problem which cuts across both the industry/distributor and the individual/viewer subject positions. "If you're a viewer, it's too hard to discover, locate, and organize what you like to watch. If you're a supplier, it's too hard, too hit-or-miss, and too expensive to find, attract and retain audiences, and the window in which to do so continues to shrink."[66] As a result, "watching television has become an 'application'—an involved, multi-step process."[67] This expands the labor of the audience which must now cull through a seemingly endless range of programming choices for what it is one wants to watch. It also transforms the labor of the programming executive, making the arrangement of their shows into schedules that "flow" seamlessly from one to the other practically irrelevant and the need to tap into or provide curatorial tools through which viewers can find and arrange their viewing diet far more important.

Metaphors of affinity: Theories of liking

Why do humans like what they like? The answer to this question is the holy grail of all free market capitalists and marketers and of course there are as many answers as there are consultants interested in being paid to create them. The conundrum of human preference and choice has been taken up by psychologists, sociologists, and economists for generations and the addition of socially mediated and motivated "liking" has merely accelerated the interdisciplinary inquiries into the possibilities.

One way to think about our motivations for choosing among varying cultural forms of entertainment is to consider the "job" for which we are "hiring" the cultural text.[68] "People 'hire' a product or service, because in the course of living their lives there are different jobs that need to be done at different times. Each job includes some combination of functional, emotional and social dimensions."[69] Therefore, as with Klein's distinctions, we may always "hire" linear television to fulfill the role of companion, time waster, background noise. But, the jobs we may hire our curated television content for will multiply—especially as our choices become more exhibited and public through our social media. The sharing of our queues or watchlists and our circulation through online and offline social worlds bring with it pressures to participate in the shared viewing choices of our fellow curators. For those seeking to theorize taste and selection the current moment makes the viewer's choices more public and discoverable than ever, while simultaneously making the reasoning behind those choices yet more opaque—it's a Big Data conundrum.

Ultimately, and perhaps essentially, we hire these texts to entertain us and perhaps fill needs not met by our daily lives. In *How Pleasure Works: The New Science of Why We Like What We Like*, Paul Bloom states: "Our main leisure activity is, by a long shot, participating in experiences that we know are not real. When we are free to do whatever we want, we retreat to the imagination—to worlds, created by others, as with books, movies, video games, and television (over four hours a day for the average American), or to worlds we ourselves create as when daydreaming and fantasizing."[70] Therefore, according to Bloom, we are, as a species, drawn to a world of vicarious experience through which we satisfy an essential desire for pleasure hard-wired into our individual psyches and also arbitrarily evolved through our uniquely human culture.[71] These pleasures "are shared by all humans; the variety that one sees can be understood as variations on a universal theme."[72] As a result, new pleasures (which Bloom suggests are represented by such varied inventions as "chocolate, video games, cocaine, saunas, crossword puzzles, reality television") are "enjoyable because they are not that new; they connect—in a reasonably direct way—to pleasures that humans already possess."[73] The essential pleasures of a love of art (whether expressed through representational painting, sculpture, or performance) and a love of narrative (whether expressed through printed novel, radio soap opera, IMAX projection, or televised screen) then, are a hard-wired aspect of our human existence.

In considering the choice of televisual texts, one might suggest that the enjoyment of narrative tropes and elements that connect to the underlying pleasures we already possess and seek is responsible for both the continued relevancy and popularity of these cultural forms, but also for the lack of substantial innovation in works meant for "televisual consumption." The content, representations, and audiences may have nichified, but the overarching narrative genres and forms of storytelling remain very consistent with the criteria of narrative and performative genres established in the first instances of human storytelling.* Thus the pleasure that we receive from the experiences and things that we choose to spend our time and energy on is "based in part on what we see as their essences. Our essentialism is not just a cold-blooded way of making sense of reality; it underlies our passions, our appetites, and our desires."[74] This essentialism is reinforced by culture in which we experience a shared familiarity with texts or activities in our public interactions—what social psychologist Robert Zajonc called the "mere exposure" effect— "Mere repeated exposure of the individual to a stimulus is sufficient condition for the enhancement of his attitude toward it."[75] The reasoning behind this is: "other things being equal, something you are familiar with is likely to be [a] safe [choice.]"[76] After all, "stories are about people, and we are interested in people and how they act. It is not hard to imagine an evolutionary purpose for why we would care about the social universe; indeed, it's been argued that one main force in the evolution of human language is that it is a uniquely powerful tool for communication of social information—and, particularly, gossip."[77] This could be one way to explain genre cycles and the popularity of shows that are perceived as similar to existing shows that have been well received.

 Curatorial culture's introduction of the "exhibition" of the choices we find pleasurable complicates this drive to satisfy essential pleasures as well as the communication of social information. Don Thompson describes how art collectors acquire different works of art for their public rooms or gallery donations than they do for private exhibition in their homes or bedrooms.[78] In this case the "signalling" value of the selection (when viewed by others) becomes of social value to the exhibitor of the artwork. The prestige value of demonstrating

---

* By this I mean the shared conventions that can be found in all widely consumed and popular narratives – from oral culture through the earliest written stories (*Beowulf, Canterbury Tales*) to contemporary offerings of *Transparent, House of Cards,* and *Designated Survivor*. Narrative conventions inhere and are reinforced in these and all texts that circulate widely. To be sure, exceptions to these conventions have been explored, but *Tristram Shandy, Memento,* and *Twin Peaks* are outliers, and one-off examples – they did not result in genre cycles nor substantial successful imitation because they fail to fulfill the essential pleasure that Bloom identifies.

one's taste and curatorial acumen to others may override personal inclination toward a less "conspicuously consumable" text.

The explosion of niche televisual content made possible by the democratization of production and distribution may make the comparison between the art and media worlds more relevant than ever. Jerry Saltz, the Pulitzer Prize–nominated art critic of *New York Magazine* has said "All art is for someone; no art is for everyone."[79] I do not think it is too far a stretch to consider this in terms of our new televisual environment. The range of human expression and the new ability of all to participate in the creation and distribution of niche content ensures that "the content is out there" awaiting discovery, curation, and exhibition by its various someones. The problem for the media industry, of course is that while: "the investment in stories and ideas that lead to the connections people make online and through social media provides the tools for the beginning of relationships" identified by Chris Anderson as "tribes of affinity," the liminal conundrum and challenge is to determine "consequence of such tribes if they do emerge."[80] Two possible forms of consequence are influence and contagion. Influence is persuasion: it is when one person presents his or her taste preferences and encourages others to adopt them.[81] Contagion occurs when neither the influencer nor the influenced is cognizant that the transmission of a taste preference has occurred.[82] However, as noted in Chapter 3, while online content, conversations, and behaviors can be observed, it remains impossible to reliably quantify the motivations or reasoning behind the sharing and definitively identify the type of influence at work.

Further complicating this transaction is that "A rule of pleasure is that it is an inverted U —when you first experience something, it's hard to process and not enjoyable; upon repeated exposure, it's easy to process and gives pleasure; then it gets too easy, and therefore boring or even annoying."[83] Thus content producers must seek to identify attractive elements within the most popular shows and find a way to replicate them that still satisfies the underlying essential pleasure that caused the tribe of affinity to form in the first place all while not innovating so much as to lose the purpose the narrative serves. In industry parlance and practice, this refers to the genre cycles discussed in Chapter 4.

Regardless of how what one likes is determined, the work of curatorial culture requires thought, planning, arrangement, and presentation. It is time- and energy-consuming labor that must be expended before the pleasure of viewing (presumably a break from one's labor) can occur. "Curation is about creating a mix" writes Rosenbaum, "a unique blend of discovered, contributed, and created content that makes your connection uniquely yours."[84] An example of this can be seen in an advertisement for CNNgo* that has been running since 2014. In this ad, a straphanger on a subway car is communicating directly with the control center of CNN. He's choosing from the selection of screens in the booth, calling out what he wants to see and in what order: "give me Anderson Cooper 360, then let's go to some sports, then I want weather and then hit me with some Bourdain, can we do that?" The control room programmer is very accommodating, directing his staff to put together this customized feed for the viewer—who is, one would think, about to experience the epitome of curated television. But—just as the control room programmer begins the countdown—"And, we're ready, in 3 … 2 … 1 …" our viewser interrupts—"Oh, hey, this is my stop, I gotta go."

CNN seems not to have picked up on the irony. This ad is not the shining endorsement of its customizeable viewing app that it intended it to be. Instead, it highlights the very real frustrations and conundrums of the viewer in a completely on-demand world, even one pre-curated by a network brand. In fact, it could well be read as an endorsement of linear viewing of professionally curated content—especially on mobile when one may want to devote one's time and attention to consuming media rather than getting ready to consume media. The economics of scarcity have shifted. Viewing options are no longer scarce. Instead, the amount of time the viewer has to consume media *and* the amount of time and energy the viewer has or wants to spend finding the media to consume in that limited time are.

What this demonstrates is that our thinking about viewing choices needs to realign to accommodate several interlocking new developments that complicate the viewer/text/distributor relationship in ways that make traditional conceptions of viewership less relevant. The first is that television/video content is now just one choice among many other media consumption options.

---

* CNNgo is a "TV Everywhere" app that allows cable subscribers to view CNN content on mobile devices. After authenticating their cable subscription, they can watch a live stream of CNN content or a curated playlist which is what this particular ad is touting.

In the time it took our straphanger to curate his consumption of CNN videos (which he never got to enjoy), he could have read the news content on a different app on his phone. So, while some sort of linear viewing will be with us so long as linear television is—the incidental viewer who has television on "for company" may now be keeping company "on" Facebook instead. The second is that curatorial culture requires more intentionality and less spontaneity than earlier forms of viewing and content discovery. This means that "why people choose" a particular text or collection of texts becomes a much more relevant question than "why people watch."

"Curating's just another word for saying 'I choose you.'" (No, it's not.)

One result of the increased attention paid to curation, both as a marketing and new media buzzword and as a professionalized endeavor within the art world is that there is now more literature on the activities, responsibilities, and effects of curators than ever before. Curation as defined and theorized by those in the art world is always about definition, relevancy-making, and information added. The curator emerges as a key figure and guide through periods of tectonic change and the questioning and realignment of traditional authorities and structures.

Curation becomes a crucial activity when one becomes spoiled by choice as well as when the boundaries of what "is" and "is not" in the pool from which choices are to be made become fluid. As visitors to the 1917 Society of Independent Artists exhibit may have looked upon Marcel Duchamp's "Fountain"* and asked "Yes, but is it art?" today we may look at a YouTube video on our 47 inch flatscreen and ask: "Yes, but is it television?" In both cases, the places of our reception of the texts affect our perception: "I am encountering this urinal in an art exhibit, it is signed by an artist, and it has been placed here by a curator, therefore it is art. I am watching this video on the same device

---

* Duchamp's "Fountain" is the found object urinal that he placed on its back, signed "R. Mutt" and submitted for exhibition. Its creation and exhibition is considered a major event in the Dada anti-art/art movement. "Fountain" resides in the permanent collection of the San Francisco Museum of Modern Art, which would seem to testify to both its continued identity as a work of art and the power of context to define "art work."

that I watch network and cable television on therefore it is television." Unlike Duchamp's "Fountain," which relies on context (we do not perceive urinals that are hung on walls in lavatories and unsigned as art); the YouTube experience works in reverse. We perceive professionally produced television shows that we consume on our phones tablets, or computers and short videos and other content that we consume on our large screen televisions as television. A professionally trained and credentialed curator may be required to transform found pieces into art by bringing them into the gallery or museum. However, the transformation of video content into television occurs when the technology of OTT viewing (especially YouTube) converges with the television set and video-capable cell phones and tablets allow viewer-curators to "pull" content across these contexts in a seamless experience. That video content has become television and retains its "televisual identity" as its site of consumption moves across multiple platforms is a result of the democratization of curation.

While contemporary artists (much like contemporary reality stars and wannabes) may rely upon shock, innovation, and assertion—"This is art, because I'm an artist and I say it is" said British artist Grayson Perry—they must still rely upon curators to contextualize their taxidermied horses, 700lbs of individually wrapped licorice candies, or life-size platinum cast of an eighteenth-century Portuguese sailor's skull bejeweled with industrial diamonds and implanted with the original skull's teeth in order to monetize these works as "art."* YouTube and Vimeo give aspirant reality television artistes a platform through which to "broadcast" themselves, a way into the context of television. Whether DIY/unbranded video becomes television when and because it is consumed on a television set or professionally produced network branded content remains television because it is consumed via a mobile app is a chicken and egg argument, the shift has occurred. To the industry, content is king, but, to the viewer/curator, context is "prime minister." The curator

---

* These three art works have all been exhibited and sold as art in high-end galleries and are (in order of description): Maurizio Cattelan's *The Ballad of Trotsky* (2004), Felix Gonzalex-Torres' *Untitled (Public Opinion)* (1991), and Damien Hirsh's 2007 *For the Love of God*. (The title of this work apparently came from his mother who is said to have uttered that phrase upon hearing a description of the plan for her son's new artwork.) More tales from the marketplace of contemporary art can be found in Thompson's *The Supermodel and the Brillo Box*.

decides the context of the exhibition of the content and how it circulates. This is of increasing importance now that everyone has curatorial power and the platforms through which to communicate and exhibit their decisions.

Curatorial activity brings with it a contextual mandate. Viewing choices are now "to be exhibited" and like catalogs of long-over exhibits, remain discoverable—in our histories, playlists, queues, "recently watched," "watch now," and "recommended for you" lists. The effect of this unavoidable exhibitionism inheres in curatorial culture—especially on the level of the individual viewer. Viewers actively add shows to their queues, their playlists, and "watch later" lists. These are curatorial activities that have varying degrees of public exhibition, some of which can be controlled by the viewer. But because of the structures of the technologies and the end user agreements, the opportunity for providers to observe these exhibitions of curated viewing inheres in the entire transaction and observation *always* changes that which is observed. In the introduction to *Viewers Like You? How Public TV Failed the People*, Laurie Ouellette cites an episode of *Roseanne* in which the Connors become a Nielsen family. Offended by the "condescending" remarks of a Nielsen rep, Roseanne mandates that they will subvert the expectations of the elites by watching only PBS.[85] While this, of course, does not ultimately work (the episode ends with Roseanne watching a *Beverly Hillbillies* marathon) it highlights one of the many challenges a curated viewing culture poses for audience quantifiers: how many of these queue choices or playlist additions are legitimately reflective of the viewing intentions and interests of the curator and how many of them are aspirational? I've added series to my various OTT lists because they've won awards, I've heard of them from friends, they're trending in the online communities with which I interact, or I feel like, as a "good" media scholar I "should" have watched them. While I'm not admitting in print to what I've been watching instead, Netflix, Amazon, and of course, the omnipresent Google know.

The convergence of social media and television, in both social media conversations and the embedding of clips from YouTube into social media feeds has also resulted in the reversals of Klein's two-stage process: the decision to use social media often precedes the selection of specific content—the selection being the curated content of your friends and networks who are simultaneously having their content selected from them by you (if you engage in curatorial activity on your social media feeds).

Cultural intermediation, citizen criticism, and the power of social networks

Professional curators are what Pierre Bourdieu calls "cultural intermediaries:" experts whose "cultural capital" gives them the authority to adjudicate matters of art and taste and thus to play a significant defining role in what is or isn't considered an art object (or cultural text).[86] "Cultural capital" in this case is the authority or the "symbolic capital" accumulated by the critic or curator in question "making a name for oneself, a known, recognized name, a capital of consecration implying a power to consecrate objects (with a trademark or signature) or persons (through publication, exhibition, etc.) and therefore to give value, and to appropriate the profits from this operation."[87] The path to this position of cultural authority for earlier professionalized critics used to be fairly clear: publication in a newspaper or magazine, membership in the Television Critics Association, a regular byline. The question of cultural authority, its achievement, and maintenance, is one that has yet to be definitively answered in the blogosphere—and probably never will be. Klout scores and page ranks indicate popularity but is popularity the new cultural authority? It is more likely that the scale of activity on the internet is turning on "social proof" and a type of crowd-sourced legitimization of either the most popular, most linked, or most social network savvy voices. It is a new stage of participatory culture in which "behaviors that were once considered 'cult' or marginal are becoming how more people engage with television texts"[88] In fact, these behaviors may be on the verge of becoming the mainstream viewing experience. The digital age is a world in need of constant curation by its inhabitants—and curatorial impulses and expertise are fast becoming a requirement for responsible digital citizenship. Ethan Zuckerman, writing about the demands of the current cultural moment emphasizes: "The Internet will not magically turn us into digital cosmopolitans; if we want to maximize the benefits and minimize the harms of connection, we have to take responsibility for shaping the tools we use to encounter the world."[89]

News aggregators such as www.hitfix.com maintain sections devoted to television (in this case, a section that aggregates television criticism (tvtattle) which was formerly its own website). Many critics maintain blogs in addition to their columns, and, of course, many are publishing in a web native environment as their publications either curtail or eliminate print circulation. Many websites currently offer a mix of "professional" "pro-am" and "DIY" television criticism while maintaining discussion boards where viewers respond directly to each other about the shows they are watching. Probably the most famous and successful of these was Television without Pity (www.televisionwithoutpity.com) which maintained a vibrant message board community, was purchased by NBCUniversal in 2007 and ceased publication as of April 4, 2014. Critics such as Emily Nussbaum (*The New Yorker*) and David Bianculli (NPR) who continue to have national venues for their work remain important to the industry for their ability to create buzz and thus search terms which push new and returning shows further into a networked public sphere were they can be found or stumbled upon by viewers. Simultaneously, as the democratization of opinion distribution fostered by the internet allows "anyone" to be a critic, new critical voices are able to emerge and find their own audiences of taste communities.

Debates about the impact of web-native journalism, DIY journalism, or citizen journalists/bloggers are not new to journalism scholars. "Popular culture" criticism is a topic particularly popular to bloggers. Alexa, arguably one of the most authoritative commercial web analytics companies (and, unsurprisingly, a subsidiary of Amazon); does not maintain a "Popular culture" category, nor index blogs separate from websites, but it does index subcategories of websites under its "Arts" category that clearly signal that the web is alive with sites on the subjects of: "Animation (6,298), Comics (2,332), Entertainment (295), Movies (25,299), Music (49.819), Performing Arts (15,261), Radio (1,759), and Television (7,400)."[90] What is clear from this list is that there is a mixture of industry and "outsider" guides but many are owned by industry insiders with a stake in controlling the content. Since these websites are themselves advertiser-supported, what we see here is an extension of the commoditized space coupled with the pre-curation of viewing choices for the viewer.

The majority of scholarship focused on the rise of the citizen critic-blogger pertains to film critics. What should be noted is that the content of a great many of these sites comes from other sites, most of them produced by professional news organizations (a detail not lost on Andrew Keen in his damning of amateur criticism). The problem for Keen is what he terms an irony "democratized media will eventually force all of us to become amateur critics and editors ourselves. With more and more of the information online unedited, unverified, and unsubstantiated, we will have no choice but to read everything with a skeptical eye."[91] This is exactly what curatorial culture requires of its citizens: the development of a discerning eye, or at least a refusal to take, wholesale, the opinions of web sources without an investigation of their provenance and authority.

Beyond the blogger or citizen journalist who is attempting to develop his or her own "brand" as a television critic, there are, of course, the citizens who use social media to talk about their favorite shows. These comprise a different type of curatorial activity and a different type of influence upon the watching habits of an interconnected public while creating different types of data streams that may or may not be useful in determining the reach and influence of a particular type of show. Their viability is a reflection and result of the challenges of negotiating the long tail of "everything": "When people are frustrated with search, they go searching for human curation" writes Clay Shirky.[92] "Curation comes up when search stops doing everything people want it to do, when people realize that it isn't just about information seeking, it's also about synchronizing a community."[93] As discussed in greater detail in Chapter 3, Nielsen and other quantification/ratings companies have begun to track this activity, but it may well be that these "virtual water cooler conversations" are being had by already-engaged fans rather than encouraging or attracting new viewership. In all of these situations inhere the problem of what Jenkins, glossing Gladwell, calls "one of the great myths of Web 2.0": the power of the influencer.[94] Jenkins does not deny the existence of influence in the web utterances of others, however, he does qualify it: "that influence typically is contextual and temporal, depending on the subject, the speaker's credibility, and a variety of other factors. Sure, there are influencers, but who those influencers are may shift substantially from one situation to another."[95]

Ben Mc Connell and Jackie Huba identify four "types" of citizen marketers in their book of the same name. These subject positions describe particular activities and operate as a taxonomy that can be used to categorize the curatorial activities of Web 2.0 users. In order from most to least curatorial they are:—filters, facilitators, fanatics, and firecrackers. Filters are "human wire services" and the type of citizen marketer whose activity is most curatorial.[96] Filters "collect media stories, bloggers' rants and raves, podcasts, or fan creations about a specific company or brand and then package this information into a daily or near-daily stream of links, story summaries and observations."[97] Websites or blogs maintained by these people become curated destinations for other webizens who have an affinity for the topic and the curatorial style of the filter. Facilitators create fan sites or moderate discussion boards. They are "like mayors of online towns" (or gallery or museum owners) and influential within their own online communities.[98] As the owners or managers of these boards they may also establish or institute guidelines for participants and thus shape the presentation of content of their site. Fanatics are filters who weigh in with their opinions. They may or may not provide filtering (curatorial) functions, but mainly, they are the active ones on the message boards. They have distinct ideas about the products they use or the shows they watch and they take full advantage of the interactivity of blogs and websites to voice them.[99] Firecrackers are "one hit wonders."[100] Firecrackers do not regularly engage in curatorial activity nor have an ongoing interest in organizing and presenting information to others. Their observable online work demonstrates "three principles of amateur content in the social media universe: 1. Memes, even latent ones, can last indefinitely on the web. 2. Social media networks accelerate the spread of memes. 3. People love to mimic what entertains them."[101] The challenge for those seeking to assess and use the curatorial evidence to further their own product's (or show's) online profile, is to accurately assess which type of marketer/curator has created the exhibition.

Ultimately, what we're talking about here is word of mouth in the digital world. How do television producers and distributors harness the power and activity of social media and the communities it engenders to drive viewers to its programming (wherever that programming may be)? The "digital commons" is a place where discussions that used to take place among people in close geographical proximity are amplified and publicized, but, in many ways, retain their intimacy and influence. This amplifies Paul Lazarfeld's theorization of "opinion leaders" in the 1940s. Lazarfeld, a sociologist, suggested that "media were less influential over public opinion than a 'two-step flow of communication'—information that flows from media to an influential friend, and then from that friend to her friends."[102] In this transaction with the public (of which the speaker is an integrated part) "authenticity contributes to authority."[103] The authority of citizen critics is dynamic because of its interactivity and it must be maintained by "continuous, productive activity."[104] (Conversely, by avoiding interaction and engagement and operating as a push media, "traditional" broadcast media and its ilk create and maintain static authority—or at least they were able to maintain it until Web 2.0.)

The impact of all of this activity is driven by what James Surowiecki refers to as "social proof." This is "the tendency to assume that if lots of people are doing something or believe something, there must be a good reason why. This is different from conformity: people are not looking up at the sky because of peer pressure or a fear of being reprimanded. They're looking up at the sky because they assume—quite reasonably—that lots of people wouldn't be gazing upward if there weren't something to see."[105] Zuckerman also highlights the effect of this saturation of opinion: "if we keep hearing about a person, place, or event, we register that what we've learned about is important, and we're predisposed to pay attention to the topic."[106] So, while certain "influencers" or "bloggers" may be particularly key in steering audience toward shows or premieres (as they have always been), the sheer numbers of participants in the online world, and the scale of "likes" possible, have an effect because "the crowd becomes more influential as it becomes bigger: every additional person is proof that something important is happening."[107] Jenkins, Ford, and Green use the term "appraisal" (another art world term) to "describe the process by which people determine which forms of value and worth get ascribed to an object as it moves through different transactions."[108] It is a particularly apt use of the term in a curatorial context since it denotes the way value is created "not through buying and selling commodities but through critiquing, organizing and displaying/exhibiting artifacts."[109]

The rise of social networking has brought both challenges and opportunities for content providers and distributors to interact with and encourage viewer behaviors and to observe their curatorial behavior in real time—since it is the crucial "site of exhibition" that distinguishes curation from merely viewer choice. One of the observable results of widespread viewer curation is that it may work against new program discovery. This is what Zuckerman, writing of "digital cosmopolitans" identifies as a "central paradox" of the networked age—"while it's easier than ever to share information and perspectives from different parts of the world, we may now often encounter a narrower picture of the world than in less connected days."[110] Zuckerman is most focused on news and information, noting that tools like Google, Wikipedia, and other online repositories of information "help us discover what we want to know, but they're not very powerful in helping us discover what we might need to know."[111] At the same time, his warnings are instructive for television viewers and the producers who seek to reach them: "As social media become more powerful directors of attention, we are encountering less media through professional curators or through our own interest-based searches. In giving so much responsibility to our friends to shape what we know of the world, we need to consider the limitations of social discovery rather than just celebrating its novelty."[112]

While our online "friends" may share their viewing habits with us, and we may share our viewing habits and "likes" publicly, the jury remains out as to whether social media popularity or metrics translate into influence or changes in activity. It is even more difficult to determine if this leads to wider discovery of new programming. Part of this is the challenge of what Eli Parisier calls the "filter bubble" which is created by insular worlds encouraged by the use of Facebook and other social networking spaces as the portal or pre-curator of our web experiences. Zuckerman warns: "As we design online spaces, we need to think through the dangers of making those spaces too comfortable, too easy and too isolated."[113]

The explosion of new programming options and the conversations around them transform the viewer into a citizen programmer/curator, responsible for discovering and engaging with new programming. To avoid falling into filter bubbles, citizen programmers must exert more energy to "seek out curators who are sufficiently far from you in cultural terms."[114] Likewise, if you want to discover new programs and alternative viewing spaces OTT and OTB, it requires curatorial work beyond one's own social community and past viewing habits.

Complicating all of this is, of course "exhibition anxiety," which I suggest is curatorial culture's version of the unreliable narrator. Because our curated choices are being exhibited via our online histories, queues, and playlists, how much do we allow the fear of missing out (FOMO) to trump the fear of revealing embarrassing taste preferences (FORETP)? Anyone who has ever tried to "hide" certain viewing choices from others who may share his or her Netflix queue or Amazon playlist, or whose innocent attempt to show a coworker a funny YouTube video has revealed a mortifying secret interest on one's "Recently Watched" list can attest: we are all curators now, not just because we have moved from "surf to search to seek" but because, intended or not, what we have sought is on display.

3

Who's Watching? When? Why? Where? The Limits and Liminality of Audience Quantification

Viewer behavior only matters if the viewers can be counted. Thus, the quantification of the audience is crucial to the fiduciary relationships between the television and advertising industries. In the United States, television has always been an advertiser-supported medium. Viewers purchase a set which comes with a tuner and the ability to receive broadcast signals through the "ether" and for that investment alone, they can receive television content via the broadcast channels, "paying" with their attention to the advertisements that are delivered with their "free" programming. While cable and satellite systems and now internet SVOD (subscription video on demand) services now collect their monthly subscriber fees, with a few paywalled exceptions (Netflix and Amazon Instant Video), televisual content of all types still carries advertisements and television advertising is still a huge business. The forecast value of the American television advertising market for 2016 is $70 billion.[1]

In an advertiser-supported medium, advertising rates are set and driven by ratings. The quantified number of viewers watching a given show determines how much networks can charge advertisers for ad spots within the show and how much product placement within the show costs. The major consumers for audience measurement data are the networks and the advertising agencies, although, now that ratings are routinely published to the public, they can also operate as a general metric of popularity which can encourage additional viewership. Streaming services do not need advertisers and, consequently (or at least according to them) have no need to externally publish their viewership. However, the importance of crowd behavior and social media influencers complicates this refusal to publicize at least *some* "numbers"—if nothing else as a way of reaching out to and encouraging those whose online friends are not engaging with the show to be leaders in new viewing circles.

The business of audience measurement, like that of entertainment, is largely oligopolized by a few major companies, such as Nielsen for television and Arbitron for radio.[2] Only in the area of internet ratings does one come across a multiplicity of companies vying for dominance. This is partially because the medium is relatively "new" and also because there are numerous ways of quantifying an internet audience. The reason for this lack of competition is that audience measurement is an extremely expensive endeavor which requires the companies that provide ratings products to make substantial investments in both the technology to capture audience activity, but also the analysts to make sense of this data and package it.[3] It also has served the needs of the principle end users of ratings (networks and production companies) to work with one set of measurements from one agreed-upon company. Additionally, as noted by Lotz, "the measurement systems that evolved throughout the network era and multi-channel transition worked because the fundamental economic and distribution mechanisms remained fairly consistent at their core."[4] In the present moment, as the site of television consumption has become contested, the costs and methodologies of ratings generation have been exacerbated by an increasingly fragmented audience maneuvering through a complex media environment. The conundrum is clear: "the television industry requires knowledge about the people who watch, but that audience is, to a great extent, unknowable."[5] As a result, the uniform adoption of and agreement upon "a" standard of audience quantification (even an imperfect one) has been the traditional covenant between the industry, its fiduciary stakeholders and the supplier of its ratings products.

It is important to note that the major users of ratings products (advertisers, advertising agencies, broadcasters, and content producers) are not always and rarely have been in agreement about the practice and aim of audience quantification methods. Broadcasters and content producers favor measurement methods that yield the highest possible numbers, since their ad rates are based on the number of viewers that they attract. Advertisers and advertising agencies favor the most "granular" measurements that quantify not just program viewership, but commercial viewership and also index-particular attributes of the viewers allowing for the most precise measurement of the "commodity audience" as opposed to the "mass audience."

The rise in popularity of web video has posed the first true challenge to Nielsen's metrics and has also opened the market to a variety of entrepreneurs and new companies. Thus the rite of passage being experienced by audience quantifiers involves the loss of a geographically fixed time-controlled audience and the need to develop ways of counting that include these viewers wherever and whenever they may be. As will be seen, Nielsen often counters these threats by acquiring companies that develop technologies or proprietary content or techniques that would seek to threaten their monopoly on all things audience quantifying.

The market for ratings products

Nielsen produces a panoply of "ratings products" for its customers and the cost of its services vary depending on the type of ratings services the customer needs. By far its biggest purchasers are the advertising agencies and media buying agencies that use these reports to determine the best media buy and advertising placement for their customers. Not far behind the advertisers are the second major users of ratings data: the television networks, producers, station groups, and independent television stations themselves. A small local broadcaster seeking only basic data might purchase a few thousand dollars of ratings reports as year, while local network affiliates in populated DMAs (designated market areas) might pay a million dollars for a more comprehensive package of local and syndicated ratings data.[6] The largest Nielsen contract to date was signed between the ratings service and NBCUniversal in 2003, guaranteeing Nielsen revenue of $400–500 million dollars for reports that met the needs of the multiple media outlets owned by this conglomerate.[7] Nielsen signs staggered multiyear contracts (Master Service Agreements) with the major television companies (CBS, NBC/GE, ABC/Disney, etc.). These ensure that the entire industry will not be in the market for a new audience measurement provider at any given time. Possible competitors to Nielsen know this and the prohibitively expensive start-up costs of starting a new audience measurement company have successfully ensured that Nielsen is both the gold standard and the lingua franca of television viewership metrics. Geri Wang, president of sales and marketing at ABC asserts: "The default mechanism is absolutely the Nielsen rating. We wake up to that report card every single morning and it is still a very useful tool."[8]

What do ratings mean? How are they calculated?

While Nielsen has, in response to industry demand and desire for greater accuracy and knowledge about the viewing populous, enhanced its data gathering methodologies, the basic approach to measurement with a representative sample (of "Nielsen families") standing in for costly, impractical, or impossible individual viewing measurement has not changed since the early days of television. The traditional television "rating" is an expression (and estimation) of the show's popularity during the timeslot it occupies and represents the percentage of households that were tuned to that show out of all homes that own a television in the United States.[9] "Share" and "demographic" are metrics that provide further information about the viewership of shows.

"Share" is the percentage of the total number of households using television (HUTs) that are tuned to a particular show at a particular time. It is useful for comparing viewership during times lots and across programs and seasons. The number of HUTs may vary from season to season or time slot to time slot, but, unless a show or channel is losing or gaining audience, its "share" should remain steady.[10]

Demographics provide descriptors of the audience based on age, gender, class, race, ethnicity, and delivery system of the signal (cable versus satellite versus OTA broadcast only). These are the holy grail for advertisers who prize the 18–34 age male, urban, educated, cable subscribers most highly. The secondary audience is upmarket women age 18–34 who presumably watch television with their male partners, and within this subgroup, women who work outside the home thirty hours per week are more valued than women who do not.[11] These highly prized segments of the audience are also known as "commodity audiences."[12] It is interesting to note that as of this writing, Nielsen's demographic quantification ends at age 49, making viewers 50 and above statistically irrelevant, a circumstance that it may behoove the television industry to reconsider given the aging baby boomers, their disposable income, and the extended lifespan of recent generations. It is possible for a show with a high rating to have a low share and thus be unattractive to advertisers.[13] Obviously this becomes much more likely after the saturation of cable since the multichannel environment provides so many viewing options that the HUT may be spread over hundreds of possible options rather than the five to seven of the broadcast era.

The most well-known rating "product" by those outside the television industry is the Nielsen Television Index (NTI) which are the national ratings of broadcast network programming that Nielsen produces "overnight" (which is how they are called by the television industry, as in "how did we do in the 'overnights.'"). This data is generated from NTI sample homes (aka the "Nielsen Families") in which PeopleMeters have been placed.[14]

The actual method of gathering and calculating data bears some discussion here since it is largely misunderstood exactly how Nielsen gathers its data and then how it quantifies it into the actual numbers on which television series live or die. The methods used to define and capture an audience affect the results that one may get. Therefore, it is not too far a leap to say that ratings themselves are largely a "reasonably believable fictional construct" that the television industry, advertising agencies, and their clients have agreed to believe are accurate in order to successfully do business. They relate to reality, but they do not capture it in all of its complexity. (Which is why an ostensibly popular and well-known show such as *Malcolm in the Middle* might have such low ratings and why it is even more important for shows likely to be consumed "off the box" and online to be able to prove their popularity and viewership to advertisers).

Nielsen ratings are based on a sample of the overall population of media consumers—since it is not possible (yet), to fully measure and quantify the usage of all people with access to a television, let alone all people viewing televisual content at any given time, Nielsen recruits a representative number of households (Nielsen families) whose television usage will representatively stand in for the population as a whole. It does this through recruitment techniques that use randomly generated phone numbers to contact and identify households that are willing to serve as part of the sample panel. Nielsen families receive PeopleMeters for each of the televisions in their homes. These PeopleMeters are attached to the television sets and the phone lines and have a dedicated button for each member of the family. An accompanying remote also contains the dedicated buttons. The PeopleMeters monitor whether or not the television is turned on, as well as the channel to which it is tuned. The members of the household, however, must take the initiative to press their dedicated button to signal their presence to the Nielsen PeopleMeter. Thus, this form of PeopleMeter is often referred to as an Active PeopleMeter since it requires action by the audience to ensure its accuracy. Every fifteen minutes, a flash of light from the PeopleMeter reminds those viewing to confirm their continued presence in the audience. National ratings include the national broadcast networks, cable networks, syndicators, and national satellite providers such as DirecTV and EchoStar.[15] These overnight ratings are the ones reported in the entertainment news, and the ones that most people refer to (if they do refer to ratings) when assessing the popularity of a favored show on network or cable. They are revised at the end of the week to include the C3 ratings as well as the "Live +" ratings.

As the American television environment is based on locally licensed broadcast television stations, Nielsen also calculates the ratings for each local market, formally defined by Nielsen as a designated market area or DMA. There are 210 DMAs in the United States, each comprised of counties that share the same set of viewing options. It is important to note that these viewing options are determined by the broadcast footprint of the television stations the FCC has licensed to local municipalities within these counties, so there are DMAs that cross state and other geographic lines. (St. Louis, Missouri, and St. Louis, Kansas are in the same DMA according to Nielsen since they receive the same broadcast signals from stations licensed in each municipality for instance.) While the DMA is determined by definitions of the broadcast footprints of local broadcasters, local ratings track the viewing of local broadcast stations and the nationally distributed programming available via the locally operating cable and satellite systems.

Local markets are measured in two ways. The largest fifty-six DMAs are measured using Local PeopleMeters (LPMs) which quantify these viewers continuously in the same way that Nielsen households that are part of the national sample do. Therefore, these viewers are measured all year long. Other DMAs are measured through a diary system, which is what "sweeps" are about. Sweeps occur four times a year, during February, May, July, and November. During this period, randomly selected respondents are asked to fill out a "diary" of the viewing habits of their household for one week. Therefore, sweep data "is actually based on four independent samples drawn in consecutive weeks. These data are combined to provide a single month-long estimate of audience size and composition."[16] While this technique has considerable room for human error or nonresponse, "if all going according to plan, Nielsen will have about 350,000 diaries to process at the end of a nationwide sweep," which would indicate an average rate of response of 30 percent.[17] As many viewers may have noticed, the networks seek to help out their local affiliates during "sweeps," by planning special guest stars, "big" episodes, or reveals during these months. Local stations might also offer special programming or contests to increase viewership during this period. Since local market advertising rates are set on the performance of shows during sweeps, it behooves the networks to help out their local affiliates in this way. This, in turn, helps the networks since national advertising rates are based on the viewership garnered during sweeps weeks.

It should be noted, however, that the fifty-six local markets in which LPMs have been installed encompass about 70 percent of television households and eliminate the need for diary-keeping in these markets. Should meter technology or its equivalent become universally accessible then diary-keeping, and thus the sweeps periods themselves, will both be rendered irrelevant.

Originally, the national sample was capped at 5,000 Nielsen family households. However, the introduction of LPMs into the largest DMAs allowed Nielsen to fold the data captured by the LPM into its national overnight ratings which increased the numbers of homes in the panel. As of the first quarter of 2016, there were 40,000 households total in the Nielsen panel, each representing an average of 2.5 individuals for a total viewership panel of 100,000 people.[18] With an overall estimation of 296.8 million persons age two and over in US TV households (children younger than two are not considered to be legitimately quantifiable "viewers");[19] each person in this panel stands in for about 2,968 viewers. It should be noted that this is the largest panel and smallest number of represented viewers in Nielsen history—traditionally a much smaller number of households was used (for example, as of 2004, there were 8,618 households in this sample, each comprised of an average of 2.5 individuals).[20] So, while still not as an exact science as a 1:1, all-inclusive accounting; today's ratings are the most specific and representative ever produced in Nielsen's more than seventy-year history.

How ratings are used

Decisions on pickups and cancellations are made on the basis of these three calculations (ratings, share, and demographic) which are presumed to represent who is watching what when, and what a show's relative popularity is in its time slot and across the television schedule at large. Shows that fall below the "cancellation threshold" can expect, not surprisingly, to be cancelled. The increase in viewing options has, expectedly, considerably lowered the cancellation threshold of shows that rely on ratings to demonstrate viewership. In the mid-1970s, when the "big three" networks attracted the majority of the viewing audience, hit shows might easily pull ratings in the thirties or higher. Thus, the cancellation threshold was in the high teens.[20] Today, "networks aspire to having a megahit with ratings in the high teens. The average prime time rating for shows on ABC, CBS and NBC is in the 6.0–9.0 range and only the highest rated shows break into the double digits."[21]

Since demographics are so important to advertisers, the emphasis on the 18–49 demographic has affected the practices of Nielsen and any ratings quantification services that seek to compete with the industry leader. All ratings companies know which measurements are in greatest demand by the television and advertising industry, therefore there is little incentive in quantifying the populations (OTA only homes, ethnic homes, older audiences) that fall outside of this group.[22] This emphasis on only a part of the viewing audience affects programming decisions and new series development since mass media requires shows that are most attractive to mass audiences. While, "audience members outside the target demographic are often treated as 'surplus' ... when these 'undesired' segments overwhelm the core demographic, they can even be seen as a nuisance, confusing advertisers about the media property's value for delivering targeted audience groups."[23] If the metrics become too confusing or the surplus demographics comprise too much of the audience, it can result in cancellations even if the show is pulling a respectable numerical rating. (A particularly unfortunate example: the cancellation of shows that are only popular to older demographics is referred to as "granny dumping.")

The primary use of ratings is the setting of advertising rates, and the goal of advertisers is to have the most accurate measure of who is actually watching their advertisements during the shows, which for most of television's history has been guesswork at best. The invention of the remote control, video home system (VHS), and other time shifting technologies such as the digital video recorder (DVR) has problematized the ratings system for shows, but even more so for advertisements since "zapping" and "zipping" inhere in and are encouraged by these technologies. The two-way communication of the DVR has provided additional data to be mined, but the Nielsen company was loathe to actually invest in or pursue this form of audience aggregation until forced to by its primary customers (the content producers and the advertisers). Additionally, the mining of viewing habits from DVRs is constrained by privacy laws as well as complicated by the outdated hardware, lack of connectivity (since several different types and generations of DVR are currently in use throughout the United States) and the fact that users tend not to power off their DVRs or cable boxes—meaning that the box may be on but the TV may be off.

The digital challenge

Karen Buzzard describes three changes that characterize the effect of the digital revolution on television advertising: increasing audience segmentation in the multichannel environment, increased time-shifting by audiences, and "place shifting" or the impact of the growing portability of televisual content through iPods, cell phones, and now, of course, tablet computers.[24] This "user revolution" challenges the traditional audience measurement system which presumed centralized viewing around a main television "set" which was receiving content through the ether, cable, or a satellite hookup. What this means for Nielsen is that it can no longer rely upon its PeopleMeter technology which identified the programs at its transmission source rather than its reception site and thus it cannot account for programming that was time-shifted, consumed on mobile, or otherwise brought into (or out of) the home. Nielsen's active/passive meter identifies programs directly off the screen that was being watched through identification codes inserted at the transmission source, and also determines how the set is being used (broadcast, cable, VCR, DVR, satellite, video game).[25] In response to pressure from networks and advertisers to provide better quantification of viewership and, as broadcast ratings appeared to decline precipitously, to figure out "where the viewers went," Nielsen has created a variety of new ratings products and metrics tailored to the unique viewing opportunities and sites of the digital age.

C3/C7 ratings

The Nielsen "C3" rating was borne of a compromise the major broadcast networks and the major media buying agencies began negotiating in 2005. Media buyers wanted Nielsen to provide detailed ratings for commercials since the active/passive PeopleMeter now enabled that information to be gathered. They also wanted to make sure that commercials that appeared in shows recorded on DVRs were accounted for during playback. Faced with growing displeasure from its customers, Nielsen created the "C3" rating in 2007 and it was adopted as an industry-wide standard in 2009.[26] The C3 provides a minute-by-minute commercial audience rating for either live viewing or up to three days of playback after the initial showing of the episode.[27] The C3 rating itself: "represents the audience size for a given TV show's commercial time. Defined by the average of all of the commercial minutes within a TV episode, plus three days of commercial viewing during time-shifted (DVR) playback. Any fast forwarding of commercials within the three-day window is excluded from the ratings calculation."[28] VOD viewing is included in the C3 rating only if it carries exactly the same commercial pods as the live version of the show.[29]

In 2014 Nielsen began generating a C7 rating which was essentially the same as a C3 rating in measurement methodology; it just quantified viewership for live + seven instead of three days. The C3/C7 ratings are now known collectively as "Commercial Ratings" (because they measure the viewership of commercials rather than that of the show as a whole).

The institution of these ratings proved to be controversial. Advertisers developed a growing dissatisfaction with Nielsen's sample-based measurement, feeling that given the changes in broadcast delivery and viewer consumption and the failure of the samples to reflect representative samples of the commodity viewer, they were unable to get an accurate measurement of the return on investment (ROI) of their media buying dollars.[30] Understandably, "advertisers were tired of paying for program ratings when programs were increasingly time-shifted and commercials fast forwarded, leaving them little assurance regarding what they were getting for their investment."[31]

The networks feared that they would lose substantial revenue if advertising dollars were calculated according to commercial ratings rather than program ratings because they assumed that ratings for commercials would be lower than the program rating average. What has been discovered since its institution is that there was practically no quantifiable audience loss between program and per-minute advertising spot ratings.[32] In fact, "for live-plus-three day viewing, it turns out that 99 percent of viewers watch a prime-time program within three days of the original broadcast, which boosts the networks' ratings over live-only data. In other words, the differences between the commercial and the program ratings were offset by the inclusion of the three-day DVR data."[33]

Total audience measurement

As this book was being completed (summer 2016), Nielsen had just rolled out its "Total Audience Measurement" tools and the first reports that used these tools to quantify "cross-platform audience measurement." This multi-platform measurement tool was first announced in 2014 and purports to measure viewership across all sites at which televisual content is viewed (with the exception of wearable portables such as the Apple Watch).[34] According to Nielsen, this single-sourced platform accounts for "all viewing across linear TV, DVR, VOD, connected TV devices (Roku, Apple TV, and Xbox), mobile, PC and tablets."[35] Recent C3 and C7 ratings indicate that linear television viewing has "flattened out" across all demographics. However, the Total Audience Report would suggest that video viewing has not ultimately declined, it has just shifted to VOD and internet connected televisions and mobile or tablet devices which C3 and C7 ratings do not count.[36] Presumably the total audience measurement is based on observation of the curatorial spaces in which viewers exhibit their viewing choices as well as the platforms through which they comment upon and contextualize those choices.

Not surprisingly, viewers in the older demographics are less likely to time and space shift their viewing (in an early test application of the tool it was discovered that only 15% of adults 25–34 watched a primetime broadcast drama live while 64% of adults 50 and over viewed it in real time).[37] Like all Nielsen products, full access to the entire report and to the interactive tools are limited to Nielsen clients and subscribers, but the tool promises to allow users to "track the overall performance [of a particular asset, network or episode] in a selected date range and all the viewers that are coming to that network."[38] It also tracks "repeat airings of an episode, VOD playback [through a DVR or a cable system] and its performance on other platforms like a network's websites and apps and SVOD platforms like Hulu."[39] The promised granularity of data is comprehensive, allowing breakdowns into categories such as: "unique audience, reach, gross average minute audience [in viewers and gross ratings points (GRP)], minutes viewed and frequency (the average number of exposures to a show or network)."[40]

David Wong, Nielsen VP of product leadership sees this new ratings product as comprehensive and advantageous for all Nielsen stakeholders: "It's going to help our clients not only be able to value their media assets, but be able to demonstrate what the value is to marketers and to the marketplace, how much interest there is in their media, but it will also help them to make better choices about how to evolve the currency. Because it gives them the flexibility to start to say, 'What really happens when I put an episode out there? What does the life of an episode look like after it first hits, and then it becomes available on multiple platforms and the windows start to open up.' This will give all the texture to a consumer behavior around a particular show."[41] What Wong is saying is that advertisers and programmers should, using the total audience measurement tools, be able to figure out precise viewership for any given minute in any show or commercial and, through a consideration of demographics and comparative engagement across other media in the moment, be able to make more informed choices about types of advertising as well as media buys. Whether this will actually occur is anyone's guess and Symphony Advanced Media and ComScore, both previously known to measure web traffic and engagement, are beginning to develop ratings systems to directly compete or even overtake Nielsen as the new ratings standard for the networked television era. All of these companies face tremendous challenges since "there has been little consensus on how, or even which, measures of engagement are valuable or how to agree on a model for business transactions around such measures."[42]

Internet ratings

The very technological nature of internet usage, with discrete IP addresses, cookies, and the like, ensures that internet usage can be more precisely tracked and traced than television viewership. Internet ratings software installed on a panel member's computer records every link that is clicked on, measures how long a user remained on a particular site, if they clicked on banner ads, and so on. At the same time, there are no program titles or time divisions on the internet, therefore "thirty day reach" (the number of discrete users who have visited a website at least once during a particular month) became the primary metric when measuring internet ratings. This metric was set as early as 1996 by PC Meter, the first metered internet ratings service.[43] In the earliest years of the internet, Jupiter Media Metrix (JMM) was the dominant internet ratings service until 2002 when Nielsen instituted Nielsen NetRatings. Nielsen's entrance into internet ratings market was criticized by JMM which noted that "when Nielsen views the world, everything looks like a TV screen."[44] While early attempts to quantify net usage did mimic TV ratings in that they focused on the conglomerated content provided by *portals* such as AOL and Yahoo! Eventually "the transparency and engagement offered by internet ratings would also shape radio and TV measurement and thereby put pressure on traditional ratings services to offer the same level of transparency and engagement."[45]

Early attempts at internet ratings treated individual sites as "properties" and recorded the number of "unique visitors" as recorded by different ISP addresses over a certain period of time (usually a month). With the rise of social media, aggregation, and hyperlinking, new forms of quantification have developed which focus on targeted ROI metrics. At the present moment, the leading internet ratings providers are Nielsen NetRatings and ComScore Media Matrix, both of which use panel systems (volunteers agree to download tracking software to their computers).[46] As no one system has yet risen to industry-wide acceptance, smaller start-ups such as Alexa, Compete, and HitWise, which operate by tracking cookies websites leave behind on general users computers, and Quanticast which uses a combination of volunteer panels and cookie quantification.[47] The inherent attributes of websites also allow for census or server-based audience measurement which examines the "log file" of a website to determine its audience.[48] As log files record the number of hits and page requests a site receives as well as the length of time a visitor stays on the site, this method provides more granular data than other methods, but, the technology can also make log file metrics unreliable as there is no way to allow for users who access the site from multiple computers or devices, and user-deletion of cookies and caches can result in misleading duplication of users.[49] But, just because a browser is pointed to a particular site on which video content appears, it is not necessarily demonstrable that that content is being viewed, nor that the content, especially if autoplaying, is being watched.

The biggest problem, of course remains how to quantify web viewing in such a way that the television and web viewers can be expressed in a metric that is statistically reliable and coherent. Technological as well as industrial barriers have hamstrung these efforts. While TNT, TBS and E! agreed to code their online ads to allow them to be tracked by Nielsen, these shows (and their ads) were only available to "TV Everywhere" viewers.[50] While "backers of the TV Everywhere initiative had tried to persuade program providers and distributors to make content available wherever viewing is watched as long as programming was secured behind the password-protected locked gates of the pay-tv providers," not all broadcasters or cable networks had "opted in" to this system.[51] The result was that Nielsen was unable to meld the online viewing measurements with its traditional TV ratings to come up with a coherent metric. While Nielsen had announced an Anytime Anywhere Media Measurement (A2/M2) initiative in 2006, it remains unable to iron out how to align these new measurements with C3 ratings, how to quantify mobile viewers, and how to compare on-air ads to online ads.[52]

OTT ratings

While neither Amazon Instant Video nor Netflix publish viewer data, Netflix has been most vocal in its insistence that there is no value in doing so. At the 2013 Television Critics Association press tour, Netflix's Chief Content Officer Ted Sarandos said: "I don't know why HBO, Showtime, any of them publish ratings. It might be for internal (reasons), or to manage the relationships with cable operators, but we don't have relationships with cable operators to manage. There's no business reason for us to publish ratings other than to create artificial pressure on a show to perform on a short time frame. We don't need to add that to the mix. There's enough pressure in creating television as it is."[53] This does not mean that Netflix does not collect viewer data—being a subscription service it not only knows how many possible viewers it has, but it can also track individual viewer behavior and use that in making long-term programming decisions. "We're going to measure a show's success on multiple metrics, but one of them will not be timeslot viewing. We'll measure viewership over the life of a license and invest proportionately to the payback in terms of customer love of the show—retention, new subscribers, brand halo."[54] This internal tracking is what led to Netflix's decision to produce new episodes of *Arrested Development*. "We had real, measurable data that proved that the audience for 'Arrested Development' was compounding in the years after it was cancelled . . . 'Arrested' was actually building an audience. I knew that if we brought it back, we'd be addressing a multiple of its Fox audience as opposed to a fraction of the audience when it was originally on air."[55] While no official metrics of *House of Cards* viewing were released following its premiere, in April of 2013, Sarandos posted that "subscribers watched four billion hours of content on Netflix in the first quarter [of 2013.]"[56] In that same period, "Richard Greenfield of BTIG Research said the Netflix users are watching an average of about 87 minutes of Netflix content per day, per household," leading an unnamed Wall Street analyst to call Netflix "now likely the most-watched cable network."[57]

Portals

Mark Zuckerberg has often said that he views Facebook as a "platform" and innovations to the website clearly demonstrate an intent to have Facebook users access the web via their Facebook pages.[58] This would create an ecosystem and an ability to monitor its users' web behavior so as to sell access to these users to advertisers. Google, long the leader in search, has sought to compete with its own social networking ecosystem, Google+ and other media conglomerates seeking a foothold in what some scholars call the "portalopoly" (originally populated by companies such as Yahoo, Excite, Lycos, AOL, AltaVista, Snap, and Infoseek). These portals function provide meta-aggregated content and a range of services and information to their users linking to other content, but generating and keeping the advertising revenue they raise for themselves.[59] The goal of these portals is to be the "home page" or "first boot," the future being "determined by those who controlled the first screen to be seen on whatever user device of the future was tuned in (i.e., computer, TV, or some combination thereof)."[60] The conglomeration that affected traditional media also affected the internet by 2001, "fourteen companies captured the largest share of the user's time and fifty percent of all time was spent with four companies."[61] By 2011, the "Gang of Four" (Apple, Google, Facebook, and Amazon) were "positioned to define commerce in the twenty-first century."[62] All four of these companies are involved in the distribution of cross-platform televisual content. Google and Amazon through YouTube and Amazon Instant Video; AppleTV through development deals for the production of original programming that will be exclusive to its distribution platform; and Facebook via embedded video on its users pages as well as "Facebook live" (a streaming service that enables live "casting" by users). Thus television in all of its new and old incarnations inheres in the capacities and offerings of all of these digital sovereigns.

Social media, engagement, and TV ratings

Beyond the "holy grail" of set-top-box data looms the question: "Does the social media conversation drive TV ratings? The answer is that there is no scientific proof that makes a direct and exact conclusion—yet."[63] Nielsen, having enjoyed a monopoly on the television ratings field for over forty years was reluctant to give too much credence to plans to incorporate social media into existing television metrics. Obviously the data is freely available since "online communication creates a textual trail of the conversations audiences have about a brand or media property which may be archived indefinitely for all to see."[64] But exactly what that archive means and how it is or is not connected to actual viewership is under contention. According to Nielsen Executive Jon Gibbs: "There's no specific reason to account for social media within TV ratings which are a specific thing: namely, the number of people who watch a program. Nowadays, there's a need in the market to understand the impact of social on driving the amount of people that watch TV, so that a TV broadcasters as a marketer can understand how to engage with social media in order to get more people to watch their program. But there's no need to actually enhance a TV rating itself—specifically with social media data."[65]

"Engagement" is one of the more granular metrics that social media measurement is attempting to quantify. This is presumably an acknowledgement that some audiences are more valuable than others, not just demographically, but in terms of their levels of involvement in a series. (Think of linear content viewers versus prized content viewers from Chapter 2.) The argument underlying this is that "viewers watched certain programs more intently or had greater passion for some shows and that advertising messages placed in such content should be more highly valued as a result."[66] Conversations and experiments in the creation of data that demonstrate correlations between social media activity and television ads (such as Shazam's 2013 Engagement Rate experiment) continue, but to date no widely accepted game-changing ratings products nor services have emerged.

As a possible attempt to create ecosystems in which social media activity driven by television viewing can be monitored and monetized, a variety of "social TV" apps and platforms have emerged. In its strictest definition, the term "social TV" names the "convergence of television and social media."[67] What this convergence yields is a lively and powerful "backchannel." This "backchannel" is "comprised of the millions of public conversations happening online while television programming airs."[68] In other words, all of the places that conversations about the shows are happening. For advertisers and marketers, this provides an important data mining opportunity; for television content producers, this provides a chance to connect with viewers and, if possible, drive viewers to new programming or loyal viewing of existing shows. Despite the challenges of the digital age, the explosion of viewing options and the fragmentation of the audience, this development actually yields positive possibilities for content providers—prior to the digital era, the backchannel existed off-line and around water coolers—away from the measurement systems of advertisers and producers. Advocates of social media note that this is merely an extension of ingrained viewer behavior since "the underlying desire to connect and share has always existed within the human race. Social media simply enables our inherent behaviors and gives us an instant means to express ourselves to a world of other people."[69] The backchannels of social media provide ratings and quantification companies with access to what, in effect, is a giant coviewing party or worldwide water cooler.

Beginning in the late 2000s, several different companies began quantifying social media activity for television shows and the ads that play on them. Some of these, such as Trendrr.tv were free services that worked from available metrics. Launching in April 2011, Trendrr.tv used "fire hose" data from Twitter, check-in data from Miso and GetGlue, and public Facebook status updates to generate "Social Television Charts," which it made available for free. In 2012 it made its Curatorr product available which lets partners like media companies and brands "*curate* a timeline of relevant tweets around a specific event."[70] BlueFinLabs was founded in 2008 and originally planned to "create a full-fledged rival to Nielsen by starting out with social analytics, aimed at telling programmers and marketers what people were saying about them when they watched TV."[71] Another industry leader was SocialGuide which published "social TV ratings and social TV analytics" culled from algorithmic analysis of publicly available social networking feeds.

The result of all this innovation was: acquisition and purchase. By 2013, all three of these "stand-alone players" in social television quantification ad been bought. Nielsen bought SocialGuide and Twitter purchased both Trendrr and Bluefin Labs. Nielsen and Twitter also announced a "research alliance" in December of 2012 which has led to the inclusion of "most tweeted shows" lists becoming part of Nielsen's ratings product line (and, presumably, the use of this data in the generation of Nielsen's "Total Audience Measurement").

The ultimate value of these metrics for content producers and how much they may be willing to pay for these measuring services is still being determined. What is clear from Nielsen and Twitter's purchase of the independent startups is that social media activity is being perceived as increasingly legitimate. These efforts to capture, quantify, and analyze social media mentions demonstrate an industry belief that: "the more people that engage on TV's backchannel, the higher the chances others online will discover and tune in, out of curiosity, to the programming getting the lion's share of buzz. The other major value proposition is that large backchannels produce a goldmine of insights that are ready and waiting to be surfaced. If TV networks and advertisers are not quite ready to make the leap by claiming that social media is good for ratings, then they can at least benefit from social ratings data as an input to strategy and planning decisions."[72] Eleanor Stribling of TubeMogul, an advertising software startup, believes that basic social media metrics are not useful: "Too often, we see a statistic such as the number of Facebook fans or Twitter followers of a media property and an assertion that this number represents value. However, these data do not indicate what those fans do once they've friended or followed in order to participate in, promote, or support the media property."[73] In order to truly determine the value of social media mentions, Stribling advocates investigating "the amount of time spent with a media property compared to others, how frequently fans interact with or around a media property, and changes in how fans interact with or around a media property over time."⁷⁴ Ways to legally, ethically, and efficiently do this remain undetermined.

A perhaps not surprising concern about the creation of new ratings products that mine backchannels of social media and set-top boxes for information is, of course, viewer privacy. While "the acceptance of surveillance is effectively a condition of participation in digital societies," the level to which audiences are willing to accept surveillance of their niche viewing choices as a condition of their access to this programming is yet to be determined.⁷⁵ There may be a degree to which audience members will accept targeted advertising and the mining of their personal information in exchange for relevant commercial messages or a price-break on access to the desired content. However, without substantial buy-in by consumers, the motives and demonstrable market activities resulting from these arrangements will be near impossible to adequately track and measure and may be of dubious validity because of the self-interest (rather than curatorial interest) which inheres in commercial transactions. Furthermore, niche markets by definition have an easier time doing consumer research so efforts to demographically quantify audiences via the triangulation of viewing, social, and purchasing activity may be redundant and irrelevant.

4

The Industry: Ritual, Tricksters, Response, and Reification

One of the key markers of a liminal period is an upending of the traditional structures and a suspension of the traditional power structures and hierarchies. Chapter 2 demonstrated how the power to employ programming strategies is being shifted to viewers, who, unlike the gatekept period of the multichannel age, now have unlimited choice of what, when, and where to watch. Chapter 3 discussed the challenges of quantifying those viewers and their curatorial viewing behaviors in a way that makes sense for and to the traditional stakeholders and financiers of the television industry. This chapter explores the major activities and actors of "the industry" itself: its organization and revenue streams; its rationalized systems of series development, production and distribution; the disruptions caused by the entrance of players from outside the traditional industry into these activities; and the ways in which all of these televisors are now approaching the distribution of their programs in screen-agnostic ways that accommodate, seek, and target the contemporary viewer/curator.

"The Industry" has long been the term used to denote the producers of televisual content. It is a metonymic term that refers to the companies, technical workers, talent, sound stages, equipment, and economic, creative, and cultural processes that lead to the production of an end product designed to entertain or inform and, for the first sixty-five years of its existence, to be consumed exclusively via the television "set." The recipients of this entertainment "paid" for the programming through their attention (or presumed exposure) to advertisements and those revenues went back to the producers for the creation of more content. As cable and satellite systems developed, some viewers paid for tiers of additional channels, but as discussed, all, except for specific subscription channels, carried advertising.

It is important to note that despite the "sky is falling" rhetoric about the "death of television" that accompanied the "Netflix surge" of 2009–2011; the traditional economic structure of the oligopolized legacy industry remains lucrative and entrenched. In *Captive Audience: The Telecom Industry and Monopoly Power in the New Gilded Age*, Susan Crawford writes "Because conventional television —a $70 billion a year advertising vehicle —offers such a lucrative marketplace, the possibility of substituting online video for cable networks poses risks to both programmers and cable distributors. Cable distributors and media conglomerates have cooperative arrangements in place that channel more than $30 billion in fees paid annually by the distributors to programmers, their largest source of revenue. The distributors, in turn, charge individual subscription rates that keep going up: a typical cable subscriber pays more than $128 a month for video, high-speed Internet access, and phone services, and the average subscription price has increased about 30 percent in the past five years, while household incomes have declined."[1] In short, the majority viewers still engage in the original economic agreements that drive the traditional television economy. Magna Global, an ad-buying and ad-market research firm forecast that 2016 TV ad revenue would "grow 0.5% to $63 billion, excluding special events such as the Olympics and election spending."[2] While OTT licensing fees, product placement, subscriptions, and season-pass models are becoming important revenue streams, on-the-box advertising sales are still a major part of legacy and cable network income and first run popularity on broadcast or cable remains one of the largest predictors of the value of "the backend" of a series.

One way to consider the recent liminal experience of "the industry" is to examine the influx of new producers (the digital tricksters): Netflix, YouTube, Amazon Studios, Hulu, Yahoo, AppleTV. All of these entities are now creating (or have plans and agreements in place to create) "original television." The similarities are clear: all of these entities were, first and foremost, distributors of video or televisual content (or, in the case of Amazon, a distributor of "everything"). In this way their evolution mimics that of the earliest days of broadcasting. The differences lie in their relationship(s) with the traditional industry producers and the ability of producers and distributors to maximize profits through lifecycle management and windowing.³ On the one hand, this is an opportunity: "the changes in the industrial norms and conditions of production ... yield substantial implications for the creative possibilities of culture industries."⁴ On the other, it requires traditional broadcasters to reconsider their identities as well as their practices. Will they continue to conceive of themselves as "entities bound to previous norms of program acquisition, distribution and scheduling?"⁵ Therefore, while liminality allows for the questioning, subversion, and reconfiguration of traditional forms of authority, new industry actors have had to grapple with many of the same challenges the legacy players did in their formative years. What may ultimately come to pass is the reestablishment and reification of the original fiduciary arrangements in renewed and transformed forms.

The structure of the linear, legacy OTB industry

As discussed in Chapter 2, the large majority of on the box (OTB) viewers experience television monolithically—a first run episode of *The Big Bang Theory* on CBS, an off net rerun of *The Big Bang Theory* on WPIX, a cable syndicated episode of *The Big Bang Theory* on TBS, it is all *The Big Bang Theory* to them. "Not so fast" Sheldon Cooper would respond—"the distributors of those three episodes are enmeshed in completely different yet related economic relationships to each other, the viewer and Chuck Lorre ... and Jim Parsons' residual check." These differing relationships depend on which traditional OTB content deliverer (broadcast, cable, subscription, or satellite) is bringing content to the box.

The structure and system of broadcast television distribution remains the same as it has been since its establishment in the post–World War II period because of its dependence upon geographically limited over the air (OTA) signal transmission. Locally television broadcasters are licensed by the Federal Communications Commission (FCC) to distribute (digitally broadcast) a television signal in a particular Designated Market Area (DMA) of which there are 210.⁶ All of the legacy networks (ABC, CBS, NBC) own and operate (O&O) locally licensed broadcasters in major markets (New York, Los

Angeles, Chicago, among others). Local stations not owned and operated (O&O) by a network are most commonly part of a Station Group but may also be owned independently. Station Groups are larger media companies that own regional collections of local stations and may negotiate network affiliation or syndication deals for all stations that they own at once. Group ownership was both made easier and favored by the 1996 Telecommunications Act and is the more financially efficient form of ownership for companies with the resources to purchase and run multiple television stations.[7] Network affiliation means that the locally licensed station (or the Station Group that owns it) makes an agreement with a network to carry its programming during primetime hours (8:00–11:00 p.m. Monday through Saturday and 7:00–11:00 p.m. on Sunday). This agreement means that the local broadcaster is receiving high-production value nationally distributed and advertised programming in return for access to its geographically fixed audience. What may be surprising to learn is that networks pay their affiliates for the time they program (a payment called "net-comp") so network affiliates are receiving programming and a payment from the network in return for carrying the network's programming (and advertising) to their audiences.[8] In addition to the programming (which carries advertisements presold by the networks), the local affiliate also receives a small amount of ad time in the show that it can use for local promotions or sell to local advertisers.

Cable companies have exclusive contracts (franchises) with local municipalities to provide cable service to residences in a particular area (and maintain the physical connections required by these systems). Cable companies are owned by multiple system operators (MSOs) which are increasingly owned by the same corporate conglomerates that own the content producers (Comcast/NBCU, Charter-TimeWarner). Cable operators buy the monthly service of cable networks (and the programming they contain) "wholesale" from channel owners based on a "per subscriber" calculation (a "carriage fee"). The MSO then bundles these channels into collections (tiers of programming) that it sells to subscribers at a marked up price. Cable networks have additional revenue streams that broadcast networks traditionally have not since in addition to carriage fees they receive advertising revenue.[9]

Satellite systems tend to operate regionally rather than locally, but their fiduciary structure is essentially identical to cable's in that they are buying channels wholesale from their owners and then retailing them to subscribers in tiers of service that contain "precurated" channel offerings. In both situations, tiers will be curated by the cable or satellite company in such a ways as to blend popular and less popular channels in a mix that is both economically fortuitous for the MSO and also encouraging of customers' subscribing to higher and more expensive tiers of service to gain access to "everything" they want to see. (In other words, a subscriber will pay for a particular tier of service so as to ensure that he or she gets AMC and the Discovery channel, but will also receive channels that he or she has little to no interest in watching (and thus does not).

For much of the cable industry's existence, MSOs could carry the signals of the local broadcasters in their areas (network affiliated or not) for free. In fact, they were required by law to carry them (the "must carry" laws). As of the mid-1990s, those laws have expired and local broadcasters now have the option to negotiate "retransmission fees" with MSOs or, they may use the granting of carriage to the MSO in return for other advantages (e.g., the free carrying of digital subchannels or cable networks that are part of their broadcast network's corporate family). This has allowed broadcast networks an additional revenue stream that has helped boost their income during the same period of audience movement to other viewing venues. The growth in "retrans" revenue has been key to the continued solvency of broadcasters through the post-network era. "It has been estimated that in the 2012–2016 time period TV stations will be paid over $18.2 billion in retrans revenues, of which the top five broadcast network owners could then be allocated over $9.2 billion. During that same period, we have estimated that TV stations would generate over $106 billion and broadcast networks could take in $91.8 billion in advertising revenue, making retrans revenue an important component of revenue but by no means the largest. By 2016, retrans revenues are projected to account for 21% of TV station ad revenues and 14% of TV network ad revenues."[10] Most recently, as can be seen by the Comcast/NBCUniversal and Charter-Time Warner deals, the distributors and the content producers are increasingly part of the same conglomerate family, so intricately linked that revenue streams from the distribution of properties and the advertising sold against them flows back to the producers who then put the money back into the production of additional content.

Pay channels such as HBO, Showtime, and Starz are retailed directly to the consumer and often subsidized by the MSO which may offer "free months" of the paid service as a selling point to increase the subscription base of its other tiers of service (since in order to receive the pay channels one must be a cable or satellite subscriber). Pay channels do not carry traditional advertising spots and therefore are more concerned with acquiring or producing properties that will increase subscriptions due to their scarcity (pay channels sharply restrict access and do not license first-run content to syndication or OTT outlets). Several key attributes distinguish these subscription or pay-channels from broadcast and standard cable networks. Most obviously, they are not advertiser-supported, nor FCC regulated in terms of content. Viewers purchase their programming as an additional monthly fee on their cable or satellite bill and thus they pay directly for the entire content of the channel each month (as opposed to an a la carte episode-based pay-per-view (PPV) pricing structure). As a result, the pay networks have revenue streams and financing models that are considerably different from those of a broadcast or cable network—the range of "targeted programming interests enables the networks to use the subscription fees of boxing fans to help finance original series, the fees of those subscribing for original series to buy movie rights, the fees of those subscribing to see original drama series help supplement documentary series' costs, and so on, thereby creating a radically different economic situation and, consequently, programming environment."[11]

The success of a pay network, of course, is based upon its subscription numbers and the nature of the subscription relationship creates different fiduciary concerns. "How many or what type of viewers watch specific content takes on decreased importance for subscription networks; a willingness to subscribe affords viewers their value rather than the possession of particular demographic features important to advertisers."[12] Thus, subscription networks are less concerned with the specific shows their paid viewers watch, and more concerned that the viewers find sufficient value in "some aspect of the programming" to maintain the subscription.[13] What all subscription networks want to avoid is "churn" or seasonal "churn" by subscribers who only subscribe to a pay channel for the period of time that a new season of a show they are interested in watching is on and then cancel their subscription once the season has ended.¹⁴ The economic threat of "churn" affects all subscription-based entities, especially those that do not accept advertising and have no other revenue streams beyond their subscriber base. Therefore, in the online SVOD realm, churn is a much bigger problem for Netflix than it is for Hulu Plus or Amazon Instant Video. Hulu Plus accepts ads and has the additional support of its industry owners behind it and Amazon Instant Video is a benefit of Amazon Prime membership which is enmeshed in the etailers other marketing activities. No one is going to cancel their Amazon Prime membership and not reactivate it until the new season of *Transparent* drops.

Television development, production, distribution, syndication

The system of television production and distribution involves three separate but linked entities: producers who work directly with teams of artists that create the shows, studios that finance the shows and networks, which deliver the shows to the viewers.¹⁵ All of these entities operate in fiduciary relationships with each other that ultimately serve whatever conglomerate/parent company owns, has a financial interest in, or is in contractual agreement with the entity.

The six major studios (20th Century Fox Television Studios, ABC Television Studios, CBS/Paramount, Sony Pictures Television, Universal Media Studios and Warner Bros) develop, finance and own the majority of scripted (meaning not "reality") television —in other words, one hour dramas and half hour sitcoms. Once the shows are completed and "picked up" for distribution by a broadcast or cable network, the network pays the studio a per-episode license fee for the right to the "first run" broadcast of the series. This gives the network exclusive right to the premiere broadcast of the series and a specified number (usually two) of on-network reruns.¹⁶ It is particularly important to note that because the producing studio and the broadcast or cable network are all owned by the media conglomerate the money stays "in the corporate family" so to speak or, even if it is "picked up" by a competing network, the revenue stream comes back to the media conglomerate (as do the rights to syndication or further monetization of the property).

This traditional funding system is one of deficit financing: the per-episode license fee paid by the network to the studio does not cover the entire per-episode cost of production. In other words, studios lose money on the first run deal for every episode of every show they produce. What the studios are banking on is that the show will be a success and go into syndication on cable, foreign television systems, OTA channel groups, local channels (and now OTT, since Netflix and Amazon Instant Video have become part of the syndication food chain). The expectation is that successful properties will turn a substantial and lasting profit in the "aftermarket" or on the "backend."[17] Successful shows pay for themselves many times over—such as early seasons of *Law & Order SVU* currently playing on the USA network. The production costs of these 18-year-old episodes are long paid for so the syndication fee is pure and lasting profit to Dick Wolf/Universal Television. Additionally, syndication deals may be geographically exclusive for local broadcast stations or station groups, but they are not exclusive for off-net cable syndication, internet, and the like. Therefore, when the fifth season of *The Big Bang Theory* is in syndication on the local OTA Fox affiliate in New York, an independent local OTA affiliate in Phoenix, AZ, national cable syndication on TBS and Hulu (among many other venues), the producing studio is receiving licensing fees from all of these media outlets. Other financing arrangements, such as barter time (advertising time given to the local broadcaster instead of or for a discounted license fee) are also sometimes negotiated, depending on the projected popularity of the show and its ability to draw an audience.[18] The main point is that when a network is considering whether or not to "pick up" a show, it is thinking about the show's "legs and repeatability."[19] How it does in its first season will be important but more important will be: will it make it to the all-important 100th episode and syndication? As will be seen, some genres have more legs and repeatability than others and some genres seem better suited to the viewing behaviors (bingeing) encouraged by particular delivery venues (web-based video on demand).

Exceptions and innovations are, of course, present (such as Amazon Studios "open submission" system); however, the basic way in which network or "industry produced" programs were/are developed follows a fairly consistent process and timetable that was developed by and for linear television: development (July–October); pilot season (January–May); upfronts (May) premieres—September, or sometime later for shows deemed "midseason replacements."[20] While the traditional "broadcast season" upon which this calendar is based (24–26 weeks beginning in September and concluding in May) has been substantially transformed by the innovations of summer reality TV premieres in the 2000s and the entrance of non-broadcasters (Netflix, Amazon Studios) into the televisual landscape, it persists as very entrenched industry practice.

During the development season, networks plan their "development slate." This is the list of projects and properties that the network has determined will maximize their viewership, reinforce their brand identity, bolster existing shows' ratings, and capitalize on the success of similar shows. There are many reasons for shows landing on development slates and many sources for ideas. Not surprisingly, many of them will be derivative or from known entities[21] (a practice that supports and is supported by the engagement of viewers via the "mere exposure" effect discussed in Chapter 2). Several interesting points to note: networks are not buying shows, they are buying ideas for shows (pitches). Also, they are not buying ideas directly from writers (or YouTube stars), they are buying pitches from studios who buy pitches from producers who buy ideas from writers (or YouTube stars).[22] Lastly, many of these shows are acquired for the following year's season, so networks may be attempting to predict what will best position them in the marketplace 12–18 months out.[23]

The sheer volume is staggering: "In a single year, a network often hears over 1,000 pitches for new comedies and dramas. Of those 1,000 ideas, each network buys approximately 100 to 130 projects."[24] Of these projects, fifty to sixty are contracted for pilot scripts (a "sample" episode of the series, usually, but not always, the first episode to be shot and aired). By January, twenty to thirty pilot scripts are selected to be produced. The economics of pilot season are even more staggering as "collectively, broadcasters often spend over $300 million per year in pilot production."[25] And, clearly all pilots are not "picked up"—in fact most of them are not. If a pilot is passed on, the producer may try to sell it to a competing network but the resale market for pilots is not particularly strong (why would a network take something a competitor has passed on when it has already invested substantial sums in its first choice shows?)[26]

While there may seem to be few guidelines for the choosing of particular pilots over others, the economies of scale involved in not just the production of the pilot, but the continued commitment of resources to the production of a series often supports the success of imitators of recent successes. This is nothing new in the world of entertainment and is part of what is commonly called a "genre cycle." Genre cycles are a way of periodizing television through an analysis of its most popular programming. What this reveals is that genre cycles are begun by an *innovation* which creates a disruption in or change to existing programming by introducing a show that deviates in a substantially big enough way to call attention to itself. If that innovative show catches on and becomes popular, the cycle will take root and *imitators* of that show will begin to be developed by competing producers and networks. As the schedules fill with these similar shows, *saturation* occurs during which an overabundance of this "type" of show can be found across multiple networks and distribution outlets. As the popularity of these shows wane, a new *innovation* is sought and the process begins again. I would argue that genre cycles are somewhat irrelevant to OTT producers, except as a barometer of what other producers are investing in. However, as will be seen, the long tail created by OTT distribution may make genre *silos* rather than genre *cycles* the more relevant way to track dramaturgical evolution.

Once a pilot is picked up, the network "commits to paying the pilot's license fee, usually about 60–70 percent of the pilot's budget (the remaining 30 to 40 percent comes from the studio; this is the deficit of 'deficit financing')."[27] While twenty to thirty pilots may ultimately be shot during each year's pilot season, most networks pick up only four to eight new shows per season. Since they expect about half of the new shows to fail, networks will initially order six to thirteen episodes including the pilot. If the show does well, the network will order additional episodes to finish the season.[28] If not, it could be replaced by another as-yet-unbroadcast pilot midseason whether or not its full order of episodes have been broadcast.

Taking the shows to market: Upfronts

The primetime upfront presentations are held in May in New York, where most of the media buyers (and advertising agencies) are located. These advertising and television industry-only events are presentations where networks reveal their fall schedules of returning and new shows to advertisers, their affiliate stations and the press. The goal is to create as much buzz and interest in their upcoming shows as possible and to sell the majority of their advertising inventory for the fall season. Upfront presentations are extravagant, usually attended by current network stars (and known names with new shows to promote) and are where the networks focus on putting their best face on and foot forward—regardless of recent or projected performance.

During the upfront buying season (which can last until August), advertisers can buy commercial time on shows airing during the fall season at a discount (usually about 15% off). The advantage for networks is that they are able to sell 65–75 percent of their prime time available spots (called "avails") and thus be guaranteed income and advertiser support prior to the fall premieres.[29] On the advertising side, media planners will work closely with media buyers and account executives to determine the best shows on which to purchase time, reviewing either past ratings performance (for returning shows) or projected target audience numbers for new shows based on talent, similar show performance, timeslot, and network ranking overall.

The agency will tell the network the client's budget as well as the desired target audience, including any particular weeks ("flightings") during which they would definitely want to run campaigns on certain shows.[30] The network will respond with a package of shows that it believes will deliver this audience and negotiations begin for a CPM rate—a cost per thousand of viewers that the network will guarantee the spots will receive.[31] Nielsen rankings from the previous season (of continuing series) are considered, but all metrics for these shows are scrutinized. As discussed in Chapter 3, since 2014 the C7 rating (commercial viewing "live" plus up to seven days of time-shifted viewing) is the primary one upon which upfront CPMs are calculated.[32] Negotiations take place on several fronts. Companies willing to commit to an entire season may receive additional discounts, networks may request advertisers to buy sometime on less-popular shows in return for prominent placement on higher performing shows. Once the program mix and CPMs have been determined, the contracts will be drawn up and the network will "hold" that time for the advertiser. Most deals struck during upfronts guarantee GRPs (gross ratings points) which are "used to measure the exposure to one or more programs or commercials, without regard to multiple exposures of the same advertising to individuals. One GRP = 1% of TV households."[33] If the advertisements do not achieve the promised number of GRPs, then the network will rerun the ads as "make goods" to "make up" the missed GRPs. The advertiser has less control over "make goods" placement as they often comprise less-attractive timeslots from the scatter market.[34] Therefore, accurate audience measurement is crucial for media buyers since: "a successful agency avoids make-goods by accurately estimating and buying time in programs for which the anticipated ratings and the actual ratings are most likely to be similar."[35] If the "make goods" are unacceptable to the advertiser, the network may actually do a "give back" and refund the advertiser's money.[36] If, by chance, the program over-delivers on the GRPs several possibilities arise: either the advertiser is happy and nothing changes, the network uses the higher performance as a bargaining "chit" in future negotiations or the network "commits to a specific number of GRPs for the season, and when the commitment is satisfied, the remaining commercial time is sold to other advertisers."[37] Of these options, the first is the most likely to happen as networks want to maintain positive relationships with their advertisers.

Advertising inventory not sold during the upfronts becomes part of the scatter market which is not discounted (and can be as much as 40% higher than the upfront market), does not guarantee "make goods" if GRPs are not met and does not allow buyers to cancel their ad buy without losing money.[38] The last market is the "spot" market which is the least desirable way to purchase ad time. While the available inventory may include desirable individual commercial slots, the spot market is limited to unsold time on hand and also much more expensive, especially for shows that have outperformed expectations.[39] If networks do not sell all of their ad inventory, or they are delivered an episode that runs short (while the maximum running times of hour and half-hour shows are forty-four and twenty-two minutes, respectively, shorter episodes are, on occasion be delivered to network by the production company) they will use the left over inventory for "make goods" or to promote their own shows or shows on their other channels. Traditionally, none of these negotiations have allowed for advertisers to choose the specific "pod" (commercial break) in which their ads will air. This is beginning to change in the wake of the C7 Nielsen which has enabled advertisers "to see not only which pods—but which positions *in* those pods—are the most valuable commercial slots."[40]

Syndication and the aftermarket

Syndication is a means of program distribution that involves the direct distribution of a show to a local broadcaster or cable network by the owner of the property. Syndication takes several forms, but the principle distinctions for our purposes here are the difference between first-run syndication and "off network" (now often called "aftermarket") syndication as it is these practices that have been most intervened upon by the explosion of OTT viewing options. Until the mid-2000s, the "lifecycle management" of a show was relatively clear and relied upon exclusive access through an established set of windows. The revolution in these practices, which spurred a complete reconsideration and reenvisioning of licensing deals was TV series video on demand (VOD) and per-episode downloads, neither of which existed prior to 2006.[41]

First run syndication

The easiest way to define first run syndication is to name representative examples: *Ellen, Jeopardy, Family Feud, Oprah, The View, The Chew* ... these shows are original productions, often produced daily or with the expectation of daily viewing which are distributed directly to station groups by their producers. Local broadcasters use these first-run syndicated shows to fill their nonnetwork programmed hours. The fiduciary relationship between the broadcast outlet and the content owner is usually "cash plus barter" so "in exchange for the right to broadcast particular programs, stations pay some cash but also surrender some advertising time back to the distributor."[42] The distributor then sells national advertising which is inserted into the episodes as delivered to the local broadcaster. It should be noted that the distributors are also conglomerated and in corporate families of the legacy broadcasters. CBS Television Distribution, 20th Century Television, and Disney/ABC Domestic Television rank among the top five syndicators to the US market.

Off-net/Aftermarket syndication

Off-net syndication is where deficit financing has traditionally paid off—it is where shows begin to turn a profit for their producers in the licensing fees paid to their content owners by local broadcasters and cable networks that seek syndicated content with a track record to fill out their programming schedules. Shows are generally not syndicated until they have reached 80–100 episodes which is sufficient for the licensee to "strip" the show five days a week at a particular time without repeating episodes for at least six months. The off-network rerun, argues Kompare, "has long been one of television's most essential program forms. It remains a viable part of syndication, even as the very nature of both 'television' and 'syndication' becomes less tangible with every new digital distribution venture."[43] "The place of off-network drama series ... has never been stable" writes Kompare, "syndicated hours have historically been difficult to schedule in daily syndication and have never drawn the size or makeup of audience that sitcoms demand."[44] One hour self-contained dramatic narratives (police procedurals like the *Law & Order* and *CSI* franchises) found off-net success on cable networks, although that market shifted as cable networks began to engage in more original prime time production from the mid-2000s onward. What is also unique to off-net syndication in the linear legacy age of television is that the "net" pretty much exclusively refers to a broadcast network. "Network shows go to cable or syndication, but there are few if any examples of shows moving upstream from cable to network."[45] The content needs of OTT television distributors and the licensing fees they have been willing to pay have expanded the aftermarkets of all television shows substantially—in ways that devalue certain parts of the syndication market while opening new venues for series previously thought to have little-to-no aftermarket besides a DVD release.

Traditional linear programming strategies: Flow, daypart, and genre

Network and cable programmers engage in a variety of strategies to arrange their programs into configurations that they think will encourage viewers to not only tune in, but to also stay with their channel for more than one show. (This is the "flow" that Raymond Williams first theorized in 1975, and which has become a guiding concept in the analysis of television and programming strategies.[46]) Network programmers have always been keenly aware of the role their work plays in making their networks' schedule of programming competitive. The strategies they employ: block booking, counter-programming, hammocking, tent-poling, and lead ins have relied upon a limited number of clearly identified competitors, whose offerings at a particular time could be quantified, analyzed, and then strategically countered. Naturally, the more dispersed the audience, the more ineffective and in some cases irrelevant these strategies have become. Nonetheless, programming decisions (where a show will ultimately "go" and what it will be surrounded by and up against) inform pilot season and pickups and are controlled and affected by a variety of traditional and new structures and practices all of which are designed to reach target audiences and strengthen the network brand.

Dayparts

Dayparts are the traditional organizing principle of the linearly scheduled programming day, and have been since the dawn of radio. They are used not only to distinguish which parts of the day will be provided to network affiliates by the network, but also in the setting of advertising rates since certain times of day have traditionally presumed larger audiences than others. There are eight major dayparts that divide a 24-hour period:

Time	Daypart
5:00 a.m.–9:00 a.m.	Early Morning
9:00 a.m.–4:00 p.m.	Daytime
4:00 p.m.–7:00 p.m.	Early Fringe
7:00 p.m.–8:00 p.m.	Prime Access
8:00 p.m.–11:00 p.m.	Primetime
11:00 p.m.–11:35 p.m.	Late News
11:35 p.m. 2:00 a.m.	Late Fringe
2:00 a.m.–5:00 a.m.	Overnight[4/]

While the particular programming carried by a particular station during a discrete daypart may be similar, the specific shows that appear on a station (and therefore, the advertising rates), are, of course, controlled by a series of interlocking criteria and depend on the individual station's relationship with a larger network. For example, WNBC (New York) being an O&O station of the NBC network, will carry network content such as *The Today Show* during the early morning daypart, and *The Tonight Show* during late fringe. An independent broadcast station in the same market may carry off-network syndicated reruns such as *Seinfeld* or *The Big Bang Theory* during the same dayparts. Additionally, the amount of programming provided during a particular daypart varies from network to network. Fox affiliates air local news at 10:00 p.m. when their network-supplied primetime programming ends, and counter program reruns during the late news daypart when legacy network affiliates are airing their local news.

Another major function that the daypart has traditionally served is to organize the broadcast day for viewers. Since the early days of radio, listeners were conditioned to expect that daytime serials (soaps) would be broadcast during the daytime, with the programming becoming more family and child-oriented toward the later afternoon, as children returned home from school, or as parents returned from work and the family prepared for dinner and the evening hours. In other words—there is (or has been) a direct correlation between daypart and genre.

Genre transformation in the post-network post-box era

It is important to consider genre as a part of programming strategy because the two have historically been linked. Dayparts communicated genre expectations to linear television viewers—conditioning them to expect first-run syndicated talk shows, soap operas, or court shows to be scheduled during the day and higher production value, bigger named star comedies, and dramas during primetime. Traditionally, genres were bounded by a fairly inflexible set of rules and characteristics that were used to contain and cohere narrative elements, ones that make—the "loglines" of *TV Guide Magazine* simple for viewers to understand for instance. This was a logical and efficient way to manage narrative in an environment with fewer viewing choices.

Genre distinctions range from the broad to the specific to the hybrid—the most obvious large categories are drama and comedy, but subgenres within these broader categories (domestic sitcom, workplace sitcom, police procedural, medical, fantasy, etc.) are often used to describe shows. Beyond content-related characteristics, there are other ways of categorizing genre common to the television industry. These usually categorize something about the show's "form" (half hour, hour, variety), which help programmers classify the show. And, there are yet other genre descriptors ("quality") that rely upon either opinion or a generally accepted, if arbitrary list of attributes rather than being tied to the narrative or thematic elements of the shows being described.

As the daypart has become increasingly irrelevant and the citizen programmers take their power, genre has been freed from daypart-based constraints. As television begins to be originated and distributed entirely off-the-box, it is also freed from the expectations and conventions of traditional broadcast forms. What we are now observing is the purported death of the longest-playing genres (soap opera) conterminously with the development of genre-hybrids and/or popularization of genres that would have been unthinkable (or commercially unsuccessful) during the traditional network era. These new niche genres have found sustainable audiences off-the-box and on the internet. Further transformations in genre and audience expectation have been fostered by the realization that different modes of delivery and accessibility encourage different forms of consumption which are uniquely advantageous for certain genres over others.

Perhaps one of the most interesting situations through which one can discuss and see the effect of the "death of the daypart" on the perceptions and practices of television producers, programmers, and their audiences is the decline of the daytime soap opera genre. Soap operas, which rely upon a consistently scheduled and continual broadcast of their sequential episodes, and which have little to no backend or aftermarket syndication revenue streams, have not negotiated the "platish or perish" transition well. While enjoying some of the most dedicated fan bases of any television genres, they have suffered audience erosion due to demographic shifts in their audiences. While their ratings performance has been equal to other daytime television offerings, the economies of scale involved in their production have made them "too expensive" for the networks to produce. The many schemes suggested to "save the soaps" have largely operated from either the traditional advertiser-supported model, or from a fiduciary model that is still traditional in its construction—such as moving the soaps to a narrowcast cable channel (although Soapnet ceased operation on December 31, 2013).

The decline of shows categorized as "soaps" has not, however, led to a disappearance of their defining generic conventions from television. In fact, I would suggest that the networks began coopting and integrating the narrative elements of daytime into their nighttime programming as early as the mid-to-late 1980s, as legacy broadcasters strove to counter a loss of viewers to an increasing number of cable networks. The resulting genre cycle, which Robert Thompson, writing in 1996, called "quality TV," borrowed heavily from the soap opera and transformed traditional evening genres such as the police procedural, courtroom story, and medical drama.

Thompson identified twelve attributes of "quality TV," the most germane for our purposes being the following:*

- Usually has a quality pedigree—creatives with track records in other high-end culture industries or, television itself.
- Attracts an audience with "blue chip" demographics—"upscale, well-educated, urban-dwelling viewers" that advertisers want to reach.
- Tends to have a large ensemble cast.
- Has a memory—characters develop and change as the series goes on, events and details from prior episodes are referred to or used subsequently to advance the action. (Another way of saying this would be "seriality.")
- Tends to be literary and writer-based.

---

* So as not to short the "completest" reader, the other four attributes of "quality TV" that Thompson identified are: "Best defined by what it is not, so *Hill Street Blues* was not your 'traditional' police procedural that introduced one crime and solved it within the forty-eight minute hour; (In the 1980s at least) The show must undergo a noble struggle against profit-mongering networks and nonappreciative audiences, or takes a season or two to find an audience; Creates a new genre by mixing old ones; Is self-conscious – may also be self-referential about being a televisual text."

- Has subject matter that tends toward the controversial or the contemporary social issue. Tends to have the perspective of liberal humanism.
- Aspires toward "realism."
- Usually showered with awards and critical acclaim.[48]

Fully four of these attributes: an ensemble cast, having a memory or seriality, being writer-based and having subject matter that addresses contemporary social issues, have inhered in the soap opera form since its inception. The emphasis on the writer and quality pedigree of its creative team foreshadows the reification of what we would now call a "showrunner" as a brand, since the first iterations of this new genre (*Hill Street Blues, St. Elsewhere, L.A. Law*) became calling cards for their creator/executive producer, Steven Bochco. The other qualities clearly describe recent innovations in original programming by Netflix, Hulu Plus, YouTube, and Amazon Studios.

If we consider the last twenty years or so, since the coining of the term "quality TV" we see a fall off in the number of shows that could be classified by this term as the reality television genre cycle came into vogue. At the same time, quality TV has borrowed at least two generic elements from soap opera—ensemble cast and seriality—which could be said to be responsible for the success of the highest rated reality programs, since one can see these characteristics in shows such as *Survivor, Big Brother, Real World*, and the like. As the reality cycle began to wane in the mid-2000s, (and alternative viewing spaces became available) there was an increase in the production of shows that could be classified as "Quality TV" by the linear networks such as *Brothers and Sisters, Grey's Anatomy, The Good Wife* and most recently *American Crime Story, Scandal*, and *Empire*.

The main commonality among all of these shows is, of course, seriality. The importance of seriality is emphasized in the criticism about quality TV and the connection between the soap opera and literary forms that encompass long narratives such as the novel. Thompson traces the movement of the serialized form into primetime series to *Dallas* which premiered in 1977, and owed its success entirely to its use of the soap opera form.[49] The success of imitators and spin-offs such as *Knots Landing, Dynasty, Falcon Crest*, and *Flamingo Road* "gave a memory to the entire medium" writes Thompson—so "many dramatic shows—even those that weren't exactly soaps—began employing ongoing story lines."[50] In fact, writes Thompson, "As the Golden Age of television (the variety shows and anthology shows of the 1950s) was rooted in the legitimate stage, quality dramas were rooted in the soap opera."[51] The complexity of these shows comes from the "slow layering of events, character traits, and other visual and dramatic details over the entire run of these series" and notes that "these slowly accruing stories could only be told in the serial form. More importantly, they could only be told on television."[52]

This last point is particularly important—they could only be told on television, because of the structure of the industry in this period. All major industry distributors abided by a twenty-six week season which ran September–May and shows ran according to fixed weekly schedules that, except for mid-season replacements, were consistent. Reruns were scheduled during summer hiatuses that gave shows that performed poorly in their first run a chance to build an audience without competing against new first-run content. This system was substantially eroded through the growing practice of premiering new content during the summer, a strategy pioneered by the "fourth network" FOX during the late 1980s and firmly entrenched when CBS premiered *Survivor* during the summer of 2000. The success of highly serialized original programming on the OTT providers and the new forms of consumption (bingeing) and distribution (the drop) is perhaps the ultimate confirmation that complex narratives are extremely viable and desirable program forms with the power to continue to attract interested viewers to new venues of televisual consumption.

Writing in *Variety* in 2013, Cynthia Littleton states that *The Good Wife*, being a "highly serialized show" was "unlikely to generate big bucks in traditional off-network syndication."[53] However, this same attribute made it "tailor-made for the new breed of digital off-network buyers looking for the soapy, social media-friendly serialized skeins that invite binge viewing."[54] Thus Netflix, Hulu, and Amazon Instant Video provide unique off-network sites that according to Leslie Moonves, "serve the content needs of best-in-class partners while realizing the full syndication value for a high-quality series. In addition, the potential for catch-up viewing across multiple platforms can provide incremental value to future broadcasts on CBS."[55] While some internet video deals are emphasizing scarcity and exclusivity (*Downton Abbey* on

Amazon Instant Video, the recent *South Park*-Hulu deal), other deals are considerably more windowed. "Nowadays, most of the time if they pay a high ticket price, they will get all the rights, but now you're looking at deals where you split it up more. You slice and dice it even more than you did before where you'll sell it to a Netflix or an Amazon and then sell it to a cable [network], then sell it in syndication."[56]

From genre cycle to genre silo—the long tail of television?

What appears to be developing now is a situation in which certain "types" of shows (those that are highly serialized) succeed on certain viewing platforms (those that encourage and facilitate binge viewing) and other types (procedurals, stand-alones, low budget slice-of-life reality) on others (OTB viewing). There is still a demonstrable market for what Kompare calls "banal" or "habitual" TV—"'just see TV' rather than 'must see TV.'"[57] Another way to look at this is that the increase in productions fostered by a multiplicity of distribution options and consumption platforms has made room for the production of content that serves all viewer needs from ambient/company viewing to focused/immersive involvement. This may result in the replacement of genre cycles spread across multiple outlets by genre silos found on one particular viewing destination and the simultaneous production of a variety of viable shows that will all eventually find an audience on net, off net, or OTT- a situation that would have been unthinkable and financially impossible during the network era of broadcasting.

The digital disruptors—interventions and new conventions

Van Gennep, Gregory Bateson, and Victor Turner theorized the mythical figure of the "trickster" as a bringer of both disorder and culture.[58] Trickster figures actually predate anthropology and exist as far back as Greek myth (Hermes and Mercury). They are, quite simply "boundary crossers" who are catalysts for exchange and trade.[59] All communities have boundaries and the trickster is always "at the gates of the city and the gates of life, making sure there is commerce."⁶⁰ The trickster stays on the periphery, not the center (for they can get more done by focusing on change rather than being the center of attention) and they "might help someone see into the heart of things, and that they therefore have a touch of the prophet about them."⁶¹ This prophetic skill is not so much the ability to see into the future and prognosticate how things will be, but rather to consider the grand possibility of the future—since the trickster is asocial and often amoral—not bound by tradition or rules. "Trickster reveals the plentitude of this world; if he then disappears, we see the same revelation repeated in the multiple ways human beings understand the plenitude of things once conventional understanding has been lifted."⁶² He/she is a liminal figure as well as a cultural hero who continues "to keep our world lively and give it the flexibility to endure."⁶³ In fact, argues Lewis Hyde, trickster is a requirement for a viable and durable culture because his/her function is "to uncover and disrupt the very things that cultures are based on."⁶⁴ Netflix's Ted Sarandos, Amazon's Jeff Bezos, and AwesomenessTV/YouTube's Brian Robbins do not necessarily embody all of the attributes of the trickster figure. After all, "actual individuals are always more complicated than the archetype, and more complicated than its local version too."⁶⁵ But they have functioned in ways that are unique to the trickster in the transformative effects they have had upon the traditional television industry structures and practices.

The successful debut of Netflix's streaming only service in the fall of 2010 resulted in the popularization of the acronym OTT ("over the top") "to acknowledge concerns that cable subscribers would use Netflix and other broadband streaming and downloading distribution services as an alternative to cable subscriptions."⁶⁶ YouTube, Netflix, Vudu, Vimeo, and other early web-streaming sites acclimated viewers to cross-platform viewing. Amazon piloted an entirely new pilot season and bundling VOD content with existing e-commerce products. While legacy OTB programmers attempted to embrace mobile and web viewing through the creation of transmedia paratexts, branded apps from OTT platforms that provided uninterrupted streaming of high-quality long-form content obviated the need to create special content for mobile, moving clips, and "spreadable media" to YouTube and the realm of social media portals and platforms.

Netflix

Netflix was, of course, the first OTT VOD system to begin creating disruptions for the traditional linear television industry. Netflix began streaming video in 2008 just as residential subscriptions to broadband began to increase.[67] Thus it created a substantial "long tail" of alternative viewing options for US viewers and a new revenue stream for television content owners and producers—at that time solely the broadcast and cable networks.* Netflix licensed entire series of current and past television shows for streaming distribution via its online platform. However, in addition to popular guaranteed money makers, Netflix was also open to licensing shows that had a very difficult time in the traditional "off-net" market, because they did not have enough episodes to make syndication fees "worth it" for channel groups and local stations, because they originated on cable as opposed to broadcast, because they were one-hour long, serialized, or because their OTB ratings performance had not been suitably high to guarantee a sufficient traditional off-net syndication audience.

Netflix internationalized the televisual viewing repertoire through deals with international producers, both English language (three seasons of *The IT Crowd*, a BBC sitcom were licensed by Netflix as well as *Top of the Lake*, an international coproduction of the BBC2, BBC UKTV (Australia), and Sundance Channel, shot in New Zealand and directed by Jane Campion) and producers working in non-English speaking countries willing to provide English-subtitled versions to the American Netflix market. (*Generation War*, a German miniseries that follows the lives of five friends through World War II was licensed by Netflix as well as *Punch* and *Pinocchio*, South Korean television shows that Netflix has made available to the American viewer.)

In addition to creating an "always on" syndication market and a plethora of choice for its subscribers, Netflix also demonstrated a vast and lucrative aftermarket for pretty much all and any televisual content. Freed from the strictures of the linear daypart, television shows from throughout the history of the medium were made available to new and old audiences in perpetual

---

* Netflix, of course, has international aspirations and is now available in 190 countries. Its first intervention was in the United States which is what I address here. The global impact of Netflix and other OTT producer-distributors on the internationalization of the television market is addressed in greater detail in Chapter 6.

"rerun" as it might be. But, of course, key to this was that these reruns were now being pulled to interested niche viewers rather than pushed out to a mass audience. This did not go unnoticed by the legacy networks who began to stream episodes of their content via their own network websites (where they could control pre-roll and other unavoidable advertising as well as receive the revenue from said advertising) and to not renew licensing deals with Netflix. In 2008, Hulu (the OTT industry venture led by NBCUniversal and FOX then later joined by Disney) launched, which further eroded the availability of television streaming licenses to Netflix.

Netflix's response to the curtailment of television streaming licenses by the legacy content producers and owners was to begin producing its own content. This entrance of distributors into production is not only not new, but it is also the reason the legacy networks were created in the first place. The Radio Corporation of America (RCA), the major producer of radio sets for the home in the early 1920s, needed a selling point to convince consumers to invest half a year's salary on a "box" for the living room that, from external inspection was inert and not very interesting looking. RCA's solution was to form NBC—the National Broadcasting Corporation which, through its red and blue networks of affiliated radio stations, broadcast shows (and advertisements) across the United States. Quite simply, the creator of the distribution platform (RCA) entered original production (via the creation of subsidiary NBC) in order to create a selling point for the distribution platform (radio) and to encourage consumers to buy one.*

So it should have come to no surprise to the OTB networks that Netflix responded to the scarcity of attractive content licenses by entering the original content business.[68] Netflix's first forays into original programming were: twenty-six episodes of *House of Cards* directed by David Fincher and starring Kevin Spacey (at a cost of about $4 million an episode); new episodes of the critically acclaimed but cancelled Fox series *Arrested Development* ($2.5

---

* To be sure, I am oversimplifying and sketching out the broadest of broad histories of the development of commercial radio and then television broadcasting here. The important points for our discussions are the industrial relationships between content delivery platform owners and content creators, which explain, in part the movement of digital "sovereigns" into the content-producing spheres. For substantially more detail on the development of broadcasting in the United States, I refer the reader to the work of Susan Douglas, Michele Hilmes, Megan Mullen, Erik Barnouw, James Baughman, Michael Curtin, and Susan Murray among others.

to $3 million an episode); and *Lillehammer,* a Norwegian-American coproduction with Norwegian public broadcaster NRK1.[69] Netflix did not "program" nor "schedule" these shows, it made entire first series available all at once to "watch instantly" even if the show also ran in other configurations. All eight episodes of *Lillehammer* became available for viewing to American Netflix subscribers on February 6, 2012, while the series ran linearly on Norwegian television. Audiences (by which Ted Sarandos means "Netflix subscribers") could choose to "binge watch" the series, or to view it at their leisure—what they were encouraged to do, and practically required to by the narrative form—was to view the eight episodes sequentially. "People need a longer relationship with a show than one or two or three weeks" said Sarandos. "What we do is provide a longer time for shows to come to life for the audience."[70] Sarandos believes that this release pattern allows for shows to find audiences, but also for audiences to view, review, and engage with the episodes and their narratives—they are experiencing, exploring, and creating new ways of viewing.

The common generic element of practically all of Netflix's first original productions is seriality, which binds the viewer to the show, creates an ongoing relationship between the viewer and the show and essentially draws upon all of the narrative and dramaturgic tropes that bound daytime viewers to soaps. The unique all-at-once distribution pattern of Netflix frees the viewer from a schedule-driven consumption of the show without disrupting the experience. Viewers do not need to worry about being "behind" or "missing" episodes—their consumption pattern (i.e., which order they view the shows in) is dictated by the narrative form. Their consumption schedule and experience (when, where, and how) they watch the serialized episodes—is up to the viewer.

The success of this experiment has demonstrated that original programming available solely behind web paywalls is, at least for Netflix, realistic and successful, and led to additional deals for *Orange is the New Black, Bojack Horseman,* and second and third seasons of *House of Cards* and *Lillehammer.* The "backend" of these shows is different from network in that once created and made available, they go into immediate and eternal syndication, remaining accessible and discoverable at Netflix for viewer recommendation in arguably perpetuity. DVD releases of these series have been timed for just before the next season becomes available, thus serving as an advertisement and enticement for non-Netflix subscribers to view, become intrigued, and subscribe.

However, the binge-watching consumption patterns for these shows has both advantages and disadvantages for subscription-based companies. Showtime and HBO have always had to contend with subscriber "churn" after their prestige shows have finished their seasons, but can count on the 12–15 week season to be a period of high viewership and structure their promotions for new programming and other appeals to viewer engagement and loyalty. An *Orange Is the New Black* viewer might consume the entire new season in one day so if the viewer sees Netflix solely as the site of destination viewing of that particular show, he or she may choose to cancel after viewing. To be sure, Netflix can start new runs of original programming whenever it wishes as well as hope that "viewers who liked X also liked" recommendations of titles from their long tail of programming will keep subscribers engaged in between seasons of their favorite original programming. This is crucial for Netflix's continued viability—while it is less vulnerable to churn than the linearly programmed Showtime and HBO, its ability to keep subscribers in between season drops of its most popular shows relies on its library and other offerings—especially in the wake of its summer 2016 price-hike for streaming-only access.

Netflix pays producers for its content based on how many people it thinks will watch a show—the success of the show is based not on Nielsen ratings, but on internal data collected from Netflix servers that show what people watched and how much of a show they watched as well as the user "ratings" that Netflix subscribers assign shows they watch to contribute to Netflix's recommendation algorithm. Since Netflix is not ratings-driven it "doesn't have a traditional network's gaggle of development executives to supervise productions and bicker over scripts. It will even take the highly unusual risk of ordering multiple seasons of a show without a pilot episode."[71] "The worse thing we'll do" according to Sarandos "is create mediocre shows."[72] If that occurs, thanks to the low cost of Netflix's long tail catalog, the shows could still find an audience of viewers who enjoy mediocre programming and have indicated this preference to Netflix's recommendation engine.

In 2013, Netflix became the first online-only content producer to be nominated for the Emmy awards. It was nominated in fourteen categories, with its "flagship" production *House of Cards* receiving the majority of these (nine). Kevin Spacy and Robin Wright were nominated for outstanding actor and actress in a dramatic series, the show itself was nominated for Best Drama, and it was nominated for several creative awards Emmys. Ultimately, Netflix won three of the awards, best Casting and Cinematography at the creative Emmys, but also the award for Best Directing, which was won by David Fincher. Netflix also brought a slate of shows to the 2013 Television Critics Association press tour, further evidence that Netflix's ultimate goal is "to take its place alongside traditional networks as a purveyor of original programming."[73] In presenting the "sizzle" reel to the TCA—arguably the largest gathering of professional television influencers in the United States, Sarandos said: "We're leading the next great wave of change in the medium of TV. We're not trying to destroy it, but evolve it for the current generation and those to come."[74]

In June 2014, Netflix signed a seven-year deal with Chelsea Handler for a series of specials and a talk show which will premiere in 2016.[75] Handler's late-night talk show on E! ran from 2007 to 2014 and averaged 600,000 viewers in its last season.[76] Sarandos said of the deal: "Netflix is looking forward to reimagining the late night talk show for the on-demand generation, starting with the late night part."[77] It is unclear how the show will be scheduled but Netflix insiders have said that "as 'a topical talk show' it would not follow the previous Netflix pattern of posting all episodes at once" and that it could be "described as 'in the style of a late-night show,' if not produced on a late-night time schedule."[78] In this way, upstart trickster Netflix is experimenting with traditional structures and patterns, to see how they might and if they should be transformed. This well could lead to the liminality of liveness.

Amazon Studios

Amazon Studios is a production wing of super e-tailer Amazon and, obviously, aims to produce content specifically for distribution via Amazon Instant Video, preferably to owners of the Amazon Kindle, Amazon Fire, or FireTV. Amazon announced its first "pilot" season in May of 2012 and solicited submissions of pitches for comedy and children's shows. It hired Joe Lewis, formerly of 20th Century Fox and Tara Sorensen from National Geographic

Kids to oversee the "crowd sourced" development process. In the first round, Amazon optioned scripts for "$10,000 within 45 days of submission and awarded an additional $55,000 plus royalties, bonuses and a small percentage of merchandise" to shows it chose to produce.[79] Amazon touted this as a "twist on the traditional closed-door approach to development in Hollywood" since decisions would be "heavily informed by feedback its users will provide when given the option via Amazon Instant Video to view animatics or video excerpts of proposed projects."[80] In 2013, the first pilot season yielded *Alpha House*, a comedy about US senators who become roommates, *Betas*, a comedy set in Silicon Valley, *Browsers*, a comedy about a web startup in Manhattan, *Those Who Can't*, *Onion News Empire*, *Dark Minions*, *Supernatural*, *Zombieland*, and the children's shows *Annebots*, *Creative Galaxy Teeny Tiny Dogs*, *Sara Solves It*, *Positively Ozitively*, and *Tumbleaf*. *Alpha House*, *Betas*, *Annebots*, *Creative Galaxy*, and *Tumbleaf* were "picked up" and went into production with between six and eleven episodes of each available on Amazon Instant Video. The second pilot season yielded *The After*, *Transparent*, *Wishenpoof! Mozart in the Jungle*, *Gortimore Gibbon's Life on Normal Street*, and *Bosch*. Of these, Jeffrey Tambour stars in *Transparent*, which is the creation of former *Six Feet Under* and *United States of Tara* producer and writer Jill Soloway, and *Bosch* is based on a highly successful series of detective novels by Michael Connelly. While the crowdsourcing of pilot selection and move to more involvement from "viewers" is an interesting move in theory, it would seem that Amazon Studios is primarily drawing from the same pool of properties, inspiration, and producers as traditional television does. In practice, it may be creating an additional development laboratory for those who have already established a track record and pedigree within the industry to develop projects rather than democratizing access to the means of production and cultivating outsider talent.

YouTube aka Netazon? Amaflix?

YouTube by design presents a challenge of definition as well as analysis—as a rebroadcaster/repository of professional and amateur created content; as a "commons" where do-it-yourself (DIY) producers can (and do) exhibit their own works; as a media buyer/ad rep for its most successful original producers, as a social media network with a robust community of commenters and curators. It also mimics the structure of a cable or satellite provider, offering a tier of over 300 "paid channels" of international and domestic niche programming to which viewers may purchase subscriptions. In 2015, it announced YouTube Red—an original content subscription service where for $10 a month viewers can get access to original programming developed by YouTube "stars" such as PewDiePie.[81] And, of course, YouTube is owned by Google/Alphabet whose corporate tentacles reach into virtually every corner of the network connected world.

YouTube never sought to become a replacement for the television industry—it is what David Weinberger calls a "meta business"—a "new category of business that enhances the value of information developed elsewhere and thus benefits the original creators of that information."[82] Ergo, it is a priori, a curatorial space. Its emphasis has always been on content sharing, even as it has, in an attempt to monetize its business model, sought production and distribution deals with industry entities, sold advertising against content it does not own the copyright to, and struck deals with amateur YouTube stars to revenue share around half of the advertising it places against their content. What we see here is a product of convergence and a demonstration that "the affordances of digital media provide a catalyst for reconceptualizing other aspects of culture, requiring the rethinking of social relations, the reimagining of cultural and political participation, the revision of economic expectations and the reconfiguration of legal structures."[83]

YouTube as democratized archive

YouTube has already offered a massive "unfiltered bottom-up cultural archive."[84] The content that comprises this archive has largely been made available "as the result of hours of painstaking labor, undertaken by the amateur collectors and curators of television who are digitizing VHS tapes in their garages, editing them for upload at YouTube, tagging and describing them, and arranging them into playlists or groups."[85] In other words, YouTube began as (and still remains) an explicitly curatorial space to which anyone may contribute, comment, and engage. On YouTube, one can review the entirety of television history—kinescopes of Milton Berle and low-quality but still watchable episodes of shows that have (and probably will) never be available elsewhere (PBS's 1973 series *An American Family*—arguably the "first" reality television series—often cited in scholarship but completely unavailable for study except through amateur or home recordings).

Users have, of course, also uploaded clips of current shows and even entire episodes, sometimes just minutes after their broadcast or cable premieres. (A circumstance made possible by the digitization of video content by DVRs and the ability of tech-savvy viewers to "rip" content from DVRs, or record content directly to their computer hard drives for compression and uploading to YouTube). Naturally this caused content owners to cry foul and sue for copyright infringement. In 2007, Viacom, CBS's parent corporation, filed suit against YouTube in the US District Court for the Southern District of New York claiming that by allowing users to upload and view videos owned by Viacom, YouTube had engaged in "brazen and massive" copyright infringement.[86] Google argued that it was protected by the 1998 Digital Millennium Copyright Act's "safe harbor" provisions and that it was not responsible for its users posting content to which they did not own the copyright. Ultimately YouTube was cleared of copyright infringement but required to take down any copyrighted material that copyright owners found on its site. YouTube also instituted a Content ID filtering system in 2008, an algorithm that combs through posted video looking for digital watermarks and other code that indicate the video is under copyright. Upon being notified of the presence of copyrighted material or finding it via content filtering, YouTube removes the offending video. According to YouTube's terms of service, users agree to not post any material that contains "third party copyrighted material, or material that is subject to other third party proprietary rights."[87] Naturally, what happens in terms of service versus what happens in practice are two different things and many shows not in the public domain can be found on YouTube.

YouTube has also provided a space for the circulation of video mashups and/or "fan videos" where fans of series have spent substantial time and energy recutting favorite clips from a particular show or film often in a music video style. This video form of remix culture has resulted in DIY "paratexts" which copyright holders may often ignore as they are, in effect, free publicity and help drive new viewers to their original projects in their monetized locales. Thus, while the onus is on the copyright holder to find and request removal of the copyrighted content, content owners who find it a benefit to have their material posted to YouTube may intentionally not request its removal. Jenkins, Ford, and Green have hypothesized the meaning of this "spreadability" of digital media, in particular its relationship with mainstream media, suggesting that these activities could be examined "to track shifts in attention and interest with greater sociocultural depth than would have been possible in an era of traditional broadcasting, when they might have counted the number of eyeballs but not understood how specific acts of reading, viewing or listening fit into larger patterns of social interaction."[88]

Not surprisingly, the professional moving image archiving community is not pleased with YouTube's "archive yourself yourself" feature.* Karen Gray, a librarian, and Rick Prelinger, a professional film archivist, have both voiced concern that the erosion of cultural authority caused by YouTube call into question both the role of the cultural institution "within society and in regard to cultural heritage" and "questions of persistence, ownership, standards, sustainability, or accountability that occupy professional archivists and their parent institutions."[89] Beyond the preservation of professionally produced (and owned) programs (which, even if in the public domain, probably exist in numerous enough copies to ensure their survival), who archives the archive of YouTube? Given YouTube's reliance on commercial viability and its terms of service, it is likely that the internet wayback machine will be the only trace of its user-produced and distributed videos. As Burgess and Green conclude: "These controversies reveal competing ideas about what YouTube is for—a social network site produced by communities of practice; a chaotic archive of weird, wonderful, and trashy vernacular video; or a distribution platform for branded and Big Media entertainment. Much of the discussion about these controversies centers around changes or perceived changes to the culture of YouTube as it scales up, makes deals with major

---

* To be fair, Prelinger in particular has a cause for concern about public domain footage being available (and rippable) from YouTube. Prelinger Archives' business model is built on his collection of licensed collections from many archives, and his ability to charge user fees for the provision of public domain footage or orphan films to documentary filmmakers. YouTube threatens the exclusivity of access and gatekeeping upon which his archive relies.

media players and attempts to create revenue from its constantly evolving business model."[90]

YouTube as DIY broadcast platform / video yard sale / video co-op

YouTube's rallying cry: "Broadcast Yourself!" is an open invitation for anyone who has a video camera to become part of the new democratized televisual environment. However, dreams of the jump from YouTube amateur to development-deal wielding television industry professional are the more akin to the dreams of lottery winners rather than the Chuck Lorres or Shonda Rimes of the world. This is not to say that one cannot get quite rich by being a YouTuber. It is, instead, to point out that the type of compensation and fame that YouTube brings favors YouTube in its retention of a large part of ad sales and encourages success in media forms (publishing, product placement, in-person appearances, brand ambassadorship) that are not televisual.

There are many reasons for this, of which the following form a nonexhaustive and preliminary list:

- The privileging of professionally produced content either due to its organic popularity with viewers or promotional placement arrangements between YouTube/Google and the content producers ensures a professional/amateur divide in the site's curated offerings.
- The genres of content that perform best on YouTube (video game walkthroughs, makeup how-tos, first person vlogs) either do not translate to linear television or have reached a saturation level on niche cable channels (prank shows for instance). One conclusion to draw may be that YouTube enables the creation of a much different televisual form which, while still consumed and perceived as "television" by its largest demographic (millennials and younger), diverges substantially in genre, length, production values, and frequency of release from linear or traditional industry-produced television.
- YouTube's striking of deals with professional showrunners creates new professional "branded" content from the likes of Jay-Z, Amy Pohler, and Anthony Zuiker which then competes with amateur talent on an uneven

playing field. If talent is moving from the professional, gatekept world of "the industry" to the democratized digital commons of YouTube and bringing its expertise, name recognition and home page "recommended video" deals with it, how can amateurs hope to reverse the process? (This might be called the "Radiohead conundrum"—in 2007, Radiohead offered its album *In Rainbows* for direct digital download and let its purchasers set their own price for the album. While this has been cited as an example of the viabilty of a democratized digital distribution model, the obvious point to be made is that Radiohead was successful with its "pay what you will" pricing for their online-only album release because Radiohead was already Radiohead and had become successful enough through traditional pre-internet industry structures to successfully exploit the online market.)

A survey of YouTube's home page indicates that amateur or even pro-am video is no longer the privileged content of the site (if it was ever). It should be noted that most people never see a "neutral" YouTube home page as if one is signed into one's Google or Gmail account or has not cleared one's browsing history, one will be served an aggregated "recommended for you" array— previously viewed videos and recommendations based on those previously viewed videos will be presented, the majority of it professionally produced (even if uploaded by persons without copyright clearance). The five "Popular Right Now" videos right now (July 18, 2016, 12:02 a.m., EST) are professionally produced. One is Katy Perry's NBC Olympics Video from her Vevo channel. The next is "We Meet DJ Khaled," which has been viewed 1.9 million times since it was posted yesterday. The third is the segment "Blake Lively Calls Jimmy Fallon her Dada" from *The Tonight Show Starring Jimmy Fallon* channel and the last two are promotional "paratexts" for the Star Wars franchise, one an "official trailer" from Season Three of *Star Wars Rebels* (from the Star Wars channel); and the other a teaser trailer for the Electronic Arts game "Star Wars Battlefront" from the "EAS Star Wars" channel. The rest of the categories, "Recommended," "Recently Uploaded Recommended Videos," feature predominantly professionally produced material (music videos from Vevo, sketch comedy from late night, or interview clips from talk shows), and the rest of the page contains rows of "Recommended Channels" that appear to be the equivalent of Google's "sponsored links": "The Tonight Show Starring

Jimmy Fallon," Jimmy Kimmel Live," "America's Got Talent," "Saturday Night Live," "Team Coco" [Conan O'Brien], "Britain's Got Talent," and "Trailers" which can be sorted by "movie" or "topic." The only category on this page that appears to favor pro-am or amateur content (aka viewers "broadcasting themselves") is "The Daily Awww" (kittens and puppies and a hyperactive squirrel, but also footage from a local New Jersey news affiliate about a bear that's been walking around on two legs over there for about a week).

A brief survey of additional pages of pre-curated categories ("Politics," "HouseholdHacker," "Sports Highlights and Great Moments," "Today's Funniest Clips") reveals that the featured clips in these categories almost without exception, trace back to a major media company or its subsidiary brands or, they are part of a collection of internet-based production companies that are creating content that circulates across their own branded websites (soulpancake.com, Omaze.com) as well as their YouTube channel; or they are a YouTube partner with their own YouTube channel (You Suck at Cooking, GiveBackFilms, Blake Grisby). These entities maintain a multiplexed social media web presence with YouTube video as the main distribution hub (and produce genres of video/televisual content that are not financially lucrative to distribute via broadcast or cable).

The YouTube Partners program allows YouTube community members to "enable your channel for monetization."[91] YouTube members can apply to monetize their videos so long as the content (including music) is solely and completely owned by the member and the video complies with YouTube's terms of service and community guidelines. Once YouTube has accepted the video for "monetization" it places ads "against" the content using the AdSense auction as well as ads YouTube has presold through DoubleClick and "other YouTube-sold sources."[92] AdSense ads "are determined automatically by our system based on a number of contextual factors related to your video" (such as user-created tags and metadata).[93] Users cannot control which ads are placed against their videos, nor can they determine the type of ads. Among the types of ads that may display are banners that run along the page either horizontally across the top or as a "skyscraper" along the right side. "Overlay in-video ads" appear over the lower part of the video and can be "closed" (if one can locate the "x" box) (these are essentially the equivalent of a "snipe" ad on a traditional television stream).⁹⁴ "TrueView in-stream ads" are "skippable video ads that are inserted before, during or after the main video," and "non-skippable in-stream ads are video ads that can be inserted before or during the main video and must be watched before the viewer can continue watching the content selected. These ads can also be placed after the conclusion of a video, in the post-roll slot."⁹⁵ Partners are paid through an AdSense account (another Google product) which handles ad sales, serving of the ads (through the use of Google AdWords), quantification of the advertising views, and ultimately payment to the YouTube partner.⁹⁶

The economics of YouTube partnerships remain shrouded in mystery— the total number of subscribers and views of various videos and channels are easily seen (and prominently displayed) on YouTube. What is impossible to determine with any certainty is how much the partners are actually making, although YouTube's analytics company SocialBlade does maintain estimated earnings based on a "lowball and a highball value based on what we know about what partners earn on average per view and multiply that by the number of views they get per day."⁹⁷ These estimates are based on daily views times a low cost per thousand (CPM) of sixty cents and a high CPM of $8 (all partners receive a CPM somewhere within this range for their monetized videos).⁹⁸ Even though Google takes a 45 percent cut, *Forbes*' "first-ever ranking" of the highest paid YouTubers estimated that the tenth highest paid, Rosanna Pansino, a "self- taught" pastry chef whose videos are shot in a traditional cooking show style, made $2.5 million in 2015.⁹⁹ The highest paid, 25-year-old Swede Felix Arvid Ulf Kjelberg, known on YouTube as PewDiePie is apparently making $12 million pretax to provide R-rated video game commentary and walk-throughs to his over 40 million subscribers.¹⁰⁰

A survey of other YouTube reveals some that may be expected (children reviewing anything, comedic parodies). At the same time, fully twelve of the top twenty earners are videogame players/commentators who record their reviews or "walkthroughs" of popular video games (Minecraft, in particular). Nine countries are represented, speaking four different languages. The Fine Bros, often thought to be two of the first "YouTube Stars" are responsible for the internet "series" "Kids React."¹⁰¹ Therefore, I suggest that the most popular YouTube stars are those that are engaged in the creation of programming that does not fit traditional televisual formats or genres and is not being produced by traditional television content producers. The short form videos that garner the most views on YouTube are perhaps unique to webcasting.

Other distribution deals that YouTube signs look very similar to the EST (electronic sell-through) arrangements content owners strike with Amazon Instant Video, iTunes, or Google Play, to provide their content for a per-episode or per-season price. Since all of these "retailers" are priced the same, there is little competition between them—they are ecosystem driven (if you have an iPad, you buy from iTunes; a Kindle, you buy from Amazon; an Android Tablet, you buy from GooglePlay). YouTube's intervention into this area is to provide an electronic-sell-through option that is platform-agnostic, web-native, and app-based.

Other deals are symbiotic partnerships, such as YouTube's contract with Vevo, "a music video and content distributor owned by Universal Music Group, Sony Music Entertainment and Abu Dhabi Media Group."[102] After months of debates regarding ad revenue splits between Vevo and YouTube, YouTube invested $40–$50 million in Vevo giving it about a 7 percent stake in the company.[103] In May 2013, "Vevo accounted for 50.2 million unique viewers on YouTube, making it the top channel partner on YouTube, according to ComScore's monthly Media Metrix report. This deal merely formalized a mutually beneficial relationship—with so many viewers, YouTube could ill afford to lose Vevo. On the other hand, the vast majority of Vevo's video views come from YouTube users."[104]

For "independent" industry professionals, YouTube can be part of a synergistic content delivery system along with "start-up" web communities or viewing destinations, such as Maker Studios, which built a substantial following before being sold to Disney for $950 million by its founder, Brian Robbins, a former child star.[105] Robbins's current project is AwesomenessTV, which "produces three to five tween-skewing YouTube videos a day" and is owned by DreamWorks Animation which paid $150 million for it in 2013.[106] While distribution via branded (non-subscription) YouTube channels has been advantageous for the endeavors Robbins has been involved in, he emphasizes the need to integrate YouTube into a broader fiduciary structure: "If your only revenue is from YouTube, yes, it's impossible to build a business... You have to have many different revenue streams, just like any diversified media company. It's harder when you're an individual YouTuber and that's how you're making your living. YouTube does take a big percentage of the revenue [typically about 45%], but they also provide a big service. If you were starting a YouTube channel tomorrow without YouTube and you needed all those servers and streaming capability and stuff, you would spend probably way more money than the revenue share that you're paying them. So I appreciate the grumbling, but it doesn't apply to us [AwesomenessTV]. We think YouTube is an amazing place to scale an audience."[107]

Many of these content producing professionals shoot YouTube-bound content at the YouTube SpaceLA in a former Hughes helicopter hangar in Playa Vista. "Everything [editing suites, recording booths, cameras, lights, mics, grip equipment, screening rooms] is lent free to those making content for YouTube—especially the roughly 200 channels the Google-owned site has partnered with and lent an estimated $250 million in exchange for an ad revenue split."[108] While Amy Poehler, Matt Damon, and other industry professionals have used the Space, it is mainly open to YouTube partners who qualify for the "Creator Class," a one month program. According to Liam Collins, head of the LA space "We'll look at your upload and subscriber base and make sure you're open to collaborating with others and are prepared to bring a crew. And we have residencies for established YouTube channels that understand how to make full use of a soundstage."[109] As YouTube is now one of a corporate family of digital businesses owned by *the* digital sovereign of our times (Google), one might see it as akin to Amazon's support of self-publishing authors—they will carry the book on their site, and as a Kindle offering, but until and unless it proves its own (monetizable) worth in the commons, they will not feature it. This is the downside of creative utopianism and yet it also highlights why the curation of content as well as talent is crucial to the continued operation of the cultural industries and their reconstitution following these transitions.

YouTube as "cable" system/alternative television distributor

In addition to its YouTube partners and other recommended channels maintained by professional television producers, YouTube also offers a range of subscription/pay "channels" that provide ultra-niche programming to those willing to pay 99 cents to $9.99 a channel per month. In creating and maintaining these channels, YouTube is, in effect, testing the economic viability of cable's worst nightmare—a la carte pricing of channels. Cable channels count on using less attractive (and expensive) choices to fill up lower tiers of service with low-cost programming that gives them the largest profit margin. A brief survey of YouTube pay channels reveals the following subscription options:

- HygroHybrid—devoted to hydroponic marijuana cultivation
- Oracle apps—"dedicated to oracle apps functional knowledge"
- Ron Figliomeni—"a channel youll [sic] love to see a channel thatll [sic] make you laugh until you pee yourself"
- Bikini G-String Thong—Beautiful Women and Shock Swimsuits Video Clips
- Community Trainer—Oracle apps supply chain management
- ScannerDanner Premium—a chance to be part of my Engine Performance class at Rosedale Technical College
- Janis Frank—Learn to knit with these easy to follow knitting videos
- HereTV Premium—an online outlet of the LGBT cable network HereTV
- Shroedinger's Box Quantum Mekanix—"hardcore auto repair"
- Bunni Channel—twerk videos
- WWGOA—wood working videos
- Sesame Street: Monthly Pass—subscribe to watch full episodes of *Sesame Street* on YouTube
- Twenty one different "Zee Channels" ranging from news to sports, to entertainment, movies, various genres of television shows[110]

One way to view this is that YouTube is providing a formalized distribution venue to material that otherwise would find neither an audience nor a revenue stream without substantial upfront investment by the producers. The content creators would have to purchase time on local stations or through station groups as "infomercials" in addition to shouldering the costs of production. The creation of these channels creates a more formalized relationship between the subscriber and the viewer than the DIY YouTube partnership—in this way the content producers get the entirety of the subscriber's payment and can sell their own ads (or opt-in to Google's ad revenue sharing scheme as partners).

The smattering of professional content producers offering subscriptions via the YouTube paid channel system merits further investigation as they may be pioneers of a new a la carte form of subscription television. HereTV is a niche pay cable channel that carries programming of interest to the LGBT community. It was launched as a premium subscription channel in 2002 and is available via traditional cable and satellite operators. It maintains a website, but does not deliver any video content via its website. Rather it refers interested viewers out to either the YouTube subscription channel or (as of 2016) Amazon Instant Video.[111] Thus HereTV is using the technological streaming capacity of YouTube and Amazon rather than investing in its own storage/streaming infrastructure and the bandwidth needed to maintain video streaming via their own site.

Sesame Street's offering is a lucrative way of reaching and monetizing parents who want trusted (aka brand recognized) media to entertain their children via cellphone or tablet while away from home. Creating a formal subscription YouTube channel (while also keeping a close eye on illegal uploads of Children's Television Workshop's (CTW) copyrighted material) is also a way to limit loss of revenue in the digital environment. It creates a revenue stream for repurposed content while saving CTW from having to invest the substantial resources that the creation of a niche cable channel would demand. Furthermore, it preserves the advertising-free distribution of CTW content parents have come to expect from its broadcast home (PBS). Finally, it acknowledges and directly serves the needs of a particular group of niche viewers—parents who want a portable, always-on, always-available precurated stream of portable media.

The twenty-one "Zee Channels" carry professionally produced shows from Zee Media Corporation Ltd., one of India's largest television media and entertainment companies.[112] YouTube is thus providing an international subscriber base with a way of seeing programming that would otherwise be behind the bundled paywalls of cable or satellite systems, if available at all. This is a situation that is unique to YouTube which has internationalized itself in ways that other online viewing sites have not or cannot without substantial corporate negotiations. Prior to internet distribution, the Zee channel or any media company seeking to provide programming to a diasporic community in other countries would have to lease time on local broadcasters (similar to the infomercial situation described earlier), or convince regional cable and satellite providers that there would be enough of a viewership of their content to justify carriage fees.

What the YouTube pay channels appear to be comprised of are channels of content that would not garner enough viewing to make their inclusion on any tier of cable programming worth the cost. Therefore, YouTube follows through on the promise of providing ultra-niche programming to those willing to pay for it which is certainly a more honest and direct interchange with the public than that of cable or satellite "bundling." It is a tacit acknowledgment that this content cost money to produce; if you want access to it, you need to compensate the content owners for the resources and labor it took to produce them. Since some of them also "may include ads," these pay channels operate as DIY cable networks that are going to a direct sell-through market rather than partnering with a wholesaler (like artisans who sell through stores on Etsy rather than investing in their own web infrastructure). This might be delivery on the supposed promise of "narrowcasting" that cable and satellite networks used as a carrot to encourage new subscribers in the 1970s and 1980s—while claiming to target underserved parts of the viewing audience with highly specialized programming, "nearly all of them offered program genres—often actual programming—already proven successful either on broadcast television or elsewhere."[113] Ergo, YouTube is filling a lacunae that the broadcast, cable, and satellite industries have always been aware of, but have been unable to deliver upon due to their business models.

The immediate dangers to "the industry" are twofold: first, viewers who are watching these paid channels are not watching other channels; and second, pricing structures like this (and iTunes Season Pass) are accustoming viewers to an a la carte payment system on either a show or a channel basis. Even if the cable company is still receiving a monthly payment from a YouTube paid channel subscriber for television service and internet access, the broadcast and cable networks are not receiving a quantifiable viewer to sell to advertisers. "Furthermore, even though YouTube is offering paid 'channels' of content, it is not (yet) legally defined as a multichannel video program distributor (MVPD). Rather, it and any and all of its internet-based video distributing brethren are classified as online video distributors (OVDs) by the FCC. These are defined, oddly enough, by their relationship with internet service providers (ISPs)—OVDs "offer video content by means of the Internet or other Internet Protocol (IP)-based transmission path provided by a person or entity other than the OVD" (in other words, an ISP—that the consumer subscribes to from an entity that is not owned by the website).[114] What is curious is that the ISPs are, of course, owned and operated by the cable, satellite, and telecom companies that are also MVPDs. (More on this in the next chapter.)

Ultimately the future of YouTube is probably dependent upon the same factor that all web-based companies face—sustainable growth. "A core challenge will be to find a balance between mass popularization (which YouTube has achieved, at least for the moment), innovation, and sustainability (which requires long-term investment and a stable and socially functioning community)."[115] YouTube's major existing contribution to culture is that it showed the industry what a video sharing site could look like and how it should function (most viewed, most liked, most recent, and the privileging of interactivity/comments/community behaviors). Most attempts at creating more curated video sharing spaces (TeacherTube) riff off of the name YouTube or brand themselves as "The YouTube for …"[116] (This of course begs the question—"in a world with a YouTube, why do we need a YouTube for …?")

It will be interesting to see if YouTubers are subject to the same sort of "innovation, imitation, saturation" content cycles that traditional television has been and how the relationship between YouTube and "traditional" television forms (and industry professionals) evolves. YouTube's Collins says "we're not competing with TV, we complement it … Over the past year, we've actually seen many of our channels partner with TV networks—Fox with WIGS and AMC with Nerdist's All-Star Celebrity Bowling, to name a few. But one of the biggest cross-platform TV successes that we've seen is with Ellen DeGeneres and Jimmy Kimmel, who are building big audiences by issuing user-generated-content challenges and featuring YouTube stars on their shows."[117] Since YouTube uses skippable ads and advertisers are only charged when someone watches the ad all the way through (which happens "between 15 to 45 percent of the time"); YouTube ads can be an economic adjunct to other media buys. And, since YouTube is now participating (along with Hulu and Netflix) in the upfront market, there is a greater awareness and consideration of it as a legitimate ad buy. Thus, the future may be convergent and symbiotic.

The industry responds

The major concern of the industry is not only the loss of eyeballs to other viewing options, but also the decline in advertising revenue caused by the dilution of the broadcast audience and the lower CPM's online viewing commands. The oft-quoted call to action (or warning cry) regarding digital distribution and the television industry is Jeff Zucker's 2008 statement: "We can't replace analog dollars with digital pennies."[118] While he did amend this to digital dimes in 2009, after Hulu proved to be somewhat successful, the sentiment behind it remained the same: "'digital' would shift audiences and therefore advertising dollars from a still-profitable medium to a different one of unknown but likely much lower future profitability."[119]

Network sites

All broadcast and cable networks maintain their own branded websites which are used as promotional sites for current and upcoming programming. They also all maintain online archives of recently aired shows, teasers for upcoming episodes, and online players. The making of full episodes available for viewing on network-owned websites has affected network ad buys overall by providing additional ad inventory. Viewers are unable to fast-forward through these ads, but the ad time itself costs about 1/3 that of broadcast spots (leading to Jeff Zucker's famous concern about "digital dimes").

The serving of these ads is also different than it is on broadcast. For instance, on ABC.com, "Brands are not able to demographically target their ads or insert them into a specific ABC show on the website. Instead, they buy a bundle of impressions that are dynamically ad served across all shows over the course of their campaign flight. An advertiser will never know when or during what shows or episodes their ad will run. However, they can ask to be omitted from certain shows that may not align to their brand."[120] This is standard operating procedure within the industry for online streaming ad sales, and networks are beginning to bundle online with broadcast and to offer all packages for sale during the upfront (or NewFront) period.*

In November, 2015 CBS announced that it would be producing *Star Trek: Discovery*, a prequel to the original 1969 *Star Trek* series. While the announcement of another *Star Trek* television series may be nothing new—there have, after all been six separate series produced as a part of this brand franchise, there is something about *Discovery* that will "boldly go where no television show has gone before." The first episode will premiere on the CBS network in May of 2017.[121] Following the broadcast/cable network premiere, all subsequent episodes will be streamed through CBS All Access, CBS's subscription streaming service which currently charges subscribers $5.99 for programming containing "limited commercials" and $9.99 a month for commercial-free viewing.[122] The restriction of access to this obviously "privileged content" will no doubt result in an uptick in All Access subscribers and it may prove to be distribution genius for this particular series. The challenge will be to keep these viewers once all thirteen episodes have rolled out—will the fourteenth week bring churn or defection to a different subscriber service as viewers "follow the content" rather than cleave to the brand? The post-network era is characterized by the erosion if not evaporation of the network as supplier of "branded entertainment." But, branding remains an important signpost for consumers since "branding adds personality, distinctiveness and value to a product or service while also offering risk avoidance and trust."[123] *Star Trek*, a brand with a fifty-year history of active and engaged viewership and fans who were on the vanguard of participatory culture when Henry Jenkins first began to theorize it is probably not a test case from which one can generalize the success of a less established franchise or an entirely new series.

---

* "NewFronts" are, quite simply "upfronts" for OTT programming. Begun in 2011, they are organized by the Interactive Advertising Bureau and take place in the last week of April/first week of May. Participation is open to any entity that produces internet videos and is deemed an appropriate participant by the IAB and the "founding partners" of the NewFronts (among them AOL, Google, and Yahoo). They also need to pony up between $12,500 and $25,000 depending on their presentation time. (Morrissey, "WTF are the NewFronts?")

What could be examined by a longitudinal study of subscriber metrics over the course of a presumed season two of *Star Trek: Discovery* would be the investor psychology of anchoring. Anchoring is when "individuals attribute a value to an object based on what they paid for it."[124] Therefore, differences in subscription pricing across seasons, coupled with similar experiments by other content producers and distributors should enable some predictions about the viability of individually paywalled distribution platforms and subscription services. How much is too much for the standard viewer to pay for content? What is the average number of individual subscriptions the viewer is willing to sustain?

Bridge content

Bridge content itself is nothing new—the carefully planted news stories speculating about "Who Shot J. R.?" in the summer of 1980 were a nascent form of bridge content. In the simplest terms, bridge content is any off-the-box show-related content devised to keep viewers engaged with a show in- between episodes or in-between seasons. In the past ten years, bridge content has been transformed by the interactivity of the web and by social media. Today, the most common type of bridge content can be found on the series-based website and series-focused pages or feeds on social media platforms such as Facebook, Instagram, and Twitter that collate and connect the accounts of the show's stars, writers, and showrunners. All of these initiatives are part of overarching transmedia strategies to keep existing viewers engaged and attract new viewers, either directly or through existing viewer's social networks—the digital word of mouth.

Digital media enthusiasts believe that this sort of fan participation and interaction will translate to increased viewership and engagement with the shows themselves as the web corollaries to the shows become less paratextual and move from extension to experience. Lisa Hsia, Executive Vice President of Digital Media at Bravo, one of the first innovators with web content, emphasizes this shift: "In the old days, it was all about digital extensions. We don't want to be an extension. We want to be a digital experience that helps drive overall viewing, whatever the platform, where the digital series is just as critical as the show."[125] The movement from passive information provider to active participatory environment has made the bridge content more important to advertisers as well as content producers. As a result, web pages will often include webisode content which may or may not feature the same characters as the show, and be more intertwined with the show's storylines, extending them across media channels and driving viewership back to the show's airtime.[126]

While linear television content producers may find the need to create bridge content a distraction or a necessary evil, it does provide a valuable service to advertisers and marketers since the value of the content is due to "choice-based impressions that result from audiences *choosing* to engage with it."[127] Therefore, although the percentage of the viewership that engages digitally with the show may be small, the viewers who choose to engage with the web-based bridge content identify themselves as opinion leaders and provide access to their social networks by their opting-in through "likes" (which helps content producers and distributors identify influential curators in the public sphere of social networking). By May 2011 over 275 million viewers had "liked" at least one show on Facebook and seventeen of the top "liked" Facebook pages are those of television shows.[128] While show-specific apps have also been developed, early data from this transitional phase appears to indicate that viewers prefer to find their tribes of affinity on large and established social media platforms such as Facebook and Twitter and incorporate their fan activity into their general social profiles.

Hulu and Hulu Plus

Hulu was launched in March 2007 as a joint venture between News Corporation and NBCUniversal (as content providers), AOL, MSN, MySpace, and Yahoo! (as internet distribution partners) and venture capital firm Providence Equity Partners. Currently the site is owned by Disney, News Corp., and NBCUniversal, but, as part of the FCC's conditions for the Comcast purchase, NBCU is a "silent partner" and may not participate in any discussions or strategies pertaining to the company for seven years. In forming Hulu, industry players created a "value added" one-stop repository of all of their shows, which also provided them with further ad inventory in addition to their network sites where their shows also were available). Hulu is a "hybrid business," composed of Hulu.com, "a free, ad-supported clearinghouse" and Hulu Plus, which carries next-day programming from its owners and content partners, as well as maintains an extensive syndication library of past series.[129] "Like many digital cinema and TV ventures, Hulu has marketed itself both in terms of convenience, promising to allow viewers to watch 'when, where and how you want,' while also promoting it as a youthful alternative to the 'old' medium of TV, to the point that Hulu came to represent an almost generational divide between passive viewership of TV and active engagement with Hulu."[130]

Basic browser-accessed Hulu is free and ad-supported, although its ad-supported model is lighter than the traditional television broadcasting load of commercials per half or full hour. As it is an "on demand" technology, it is not beholden to the strict scheduling timeframes that linear television is. Therefore, it might put only a three minute roll-in of commercials into the beginning of a twenty-two minute sitcom rather than interrupt the show for eight minutes of commercials as is standard practice on broadcast. Hulu offers a range of advertising opportunities at prices currently 25 percent that of broadcast or cable.[131] Advertising on Hulu costs less per CPM than broadcast yet "based on data from Nielsen/IAG," the company has stated that its advertising effectiveness is twice that of broadcast television commercials. Hulu offers advertisers and viewers advertising choice. Advertisers can choose from in-stream video, pop-up banners, or they can brand the screen around the Hulu player while their ads play. They can also choose a "branded slate" which displays a card with the sponsor's art on it accompanied by a voice-over stating "The following program is brought to you with limited commercial interruption by" their name.[132] This is an interesting throwback to the single-sponsorship days of the early days of television. Hulu viewers can also use an "ad selector" which provides viewers with a choice of three options of video ads and can even "swap" ads once an ad has begun to play. The ad selection is based on "relevancy" to the user's Hulu profile and these ads are valued by advertisers who think that viewers "will be more receptive to viewing the ads, since they have been empowered with a certain level of control over them" and the selected or swapped ads do yield higher click-through rates.[133] Hulu purports the fact that it generates more ad revenue per half-hour TV episode than cable and DVR (but not yet broadcast), and that its ability to better target audiences increases relevancy and eliminates wasted impressions.[134]

Hulu Plus is a subscription-based version of Hulu which allows mobile viewing via apps and application program interface (API) integration for seamless viewing on smart TVs. It offers next-day viewing of current episodes on its content partners' broadcast or cable channels and an extensive archive of video holdings including shows that were never released as DVD box sets or ESTs. Hulu Plus carries a smaller advertising load but still places ads against its subscriber-only content. Ostensibly this ad revenue subsidizes the licensing costs of the extensive collection of next-day first run programming, thus helping to keep subscription fees down. Since Hulu Plus is also partially owned by its major content providers and has revenue-sharing partnerships with a host of other content producers, this strategy may be more about increased revenue and revenue streams than concern for subscriber cost. What it also suggests is that Hulu expects that its Plus subscribers are used to ads in their television and is proceeding with a cable-like hybrid fiduciary model.

TV everywhere (with us!) and the reification of control

"TV Everywhere" is not the freeing rallying cry that it may sound like—it is, plain and simple, a marketing ploy and an attempt by the industry "to protect the last remaining business model in the industry—cable [and satellite] TV—not yet destroyed by the wrath of digital audiences."[135] "TV Everywhere" is about "TV Ecosystems" and ensuring that cable and satellite subscribers stay within their DishTV, Comcast, or TimeWarner cable bundles when they take their viewing mobile. Technologically, it is the marriage of cable or satellite content with off-the-box viewing via a mobile device attached to the web via a home broadband connection supplied by the cable or satellite provider. While the term "TV Everywhere" was coined in 2009 by then Time Warner CEO Jeff Bewkes to name a particular initiative of Time Warner Cable, the term has become generic for any and all authentication-based viewing apps or technologies. The creation of these technologies was the cable and satellite industries' response to the growing popularity of Netflix, YouTube, and portable devices (tablets, smart phones) that allowed viewers to space-shift. This "caused cable operators, satellite providers, and telecommunications companies to realize that tethering their programming to the set-top box in the living room was starting to feel archaic relative to consumer expectations."[136] More importantly, "cable companies were especially alarmed that cable programming, such as Comedy Central, FX, and the SyFy channel, could be viewed on the internet by all, subscribers and nonsubscribers, and worst of all, for free."[137] Thus, TV Everywhere apps (Xfinity, the Hopper, CNNgo, sign in protocols on ESPN viewing sites) put programming behind authentication systems that permit web and mobile access only to existing subscribers. They allow for time and place shifting, but only for those who have already paid for the content. Individual cable networks have taken this a step further by incorporating authentication protocols in their live-streaming features. For example, CNN began to include live-streaming with authentication in its iPad app in July of 2011. Users of the app who can authenticate their cable subscription to an MSO that carries CNN on its system can watch CNN's live broadcast including commercials on their iPad or iPhone.[138] This extends the reach of Television Everywhere since it makes the most traditional of the televisual forms (the live broadcast) portable through the internet rather than the broadcast spectrum and at the same time, it maintains a paywall that restricts access to those who are already subscribers to the more "traditional" form of television delivery (cable). "The genius underlying TV Everywhere is that most pay-TV subscribers will believe that their cable provider's online aggregation of content is free, whereas they will perceive that they have to pay extra for, say, Netflix."[139]

While the TV Everywhere/authentication viewing platforms come with EPGs from the cable and satellite companies, cable companies are beginning to integrate personalized recommendation functions into these technologies. This is part of a move to make TV Everywhere/authentication viewing easier for the viewer since "implementation"—despite the hype—has been slow and haphazard. Many customers have found it difficult and confusing to get content on their computers, tablets and phones even after they pay for it.[140] New, easier authentication systems, an increase in publicly placed "Wi-Fi hot spots" that seamlessly connect authenticated subscribers' devices and software that maintains personalized recommendation profiles for all viewers in a subscription household have been developed. The recommendation engines "learn," based on individualized viewing patterns "what you have watched, what you have recorded on your DVR, and determines what you like."[141] For those who think this use of information (that the cable company already collects on you) is too intrusive, an opt-out option is available. The goal, of course is to "get customers so involved and integrated into the cable company offerings that it won't be desirable to cut the cord or switch to satellite or over-the-top providers who can't match the full cable bundle of services."[142]

Most recently HBO has launched HBO Now, a "stand-alone" streaming subscription service which breaks with the paywall/authentication protocol that restricted "Television Everywhere" access to cable and satellite subscribers. What is interesting is that subscriptions to HBO Now are handled through its "subscription partners" who either are, or are enmeshed in paywall/authentication ecosystems. As of this writing, there are eleven HBO Now subscription partners, six of which (Frontier, Google Fiber, Liberty, Optimum, Service Electric (Cablevision), and Verizon) are ISPs/MSOs, three of which (Android, Apple, and Samsung) are mobile device makers, and one of which (Roku) is a streaming technology producer. The eleventh is Amazon, e-tailer of everything. While HBO Now has not sparked an explosion of other stand-alone direct subscription apps (although one could ask how "stand-alone" it actually is, given the "subscription partners") it is clearly an interesting test case of how much viewers are willing to pay for access to exclusive content.

Second screen apps

Second screen apps are the industry's attempt to come to terms with the fact that according to Nielsen, 60 percent of Americans use the internet while watching television.[143] Therefore, if viewers are going to be distracted by another screen, why not have the content on that screen drive them back to the first screen, or engage them in active viewing, and possibly social media activity that will increase viewership among their friends? Interactive television, in its traditional sense, has never fulfilled the potential industry advocates and developers long lauded it to have. Smartphones and tablets fulfill the promise of interactivity as they operate as familiar companions to the viewing experience, rather than an immersive interactive experience. What distinguishes the second screen apps and experiences from network websites and social media is that they *synchronize* to the first screen, to provide a true real-time "companion" to the viewing experience.

Since 2010, three main types of second screen apps have been produced by various television content providers: series-, event-, and network- specific apps, and almost all of these are primarily developed for the iPad and iPhone platforms.[144] Lisa Hsia, executive vice-president of Digital Media for Bravo Networks sees these apps as a way to target particular engaged demographics: "The most important thing about these products right now is that we can create a curated important conversation with people of influence versus some sort of fire hose that provides a less meaningful conversation."[145] BravoNow, the first network-specific iPad app, allowed users to interact, share, and engage with additional content during certain Bravo episode premieres. Hsia emphasizes that these second screen apps have to "offer something that's really exceptional—like a filtered community, insider knowledge, or a celebrity that's tweeting along with you. There has to be some unique hook."[146]

Early research by the creators of second screen apps such as Miso has revealed that "every type of show requires a unique second-screen experience in terms of the companion content's type, frequency, delivery and timing."[147] Naturally, the issue comes down to market share even of the apps since what appears to have happened is a "Tower of Babel" with thousands of series- or network- specific apps that deliver the same "companion experiences" but do so solely within themselves.[148] This sort of balkanization works against the formation of or engagement with a mass audience as well as the opening up of viewer experience to other options. It is akin to a museum of modern art restricting its patrons to only one room in which hang multiple works by the same artist or, even more confining, only one work by one artist, displayed in multiple forms. The effect is creation of a "filter bubble" by the second screen, which, because "app culture" is organized by operating system ecosystems, is already a possible stricture to wider engagement or program discovery.

Wider engagement and/or program discovery are not, however, the goal of second screen apps, so this may be an irrelevant complication. Ultimately, the goal of the second screen apps is ad interactivity—which then creates the traditional challenge of audience opt-out (zap the channel, close the app). Advertisers and app developers seem to believe that targeted, "relevant" advertising will yield engaged viewers of the commercial message. Cory Bergman of *Lost Remote* calls this the Holy Grail: "to have a feedback loop with television. So that when I'm watching something, I am able to not only interact with the TV show; I can also interact with the ads. That's been what interactive TV has promised, but has never delivered on. When that happens on a truly scaled basis, there will be so much new value creation in this business that it will really be the second coming of television."[149] Among the innovations being explored is the "sync ad"—which would provide a traditional commercial "spot" on the first screen to provide "emotion and immediacy" synchronized to a digital ad on the second screen that provides interaction, transactions and data collection.[150] However, the key to this would be establishing large second screen partnerships with major advertisers and advertising agencies, which has not happened. Therefore no second screen experience has yet yielded a substantial audience or demonstrated mass reach.[151]

A *TV Guide* research study reported that half of Twitter users tweet about the shows they are watching on television while they are watching them, about one third of Facebook users post about their television watching in real time, and the average Facebook user has "liked" at least six shows.[152] Content producers have recognized this activity and many have begun to display onscreen Twitter hashtags to encourage (and also control) the social media backchannel, as well as to set up official showpages on Facebook in addition to their own dedicated websites. Twitter reports that there is a two to tenfold increase in tweets about shows that include onscreen hashtags.[153] Some shows have experimented with "live tweeting" during the premiere broadcast of particular episodes, or as sweeps week specials in an attempt to increase live viewing—since "Social media amplifies the feeling of being connected and part of something bigger when watching television."[154] While social media can be an important force, it is important to note that "social media cannot and will not save a bad show or make poor products and services 'look good.' But social media absolutely has a powerful amplification effect in the presence of resonant content."[155] What it can do is encourage and increase "live" viewing. According to *TV Guide*, 20 percent of tvguide.com users surveyed "reported that they are watching more live television broadcasts because they do not want the potential of people within their social networks to ruin the plots of their favorite shows."[156] The real-time web has, of course always created a dilemma for content providers and schedulers as it frees content from the "windowing" of time zones. The social media backchannel knows no geographical boundaries and a single Tweet could "spoil" a reveal for millions of viewers since its resonance can be multiplied through retweeting.

A further convergence of web-based technologies embeds viewers within social sites so as to provide for immediate real-time sharing of viewing choices as well as community viewing. Facebook is the leader in these innovations, allowing users to watch television episodes from Netflix and Hulu "within" Facebook. As a result, these viewing choices are immediately shared with the user's Facebook friends and appear in the newsfeed post. Friends can then tune in to these episodes directly from Facebook by clicking through their friend's newsfeed posts.[157] Facebook calls this "frictionless sharing" but, of course advertisers call it a gold mine given the level of data it reveals about users and the ability to micro-target these viewer/consumers.[158]

Still liminal or passage complete?

Liminality "refers to moments or periods of transition during which the normal limits to thought, self-understanding and behavior are relaxed, opening the way to novelty and imagination, construction and destruction."[159] While we have definitely seen the traditional understanding of producer, distributor, and television change throughout the past eleven years, the ultimate power structures (and strictures) have remained largely unchanged, they have just expanded to include new participants, also oligopolized and conglomerated media entities whose creativity and innovation during the liminal stage were the driving forces of a carnival that has now ended with the reification of the traditional power structures.[160] The destruction of the stranglehold linear television providers had on the creative structures and activities of the producers has successfully been achieved, as has the limiting of access to previously aired shows—infinity, which "appears in the horizon of the liminal" has been achieved to provide the curatorial viewer with choices worthy of his or her curatorial investigation and intermediation.[161]

Platform agnostic digital distribution seeks not to undermine the traditional release patterns of "windowing," but actually aims to completely replace it with a different fiduciary market that ultimately benefits the same entities as the old system. Rather than structuring release dates sequentially across a variety of different largely incompatible or nonsimultaneous venues, digital distribution results in simultaneous and universal accessibility across multiple platforms. Therefore it "allows each medium to compete for its share of audience using the same content, but addressing distinct viewer technology and lifestyle preferences."[162] Even though it appears to be a digital disruptor, it is not outside the realm of possibility to consider Netflix as a "next step" in the evolution of the television rather than the information industries. Its "economic and narrative structure" is identical to that of premium pay television channels such as HBO so perhaps it has merely "established a third distribution track."[163] "There was, in fact, rather little that Netflix depended on from the digital system of networked traffic and advertising revenue, whereas it was entirely dependent on its ability to license television content and to attract top writing, acting, producing, and directing talent" notes Michael Wolff in *Television is the New Television*.[164]

The change, may therefore be driven by viewer behavior, but the industry response has been to counter lost revenue and opportunity through economic acquisition, partnerships, negotiation or, as will be seen in Chapter 5, regulatory protections. When all distribution sites are paying license fees to the content producers or, in the case of Hulu, are partly owned by the producers, they remain revenue streams—so long as the viewers stay within these digital viewing ecosystems, they are still patrons of the legacy television industry (or of "new" producing and distributing entities that have employed those with track records in the legacy television industry). Thus, as long as viewer attention can be captured by a viewing platform that feeds back to the industry (and all of them ultimately do); the essential health of the legacy television producers and distributors themselves is not unduly compromised, the back end and/or viewing transactions are merely made more complex. The agents of change—those innovative OTT tricksters—are the ones who, having altered the televisual landscape and entered the television "market" will now have to ensure that they can stay relevant and viable in the infinite choice of long tail syndication.

5

Containment, Common Carriage, and Net Neutrality—Regulating the Long Tail of OTT Television

There may be no more-perfect site in which to study the unfinished, transitory, and transformative nature of the liminal than government regulation. While charged with the protection of the airwaves from monopolization by special interests, the use of those airwaves to create a national mass media culture required substantial investment by big business. This conundrum of how to encourage innovation and advancement while not creating unfair advantages or market shares for the corporations with the resources to innovate and advance has been a hallmark of American broadcast regulation since the early twentieth century. The internet—which knows no national boundaries and yet relies upon geographically based wired and wireless communication technologies—has further complicated the issues with which regulators, industries, lobbyists, and citizens must contend.

To begin, there are a few points that should be noted about the US regulatory system and its primary policymaking mechanism, the Federal Communications Commission (FCC). First, "the American approach to regulating new communication technologies and their impact has generally been more reactive than proactive."[1] Thus, technologies have often developed and entrenched themselves in industrial and user practices before being assessed in relation to existing federal communications law, or without exploration of alternatives to incumbent patterns and practices.* This, of course, shapes

---

* An illustrative historical example: the regulatory and geographical structure of the mature radio industry (originally established in the 1920s) was the groundwork for the nascent television industry that developed in the post–World War II era, an arrangement that favored the interests of the corporate entities that controlled and programmed radio. These companies argued that they were

regulatory intervention particularly when certain practices or technologies are defined and deployed by corporations with substantial resources long before they have reached market saturation and before or during regulatory deliberation.

Second, FCC commissioners have historically had unusually close relationships with the industries they regulate. A large percentage of former FCC commissioners have gone directly into positions in the television, cable, or information services industries following their terms. Michael Powell, a Clinton appointee to the commission in 1997 and FCC chairman from 2001 to 2005 is the current president and CEO of the National Cable Television Association (NCTA).* Current FCC Chairman Tom Wheeler has gone "the other way," having previously been president and CEO of the NCTA and the Cellular Telecommunications & Internet Association (CTIA); lobbying arms of the cable and wireless industries, respectively.[2] Meredith Atwell-Baker, an Obama-nominated FCC commissioner, served on the FCC from 2009 to 2011. She left the Commission four months after the Comcast/NBCUniversal merger for a new position as senior vice president of governmental affairs at NBCUniversal.[3] In 2014 she became president and CEO of CTIA—The Wireless Association, an industry trade group that lobbies on behalf of the wireless communication sector.[4]

Finally, while the decisions of the Commission are ostensibly justified by the contributions wired and wireless communication make to the public interest, they are often driven by and in response to free market forces and exigencies. As Thomas Streeter writes in his history of broadcast regulation: "Much of what broadcast regulation is about in the United States is crafting the mix of rights, privileges, and restrictions that form the conditions of operation, the bargaining power, and thus the market value of stations, copyrights, and audiences."[5]

---

the ones who had the resources to develop the new medium as well as the understanding of broadcasting to bring the new medium to fruition. Therefore, television in the United States was "superimposed on the existing pattern rather than basically altering it" (Sterling and Kitross). (And the Commissioners during this time went to work for NBC, CBS, and ABC at the end of their terms.)

* While the same cannot be said of Powell, it should be noted that current FCC Chairman Tom Wheeler has not shied away from confrontations with his former employers, nor from taking positions in opposition to them. This is particularly evidenced in his advocacy for reclassifying ISPs as "common carriers" in the net neutrality debate as well as his current efforts to create an open market for set-top boxes.

A brief history of regulatory legislation

1934 Communications Act

Although revised by subsequent legislation, the 1934 Communications Act remains the "Ur-text" of American wired and wireless communication regulation. It brought all services that "rely on wires, cables, or radio as a means of transmission" under the regulatory control of the FCC (which replaced the Federal Radio Commission).[6] This act also codified the tenets of diversity and localism as key to the regulation of the scarce electromagnetic spectrum and mandated that licensees were to operate in the "public interest, convenience and necessity."[7] However, this codification ended at the inclusion of these terms and phrases in the act. Nowhere does the act provide operative or even interpretive definitions of "diversity," "localism," or "public interest, convenience and necessity." As a result, the meanings of these terms have been defined and redefined according to the interests (and usually special interests) of the sitting FCC commissioners who of course act in the best interest of their favored constituencies.

1965 First Report and Order on Cable/"must carry" rules

This first substantial piece of cable regulation by the FCC was designed to "ensure local stations equal access to viewers who might be cable subscribers."[8] As a result, all cable companies were required to carry all over the air (OTA) signals that were "significantly viewed" within their coverage area but did not have to compensate the broadcasters for the retransmission of their signals.[9] As the number of original cable networks that could be utilized to "light up the dial" of cable providers expanded, these requirements were challenged by providers who wanted to carry more profitable niche networks on their limited systems rather than being forced to retransmit all ultra high frequency (UHF) and very high frequency (VHF) signals in their operating areas.* While the original raison d'etre of this legislation was to protect

---

* What should be noted about the "must carry rules" in this earliest period—while one may think that this pertained solely to local affiliates of the "big three" networks at the time, the term "significantly viewed" is significant. Most municipalities had several independent VHF stations as well as a bevy of stations on the always-disadvantaged UHF channels. Therefore, the number of channels that

broadcasters from being excluded from cable systems by forcing cable systems to accommodate them and their advertising-supported programming as cable networks began to proliferate—funded by both advertisers and carriage fees—broadcasters began to lobby to eliminate the rules so that they could also receive "retransmission fees."

1992 Cable Television Consumer Protection and Competition Act

This act altered the "must carry" rules by allowing broadcasters to renegotiate their multiple-system operator (MSO) carriage agreements and to choose whether they wanted to receive "retransmission fees," or "retrains," (a per-subscriber, per-month payment—as was paid to cable networks) or another type of "compensation in kind."[10] This "compensation in kind" could be the waiving of retransmission payments in return for the carriage of an additional channel on the cable system and some barter advertising. If one considers the "families" of channels that are owned by companies that either are primarily broadcasters or have substantial broadcast holdings, one can see how this shifted the balance of power toward broadcasting conglomerates who can leverage the carriage of their nationwide programming to ensure the distribution of their niche channels to the cable and satellite subscribing public. If MSOs balk at these deals, broadcasters can withhold their signals until the carrier offers them acceptable compensation. This imbalance of power can be solved, of course, by the MSO's purchase of the broadcasting company.

1996 Telecommunications Act

The Telecommunications Act of 1996 was heralded by the FCC as "the first major overhaul of telecommunications law in almost 62 years."[11] The goal of

> qualified for "must carry" could easily be in the teens. While this did create a multichannel viewing experience for the subscriber, it was also a financial challenge to cable systems, especially those with smaller channel capacities.

this legislation was to create an open market for telephone, cable, broadcast, wired, and wireless information services—"to let anyone enter any communications business—to let any communications business compete in any market against any other."[12] Poised as it was on the brink of the internet's maturation as a multimedia information network, it was an interesting moment for the legacy entertainment industries that could be viewed as the culmination of their lobbying efforts to have ownership rules relaxed in order to engage in the empire-building that media companies have pursued since the earliest days of the film industry. In many ways, the act may have been inevitable since in the years preceding its passage, "the final regulatory obstacles were removed, ideological consensus achieved, political will solidified, and significant deals struck. By 1996, the political landscape was no longer hostile to common ownership of telecommunications, cable, broadcast and film."[13]

The 1996 Telecommunications Act "launched a free-for-all in the TV marketplace because regulation that had been in place for decades was lifted. Broadcasters, cable TV operators, and local and long distance phone companies were now permitted to increase their market power within their traditional markets and to enter one another's markets."[14] This allowed telecomm companies such as AT&T and Verizon to begin to enter the multichannel video programming distributor (MVPD) market. While this act increased the options consumers had for how they accessed the multichannel environment in theory, in practice, the situation was much different. There were no provisions in the act against the MVPDs engaging in "clustering" in which they preserved regional monopolies by dividing the country up among them. ("You take the Southwest, I'll take the Pacific Northwest.") Ownership caps of broadcast television stations were relaxed, which resulted in the increased power of "station groups" or large holding companies that own multiple locally licensed stations across the United States, and use their market-power to negotiate more cost-effective off-net syndication deals with content producers. In short, writes Jennifer Holt: "The Telecommunications Act of 1996 was the ultimate deregulatory initiative to complete the structural convergence of the media industries that began during the 1980s ... and the last piece of legislation necessary to solidify the blueprint for the new millennium entertainment empires."[15]

Current FCC issues and actions

At present there are four separate yet interconnected regulatory issues that have, do, or will affect the shape and operation of the television industry/ies:

- Net neutrality
- Ownership
- Spectrum allocation (in particular the incentive spectrum auction)
- Definitions of MVPDs

As many of these will have been decided or the conversation may have shifted by the time this book is released, my purpose here is to sketch out the stakeholding positions of those who stand to benefit or be disadvantaged by particular rulings on these topics, as well as explore some of the implications of the more likely outcomes of these regulatory actions.

Net neutrality

The term "network neutrality" was coined in 2003 by Columbia Law Professor Tim Wu in a journal article that highlighted potential problems with "broadband discrimination." Wu sees network neutrality as an end goal of policy that should prioritize innovation in a dynamic communications environment whose fundamental industrial organization has not yet been concretized.[16] Because "cognitive biases" toward existing schema or traditional protocols may stifle innovation, especially by those who may already be established on the platform (in this case the internet) it is crucial "that the platform be neutral to ensure the competition remains meritocratic."[17] In specific terms of what net neutrality means for the end consumer, it ensures that all traffic carried over an internet service provider's service network and into the subscriber's home be treated equally in terms of access and delivery efficiencies. For example: the principle of net neutrality would not allow Comcast to slow down the movement of Netflix's information packets to Comcast internet subscribers (as it did in 2013) while optimizing the Comcast subscriber's reception of video over Hulu (in which Comcast subsidiary NBC owns a controlling interest).

On February 26, 2015, the FCC elected to codify net neutrality as a fundamental principle of broadband network regulation.[18] Its "Open Internet" ruling reclassified broadband internet as a "Title II telecommunications service" under the 1934 Communications Act.[19] This means that broadband internet providers (both wired and wireless) are now legally defined "common carriers"—just like the (wired) phone companies. As such, they have responsibilities to "act in the public interest" and cannot "make any unjust or unreasonable discrimination [or undue or unreasonable preference] in charges, practices, classifications, regulations, facilities or services."[20] This means that internet service providers may not engage in blocking, throttling, or paid prioritization—in other words, all websites, regardless of owner, content, or bandwidth usage must be delivered to consumers without preferential or prejudicial altering of their load times.[21]

The open internet ruling also invokes Section 706 of the Telecommunications Act of 1996 which states that "advanced telecommunications services" must be utilized "in a manner consistent with the public interest, convenience, and necessity, price cap regulation, regulatory forbearance, measures that promote competition in the local telecommunications market, or other regulating methods that remove barriers to infrastructure investment."[22] Section 706 also seeks to extend "advanced telecommunications capability to all Americans" but particularly "elementary and secondary schools and classrooms."[23]

It appears that the FCC invoked Section 706 in its classification of broadband as a common carrier under the original Title II so as to refute earlier judicial rulings in the 2014 *Verizon v. FCC* case. In this case, Verizon stated that because the FCC had previously defined broadband as an information service (under Title I of the 1934 Communications Act); it could not reclassify them as a common carrier. If Verizon and other internet service providers (ISPs) had remained information services, they would be free to engage in competitive speed capping as well as avoid the much stricter regulatory requirements that adhere to common carriers. Section 706 softens the language of Title II by emphasizing the promotion of infrastructure investment and preservation of a competitive market for advanced telecommunication capacities that preemptively strikes at industry complaints that common carrier status will prevent innovation and expansion.

In what can also be interpreted as a preliminary strike against legal challenges by the industry, the FCC also explicitly claims "broad forbearance" in the parts of Title II that apply to ISPs. It states: "In finding that broadband Internet access service is subject to Title II, we simultaneously exercise the Commission's forbearance authority ... to establish a light-touch regulatory framework tailored to preserving those provisions that advance our goals of more, better, and open broadband. We thus forbear from the vast majority of rules adopted under Title II."[24]

The sections that the FCC specifically/explicitly does *not* waive are "sections 201, 202 and 208 (or from related enforcement provisions), which are necessary to support adoption of our open Internet rules."[25] These sections of the 1934 Communications Act pertain to interconnectivity (the ability of ISPs to make arrangements with each other to carry each other's traffic across the internet until their proprietary "last mile"); discriminatory provision of services (throttling, paid prioritization, etc.); and the right of persons with complaints about the common carrier to petition the Commission, who will follow an information-gathering process to ensure fairness to all parties involved. Therefore, these parts of the act protect consumers, preserve competition, and encourage growth without creating ownership caps on MSOs or engaging in rate-regulation. (ISPs may set their own rates in accordance with whatever the market will bear.)

Other Title II regulations of the 1934 Communications Act that remain in effect in this ruling are sections 222, 224, 225, and 254. These pertain to privacy, accommodations for persons with disabilities, and the requirement that local utilities grant the ISPs access to their infrastructure (poles, ducts) so as to encourage the growth and development of universal service.

One interesting feature of this ruling is that it redefines both wired and wireless broadband services as "common carriers." Therefore, wireless ISPs (essentially cell phone providers) are now subject to the same rules as are their wired ISP brethren (the cable companies). In this case the forbearances have much more direct advantages for the wireless ISPs as "data caps" are expressly not forbidden so as to encourage the universal spread of internet access to mobile-only users. Thus, wireless providers may provide different "tiers" of data plans with different pricing points as presumably this supports universal access through different price points. It should be noted that this is a capping of amount of data one can receive a month for one's set fee, not the capping of the speed of the delivery of certain kinds of data.

A less clear wireless data initiative is that of "zero rating" particular apps or families of apps that stream content. Zero rating means that customers use of these apps does not count against their monthly data allowance. The FCC has yet to rule on a case about this, but it would seem to fall into a grey area, particularly if it favors the streaming consumption of one company's service (e.g., YouTube) over another's (Netflix). (This is also where programs like T-Mobile's "Binge On" may be vulnerable to challenge.)

As was predicted, the industry majors immediately filed suit against the FCC open internet regulations claiming that the agency had again exceeded their power in reclassifying wired and wireless broadband as common carriers and insisting that the ruling not only violated the First Amendment rights of the corporations involved, but also would retard innovation in the field. On June 14, 2016, the District of Columbia's Appeals Court rendered a decision upholding the network neutrality rules finding that the Commission was acting within its powers to reclassify the service providers as common carriers.[26] While AT&T, Verizon, and the other plaintiffs have vowed to take this to the Supreme Court, it is unlikely that this will occur in the immediate future. FCC Chairman Tom Wheeler said of the ruling "It is a victory for consumers and innovators who deserve unfettered access to the entire web" and that it would "ensure the Internet remains a platform for unparalleled innovation, free expression and economic growth."[27]

Ownership

As repeatedly noted, due to market realities and the economies of scale traditionally required to create and sustain the production, distribution, and exhibition of entertainment, these industries tend toward oligopolies. The role of regulators has been to control conglomeration by maintaining ownership caps or prohibitions against purchases that would create too large a controlling entity in any industrial segment so as to ensure a diversity of voices in the marketplace and to prevent one corporate perspective from gaining too much exclusive or exclusionary access to the viewing population. Station caps and ownership limits were inscribed in the original 1934 Communications Act but, as we have seen, these caps have been revised in subsequent legislation to respond to the multiplication of choice with regard to viewing options and presumably voices that are now available to the citizen-consumer.

Patterns of corporate acquisition can take several forms. The overall goals were originally vertical and horizontal integration. Vertical integration brings companies involved in all phases of production—distribution—sale together while horizontal integration is the accumulation of multiple companies whose primary economic activity is at the same phase or stage of industrial activity.[28] Now we have reached a stage of transindustrial conglomerates—"firms that vertically and horizontally integrate multiple media operations within and across multiple media industries."[29] The result of this is an "increased concentration of ownership across all media, with fewer companies involved in more media oligopolies."[30] The easiest way to understand this is to consider the holdings of any of the six global conglomerates that controlled 90 percent of media markets in 2011.[31] Among the holdings of each of these companies (Comcast-NBCU, News-Corp, Disney, Viacom, TimeWarner, and CBS) one finds not only film studios, television production companies, television and cable networks, station groups, and O&Os, but also publishing companies, music, theme parks, newspapers, and magazines—all in the same corporate family.

For example, in 2011, the merger of Comcast and NBCUniversal united the largest cable MSO in the United States and a large diversified entertainment company with many broadcast and cable holdings. More recently TimeWarner, a highly vertically and horizontally integrated media company with holdings across television, film, music, and publishing, merged with Charter Communications (the number two MSO in the country). Shortly afterward, Altice, the fourth largest cable provider in Europe purchased New York-based Cablevision (more on this in the next chapter). The implications of this new wave of conglomeration which brings together massive content creators with cable and internet providers are massive for both the market and the consumers.

Prior to the merger, Comcast was the largest cable operator in the United States, the largest residential high-speed internet provider in the United States, the third largest home phone company, the owner of key content properties including eleven regional sports networks and the manager of a large video on demand (VOD) concern.[32] NBCUniversal was a content conglomerate that owned one of the largest national broadcast networks as well as some of the most popular cable networks in the United States, owner of NBC Sports, seven production studios, twenty-five television stations in all major US DMAs and had interest in several internet properties, including iVillage and 1/3 of Hulu.[33]

Writing shortly after the merger, Susan Crawford noted that the merged company controls "one in five hours of all television viewing in the United States ... and more than 125 media outlets (cable channels, television stations, film studios, web sites)."[34] But more important than the content library and branded channels that NBCUniversal brought to the table was Comcast's broadband service—a primary provider of broadband connectivity in most major US cities.[35] This bears further examination in light of the "sky is falling" rhetoric that has been employed with regard to the "threat" of OTT producers and distributors to traditional television "because no other widely available privately provided wired Internet access product is fast enough or can be installed cheaply enough to compete with cable, each of the country's large cable distributors can raise prices in its region for high-speed Internet access without fear of being undercut."[36] While cable subscriptions may have declined in recent years, "80% of Americans buying a wired high-speed connection these days sign up with their local cable incumbent" and in fact, "for 75% of Americans, the only choice for globally standard high-speed Internet access will soon be the local cable guy."[37] So, if the traditional "legacy" broadcast and cable television companies are part of these large wired internet service-providing conglomerates, how much do they really have to worry about cord cutters or cord shavers? If "broadcasting" and "cablecasting" moves predominantly to IPTV platforms, it is their same content, same advertising, just served via a different pipe, which they still own and receive revenue streams from. And, of course, cable companies can, have, and will "push subscribers toward bundles of pay-TV and Internet access by pricing Internet-only subscriptions at a higher rate than that of the bundle."[38]

Spectrum allocation and auctions

Among the lesser-discussed mandates of the 1996 Telecommunications Act was the transition of all analog television broadcasters to digital. The presumed and widely publicized reason for this conversion was to "free up parts ('bands') of the scarce and valuable broadcast [airwaves], allowing these bands to be used for public safety and emergency services, such as police, fire and medical services, and new wireless, services, such as wireless broadband."[39] This conversion was pushed back several times, from 2006 to 2007 to 2008, until analog television broadcasting ultimately ended on June 12, 2009. The spectrum that was freed by the transition was sold through an FCC-administered auction and netted the government $19.5 billion, $16.3 of it from wireless mobile providers Verizon and AT&T.[40] Verizon, AT&T, and US Cellular have utilized their new spectrum to enhance the speed of their wireless broadband coverage in urban areas, rather than enhancing coverage in less populous area.

As I write this, the 600MHz spectrum is imminently going up for auction by the FCC. This auction is actually composed of two separate actions, one of which is a "reverse auction" (Auction 1001) in which current license holders (television broadcasters) will sell their spectrum back to the FCC. This repurchased spectrum will be bundled with additional spectrum currently controlled by the FCC and then offered in a "forward auction" (Auction 1002) which will offer this spectrum for reprovisioning as wireless broadband infrastructure. The FCC states explicitly that the goal of this buy-back/sell-forward is to "expand the benefits of mobile wireless coverage and competition to consumers across the Nation, offering more choices of wireless providers, lower prices, and higher quality mobile services."[41]

The major participants registered for both auctions are, not surprisingly, Verizon AT&T and T-Mobile US; it is assumed that they will be the winners of the largest amount of spectrum. This particular part of the spectrum is technologically attractive to wireless providers because it "offer[s] both distinct propagation characteristics for deployments over long distances and strong in-building penetration."[42]

It is instructive to note that Chairman Wheeler emphasizes the fact that broadcasters' participation in his auction process will be "purely voluntary, and participation ... does not mean they have to leave the over-the-air TV business entirely. New channel-sharing technologies offer broadcasters a rare opportunity for an infusion of cash to expand their business model and explore new innovations, while continuing to provide their traditional services to customers."[43] How this will be accomplished, both technologically and in a regulatory sense, remains to be determined.

What this means is that there may be locally licensed broadcast affiliates or independent stations that are going to sell back all of their spectrum allocation to the FCC—in effect ceding their identities as traditional broadcasters. This would free them from certain legally defined responsibilities of FCC-licensed OTA broadcasters such as main studio rules, local programming, and the nebulously defined "public interest" services and force them to rely upon carrier agreements with cable and satellite MSOs as well as their own IPTV websites to distribute themselves to viewers.

What is important to understand about the spectrum auction is that while it will increase the industrial size and capacity of wireless providers, this does not pose a major threat to the wired broadband providers. Wired high speed internet and wireless services do not currently compete with each other directly. They are complementary services.[44] Therefore, "there are two enormous monopoly submarkets—one for wireless and one for wired transmission. Both are dominated by two or three large companies."[45] In many of the largest markets, the same companies (Verizon and AT&T) might be dominant in both the wired and the wireless broadband markets, making such distinctions irrelevant except to those interested in antitrust legislation.

Because spectrum is a limited resource, wireless is inherently a limited technology. Wireless might seem to be the antidote for the stranglehold the cable companies have on wired internet access but coaxial cable and fiber optics are 20–100 times faster than a 4G wireless connection.[46] According to Crawford, "In order to build a wireless network that could be used by everyone and that would perform as well as wired high-speed Internet services there would have to be a wireless tower on every rooftop—connected to a wire—that no user shared with any other."[47] Therefore, while AT&T and Verizon must abide by net neutrality rules in their provision of wired high-speed internet, the very nature of their wireless technology (use of the scarce spectrum) ensures that they will not challenge MSOs broadband services in the marketplace, particularly not in the delivery of IPTV.

Wired distribution systems such as telephone and cable are what Crawford calls "natural monopoly industries" because "up-front capital costs are high and the marginal cost of serving one additional customer is low."[48] Once the major wiring has been installed and the necessary deals made with the municipalities through whose infrastructure the wires run, additional customers "will not only mean more revenue for the provider, it will also reduce the company's average cost of serving its entire customer base."[49] This obviously favors incumbents, especially if they already have monopoly control over particular regions and markets—and it also dissuades competitors from attempting to enter the market.[50] This is what caused the "nationwide rollout" of Verizon FiOS to stall as well as what makes Google Fiber unlikely to spread beyond its experimental run in Kansas City.[51] The incumbent cable systems already have formed a natural monopoly and the cost of running fiber into these communities is prohibitively expensive when compared with what the market will currently bear, even though a large-scale capital investment in this infrastructure now would yield much higher profits for Verizon and Google in the long run.

MVPD vs. OVD—What's in a definition?

The legal definition of a "multichannel video programming distributor (MVPD)" is "a person such as, but not limited to, a cable operator, a multichannel multipoint distribution service, a direct broadcast satellite service, or a television receive-only satellite program distributor, who makes available for purchase, by subscribers or consumers, multiple channels of video programming."[52] This includes all existing cable and satellite MSOs. As a result, content providers such as AT&T/DirectTV, Comcast, Charter-Time Warner, Cablevision/Altice, and Verizon FiOS (the five largest MVPDs in the United States)[53] are subject to regulations that exclusively online video distributors (OVD) such as Amazon Instant Video, Hulu, and Netflix are not.

The primary point of contention here is the financial challenges that the regulatory requirements of MVPD classification would create for OVDs, particularly those seeking to enter the market. Among these regulations are cable program access, Equal Employment Opportunity Commission (EEOC) obligations, mandatory closed-captioning/video description, and, most importantly, retransmission consent fees.

The FCC released a Notice of Proposed Rulemaking on the topic in 2014, in which it advocated the reclassification of OVDs as MVPDs, arguing that the designation MVPD should apply to any "services that make available for purchase, by subscribers or customers, multiple linear systems of video programming, regardless of the technology used to distribute the programming."[54] Presumably the FCC is seeking to primarily address one reality and one industry/market-based concern with this proposed redefinition. The reality is the acceptance that "television" can no longer be technologically defined as "broadcast, cable and satellite"—it is now "platform everywhere" and its definition in practice is more based on the characteristics of its content rather than the container through which it is delivered to the viewer. The market-based concern (according to Chairman Wheeler) is that "efforts by new entrants to develop new video services have faltered because they could not get access to programming content that was owned by cable networks or broadcasters" and that "big company control over access to programming should not keep programs from being available on the Internet."[55]

That being said, the validity of the market-based concern raises more questions than it addresses. The majority of OVDs are owned and operated by big companies anyway—as such they are already operating in the collaborative cross-licensing economy that is part and parcel of the operation of the entertainment oligopolies (you pay me for my content and delivery, I'll pay you for yours and do likewise). When "big companies" have restricted access to their content (as NBC and ABC did with Netflix in the lead up to the Hulu launch), Netflix's response was to expand its licensing deals of overseas English-language programming and to enter the original production realm. This was possible because it already had the revenue streams and capital to invest in this competitive action. If it were classified as an MVPD, NBC, and ABC would have been forced to negotiate carriage fees with Netflix, but could have made these negotiations prohibitively expensive or stalled them until it had sufficiently benefitted Hulu.

The position that OVDs should be recategorized as MVPDs to encourage competition and new entry into the market is interesting in the wake of the Supreme Court decision on Aereo in 2014. In 2012, Aereo began offering OTA viewers in New York City access to broadcast channels via a remotely located dime-sized antenna and DVR service that the viewer accessed over the internet via his or her computer, tablet, phone, SmartTV, or streaming device.[56] The viewer leased the remote antenna for about $8 a month which included twenty hours of cloud-based DVR storage. Technologically, Aereo worked by tuning the individual subscriber's antenna to the broadcast feed of the channel that the subscriber selected to view, began recording the broadcast feed of that channel to a remote DVR on a cloud server and then streamed the programming from the cloud-based DVR on the device to which the subscriber was viewing. Therefore, the subscriber was not receiving a direct live feed of the OTA broadcast signal, but rather a seconds-delayed replay of the content from the remote DVR.[57] Aereo was thus technically an OVD—while it relied upon the OTA broadcast signal for initial reception of the content, its use of broadband and wireless connectivity made it an online video distributor of sorts.

Aereo's design was widely critiqued as being "barely legal" from the start. Writing in the *Harvard Business Review's HBR Blog* in 2013, Larry Downes said "the entire business is engineered to exploit existing copyright law."[58] It did so mainly by relying on a combination of one of the central unchallenged tenets of American broadcasting—that "over-the-air television [is] free to anyone who puts up an antenna and connects it to a receiving device" and legal precedents set by the 1984 Sony Betamax case that said individual consumer use of video recording devices to time-shift the viewing of video programming was "fair use" of the content.[59] The Betamax decision was further complicated by a 2008 case in which the television networks sued Cablevision for its development of a "'Remote Storage' DVR." Cablevision wanted to maintain "virtual DVRs" for each of its subscribers to which the subscriber would record his or her time-shifting programming via home remote. While "from an engineering standpoint it would only have needed one [recorded copy of the shows] to handle the replay," the Cablevision system made an individual copy of each show on its cloud servers as the show was aired for each subscriber who requested it.[60] Thus, the Cablevision customers were watching "their" copy of the show during playback. The Cablevision system looks very much like what Aereo offered. The networks argued that the virtual DVR system as "really just a ruse to let Cablevision offer their content as on-demand programming without paying extra for it. The difference between a home VCR and a remote DVR was legally significant, they said. Indeed, it was the difference between fair use and an unauthorized rebroadcast."[61] The court ruled in favor of Cablevision saying that as long as separate viewer-initiated recordings were made and maintained by Cablevision on its hard drives and served individually to customers, the service was within the boundaries of Betamax.

The television industry argued that Aereo was operating as a cable or satellite provider—providing "retransmission" of their content without paying "retransmission fees," which were established by the 1992 Cable Television Consumer Protection and Competition Act and are federally regulated. The specific charge made in this case (*ABC Television Stations v. Aereo*) hinged on the interpretation of the definitions of "public versus private performance" in US copyright legislation.[62] Central to this question was "when private consumer technology crosses the line into becoming a public performance."[63] According to the Copyright Act of 1976, an indirect public performance (as opposed to a direct one, such as a movie screening) is when "members of the public capable of receiving it did so 'in the same place or in separate places, and at the same time or at different times.'"[64]

Aereo claimed that its activity was within the "fair use" rulings of the Betamax and Cablevision decisions because its service was based on the individual—"hundreds of thousands of tiny antennas ... one for each of its customers. It's just like having your own antenna and a DVR at home, the company argues, except that the antenna and the DVR are both remote, and you control both through the Internet and not your television. It's not just time shifting. It's place shifting."[65] The assigning of an individual antenna to every subscriber thus made the transmissions private performances.

The Supreme Court disagreed and in a 6–3 decision said that Aereo had violated the copyright of the broadcasters. Writing for the majority, Justice Breyer said that Aereo was "'not simply an equipment provider' but acted like a cable system in that it transmitted copyrighted content."[66] As for the private performance argument, Breyer stated "You can transmit a message to your friends whether you send identical emails to each friend or a single email all at once."[67] Justice Scalia, writing for the dissent objected to Aereo's entire business model saying it was one that "exploited a loophole" and that it was the job of regulators and legislators, not the Court to plug loopholes.[68]

CBS CEO Leslie Moonves, one of the most outspoken television industry leaders said of the decision: "We expected to win, but it certainly feels good to win as decisively as we did."[69] He was blunt about what was expected of the Aereo-like service: "all that's important here is that broadcasters and cable content companies and everyone who's involved with the content producing business gets paid appropriately for their content. And that somebody can't come and take that content, charge for it, and not pay us back for that content."[70] Other industry entities from networks to unions and guilds voiced much the same relief at the exit of Aereo from the market since it protects a valuable revenue stream that supports new production.

In 2014, Aereo filed paperwork to be reclassified as a cable company.[71] This reclassification would have required Aereo to pay retransmission fees to the broadcasters whose signals it provides, which begged the question of Aereo's viability as an MVPD. At the end of 2013, Aereo had "77,596 subscribers, spread out among 10 cities."[72] With a maximum subscription of $12 per month, Aereo would not have been able to cover the cost of retrans fees for all the signals it was rebroadcasting. Additionally, although Aereo claimed to have the technological capacity to serve hundreds of thousands of subscribers, its market performance indicated that the majority of viewers were unwilling to pay a monthly fee to get programming that is usually available (along with many other options) for next day viewing via online outlets like Hulu Plus or the networks' own sites. This left locally originated programming (primarily news) as the unique programming Aereo was able to provide. Regulatory issues aside, as all local television stations maintain websites that include streaming video, Aereo was ultimately providing a redundant service without sufficient value-added for all but a small group of viewers. After filing for bankruptcy, Aereo was acquired by TiVo for $1 million and briefly used in an attempt to sell its now-defunct Roamio OTA DVR system.[73]

The use of Aereo-like technology to offer access to broadcast signals has just now begun to be explored by cable MSOs. Optimum is offering a $24.95

subscription package that essentially provides subscribers with a digital antenna that receives all broadcast signals in their service area plus a DVR. This, however, is a bona fide retransmission-fee-paying MVPD utilizing this technology to bring cord-cutters back into its subscriber fold. This convergence of cable and OTT seems primed to continue as Comcast has recently announced the integration of Netflix subscriptions into its new set-top boxes in late 2016.[74] This would seem to indicate a tacit acceptance of the OTT platforms by the traditional video industries—and it legitimates them as another form of television. Whether this will be subject to FCC intervention at a later date (the set-top box issue is currently moribund but may rise again) remains in a liminal state.

Regardless of parent company ownership, it behooves OVDs to be excluded from the MVPD definition. While some may find future OVD retransmission markets to be lucrative, the requirements to carry OTA content would create needless duplication as well as raise further questions about the relevancy (and definition) of "local broadcast footprints" in an era of IPTV. The comment-period for this rulemaking was extended into spring 2015, but as of summer 2016 it remains in a decidedly liminal phase while OVDs continue to behave like (and be acquired by MVPDs).

What we can say of the contemporary moment in US communications regulation is that it appears to favor an expansion of viewing options through mandated "equal access" of content via the internet. At the same time, spectrum auctions seem destined to sharply contract the technological existence of "broadcast" television and to move that distribution to wired and wireless broadband common carriers. The ability of the on demand audience to engage in substantial mobile viewing will be directly affected by the strength and expansiveness of high-speed next generation wireless systems, as will the building of a reliable nationwide wireless system with capacities suitable to provide universal service to urban and rural populations equally.

6

Curatorial Culture Goes International

The entertainment industries have always been internationalized and content has flowed across national boundaries for profit since the first Lumiere films appeared on American nickelodeon screens in the 1890s. Television has been no different and the spread of televisual content across national boundaries has occurred since the founding of the medium—in part because broadcast signals do not turn back at national borders and, of course, because lucrative foreign aftermarkets developed for domestically produced products.

As should be obvious, content distributed by the internet is, unavoidably, internationally distributed. While Netflix and other video distributors can and do use IP geoblocking as a way of controlling access to content that is not licensed for the countries in which the IP is located, it is far from a foolproof method of control. There are numerous ways around this technology for the determined that require less technological know-how than setting a VCR did.[1] While the global effect of internet protocol television (IPTV) on televisual practices could easily yield many more books, I attempt, in this chapter, to provide a very brief survey of how the main concepts related to curatorial culture operate internationally

The most important things to keep in mind when considering curatorial culture in an international context are listed below:

- Curatorial culture's context is, by definition, international. The plethora of offerings available via internet-distributed video knows no international boundaries.
- Curatorial culture is global but not globalizing. Because it is created by a long tail distribution it does not operate in an environment in which scare spectrum space is saturated by foreign programming. Online distribution platforms can and do offer programming from all countries' professional

- and amateur producers in the same long tail and that tail has endless opportunities for expansion.
- OTT producers have, by and large, piggybacked on traditional television marketplaces and enmeshed themselves in these well-established trade practices as just "one more producer" and just "one more distribution platform" in the transactions that take place there.
- OTT development in any one given region is largely determined by technological infrastructure and the development of a home market for information service products. OVDs rely upon broadband connectivity to provide their programming largess thus the spread of the long tail of television programming internationally (a precursor to the full flowering of curatorial culture) may be constrained by local or regional limits. (Note that I say "may")
- Almost every locality on earth with a preexisting television system now has some sort of OTT video offering even if those offerings are highly localized and ad hoc—the movement to IPTV and the availability of an internationalized long tail television library is well underway.

The markets themselves

While the same television distribution systems of broadcast, cable, satellite, and now internet, can be found in every television market that participates in the global circulation of television, individual regions and countries have different histories, institutional structures, and regulatory bodies and practices. Obviously it is not possible to treat the economic, regulatory, technological, and cultural ecosystem of every country's television environment individually here. For the sake of clarity, I use the geographic and supranational divisions that are traditionally used in the selling of rights which are: North America, Europe, Asia Pacific, Latin America, and Africa/Middle East.

One major difference from the US market

Public Service Broadcasting (PSB) was the original form of television (and radio) in Western Europe and this model (of which the BBC was the first) spread through most other industrialized countries, spawning similar systems such as NHK in Japan. In almost all cases, the former colonies of a European nation will have retained to some degree the vestigial structures of their previous government's broadcasting, so nationalized PSB channels can be found through the Asia/Pacific and African/Middle Eastern markets.

PSB differs from the commercial broadcasting model of the United States in its funding sources as well as its articulated responsibilities to the nation state and civil society. While debates on the actual achievement of these goals and ideas persist, in general it is agreed that public service broadcasters share the following characteristics: "some form of accountability to political representatives of the public via administrative organization; some element of public finance; regulation of content; a universal service which addresses citizens; a degree of protection from competition."[2] Note that while these broadcasters are funded in part or in whole by public subsidies (taxes, license fees on television sets, tax levies), they also accept a certain amount of paid advertising which is usually regulated by the administrative organization that oversees their operation. Nonetheless, their relative independence from advertising money has resulted in an approach to programming that is less immediately responsive to viewership numbers than it is in the United States. Shows can attract smaller audiences and programming can be much more explicitly "public interest" or "civil society oriented" because it fits the mandate of the PSB rather than because it panders to current commercialized programming trends. It is important to note that the original PSB entities have evolved with, to, and through new technologies—therefore the BBC maintains a worldwide cable and satellite presence through a variety of international channel offerings, distributes its domestically produced content via traditional markets (*Are You Being Served?* and *Downton Abbey* to the US market via PBS) and OTT distributors (*Father Ted* and *The IT Crowd* via Netflix), *and* maintains a substantial website of content from its news and entertainment divisions which includes on-demand IPTV offerings.

PSB-dominated television markets have not been immune from competition nor international trends toward deregulation and thus, since the 1980s, a large increase in "commercial" or "independent" channels and networks can be found across the globe. Not surprisingly these have usually taken the form of international PSB brands (BBC) as well as the internationalization of US-based networks such as MTV, Bloomberg, and CNBC. Due to the proximity of nations and shared or multiple languages in other regions of the world, viewers can often receive content from several countries via their terrestrial, cable, or satellite service. In some cases the carriage of domestic channels on regional multicountry systems is mandated by supranational organizations (e.g., the European Union's "Television without Frontiers" directive).* Again, this topic could easily spawn several other books—the important point for our purposes is that the "multichannel age" wrought by cable, satellite, and alternative forms of terrestrial (digital) broadcasting is a worldwide phenomenon and all contemporary viewers experienced a vast increase in channel inventory prior to the rise of internet protocol delivery.

Countries that do not have democratic or free market economies generally have television systems that are completely state owned and operated, although even they may have opened borders to international television products. China has allowed certain international cable and satellite services to enter its market provided, of course, that the content be subject to regulation by the State Administration of Press Publication, Radio, Film, and Television. While technologically possible, the reception of unapproved television signals via satellite is a crime in China.[3]

Some similarities and some statistics

While the international television market may have been dominated by US product, the US television market is statistically smaller than both the Asian Pacific and European markets in number of television homes. A bit more than half (52.5%) of television homes are located in Asia Pacific (not surprisingly

---

* The EU's "Television without Frontiers Directive" is the cornerstone of the EU's audiovisual policy. It was adopted in 1989 in response to the expansion of the television systems and offerings of EU member states in the wake of deregulation and commercialization as a way of protecting the European market from foreign domination. The directive "rests on two basic principles: the free movement of European television programmes within the internal market and the requirement for TV channels to reserve, whenever possible, more than half of their transmission time for European works ("broadcasting quotas"). It was, in short, a directive that supported the distribution of locally originated programs and the protection of "European television" in response to the rising power of international television markets and the increased incursion of foreign (in this period, predominantly American) television onto European broadcasting schedules (European Union).

63% of this 52.5% are located in China).⁴ Europe comprises 22.6 percent of the world television viewers, followed by North America (10.3%), Latin America (9.7%), and the Middle East/Africa (5.0%).⁵

Internationally, there are four ways in which viewers receive television signals: terrestrial,* cable, satellite, and IPTV. In 2013, out of an estimated 1.33 billion worldwide television homes, it was estimated that 438.5 million relied on terrestrial delivery for the majority of their programming, 489.2 million on cable, 339.2 million on satellite, and 60.6 million on the internet.⁶† The movement from other television delivery modalities to an internet-based system is an international one and the convergence of internet and television appears to be an inevitability, particularly for highly industrialized nations.

At present the percentage of internet users is 46.1 percent of the world population, or 3,424,971,237 people.⁷ The division of internet users by country/region is proportionally similar to that of television—48.4 percent of users live in Asia, 21.8 percent in the Americas (South America is bundled in with North America); 19 percent are in Europe, 9.8 percent in Africa, and 0.9 percent are in Oceania (which for these purposes includes Australia).⁸ "China, the country with most users (642 million in 2014), represents nearly 22% of total, and has more users than the next three countries combined (United States, India, and Japan). Among the top 20 countries, India is the one with the lowest penetration: 19% and the highest yearly growth rate. At the opposite end of the range, United States, Germany, France, U.K., and Canada have the highest penetration: over 80% of population in these countries has an Internet connection."⁹ What is important to consider about these stats is how they overlap and thus create a roadmap for subscription video on demand (SVOD) and online video distributor (OVD) providers looking to expand across a global market of programming distribution.

---

* "Terrestrial" is also referred to as DTT (digital terrestrial television) in regions that have converted to digital broadcast systems, and is what the United States would call OTA (over the air) broadcasting. As previously noted, terrestrial broadcasting is the first and oldest form of radio and television signal delivery.

† It should be noted that the qualification "majority" allows for the possibility of hybrid reception in which one mode is primarily used. Due to program duplication and the nature of the technological delivery system, it is highly unlikely that satellite, cable, or traditional terrestrial signal recipients engage in multiplatform reception. Therefore, out of the estimated 60.6 million "IPTV homes" one can imagine viewers who still use an antenna for local signals (as American cord cutters, who are included in these statistics) do.

Programs go to market

There are four major markets at which American programs have traditionally been sold to foreign markets and distributors: MIPTV (Marché International des Programmes de Télévision, April, Cannes); MIPCOM (International Market of Communications Programmes, October, France); AFM (American Film Market, November, Santa Monica), and NAPTE (National Association of Television Programming Executives, January, Miami).[10] These are part of the oh-so-crucial aftermarket that makes deficit financing worth the risk—international sales can guarantee additional orders for series that are approaching the "cancellation threshold" in their American ratings, they can also create substantial after- aftermarkets as they move through the syndication food chain of foreign television stations. Not surprisingly, there is a substantial body of scholarship on the global television markets and its related topics such as cultural imperialism, trade agreements, GATT, and the like.

For our purposes, the important thing to know is that these markets remain crucial for legacy producers and have become so for OVD companies. While they began trading in legacy television product only, they now are often the site of licensing deals for Amazon Instant Video and Netflix original productions—so these OVD platforms have been able to monetize their content through international distribution before rolling out their services in these regions. John Penney, Starz chief strategy officer states: "OTT is a real part of the ecosystem at this point. It's no longer a second or third choice or window for a market; it's considered right along with the cable channels and broadcasters. It's not a scary thing so much as an opportunity—an opportunity to grow the pie and reach more people."[11]

One of the things this new market reveals is the way in which curators/viewers enabled and empowered by the long tail offerings of OTT have created a new iteration of television. According to Hulu CEO Mike Hopkins, "We and others are racing to meet demand from consumers, demand that has really existed for decades, (as consumers want) to have more control and flexibility around their television."[12] This control and the demand it has created makes ownership of content and licensing deals even more important—especially for those who have already signed deals with OVD leaders Amazon Instant Video and Netflix. "Without the ability to distribute your series—those guys take worldwide exclusive rights—you're not maximizing worldwide revenue on the show. You may not have a backend."[13] Or, that backend may be compromised through a multiyear exclusive licensing deal with Netflix that coincides with the period of highest interest and popularity of your product. Netflix itself has been caught in the premature licensing of its own programs to the worldwide market since it signed licensing deals for *House of Cards* and *Orange is the New Black* with Asian OVD companies with whom it now seeks to compete.

What is also being revealed via the sales at these markets is that American product, while still dominant, no longer has claim to assumed worldwide popularity—regional markets are reflecting niche tastes, such as the popularity of Turkish soap operas and K-pop in South America.[14] This creates exposure but also new revenue streams and market opportunities domestically and foreign—according to Hans Van Rijn, Netflix's VP of digital media and business: "OTT is a great testing ground. If it works well in a local market, we can move content to other markets. We've taken talent (in local markets) and moved them into OTT; if that works we move them to a linear sphere. It's a road map for talent."[15] That road map has also led back to legacy network productions as evidenced by ABC's casting of Priyanka Chopra in a starring role in *Quantico*.[16] Chopra, thirty-four years old, is a massive international star, just not in the United States (which is now quite possible). She made her career in Bollywood, and has appeared in over fifty Bollywood films including the top box-office grossers of the recent decade.[17] She also has won the Indian equivalent of the Oscar and was named one of *Time Magazine's* "100 Most Influential People" in 2016.[18] Given the international popularity of Bollywood and the size of the Asia Pacific television market, it is unlikely that this is a coincidence, even though ABC president Paul Lee downplayed the multinational fan base that Chopra has already established: "We looked at Priyanka and thought she's a fabulous actress; she's incredibly relatable to our audience; she's empowered and fierce the way only ABC heroines are empowered and fierce." This places Chopra among the pantheon of domestic female stars from ABC's "genre silo" of shows featuring strong female leads.[19]

Platforms go international

The integration of OVD producers and distributors into existing international television licensing protocols and practices has prevented much of the transformative power of the liminal to take hold in this sphere. Nonetheless, the challenges, opportunities, and interventions of the largest US OVD platforms to existing foreign markets is instructive. Some, like Netflix, are merely attempting to "port and replicate" their North American technologies and practices into other markets with little to no change. Others, like Hulu and Amazon are either forgoing international expansion altogether in the short term, or providing limited roll out of their streaming capabilities in response to local or regional regulations that make market entry difficult. It should be noted, however that although Hulu is not entering international markets as a platform, its parent companies are already major players in the international content market. Therefore, their original productions have a clear pipeline to the international markets. Amazon Studios has licensed the distribution rights to its original programming to local OVD outlets in certain territories where its Amazon Prime membership does not include instant video access. YouTube, always the outsider, appears to be having some growing pains in its video distribution/monetization strategy, despite being the second most visited website in the world after parent company Google.[20]

Amazon

When enmeshed in a consideration of Amazon Instant Video, Amazon Studios, and *The Man in the High Castle*, it can be easy to lose sight of the fact that Amazon is first and foremost an international e-tailer of everything from books to soup to nuts. Amazon Prime (called Amazon Premium in some countries) is an international service that provides free shipping, cloud storage, and other benefits to customers in the United Kingdom, Spain, Japan, Italy, Germany, France, Canada, and Austria. What is key to note is that because Amazon's primary business activity is the distribution of consumer goods, its internationalization has been driven by different company goals. As such, "countries where deliveries can be slow or have significant rural populations aren't useful for Prime's very suburban/urban consumer-centric version."[21]

Therefore, Amazon Instant Video is not internationalized—Canadians do not have access to Amazon Instant Video but Amazon licenses its original productions to local Canadian OVDs for distribution to this market.[22] Italy and Spain have a stripped down version of Prime that primarily offers free shipping but no other streaming services or access. French customers do not have access to prime streaming due to licensing and regulatory issues.[23] Given France's history of fierce protectionism of its film and television production (e.g., its insistence upon the "cultural exception" in the 1993 GATT talks) this should come as no surprise.[24]

Germany and Austrian Prime members receive instant video as part of their subscription package. In Japan, Amazon Prime Video debuted in 2015 and Amazon views the Japanese market as so important to its international content production success it is beginning to investigate deals to develop original programming for the Japanese market.[25] The United Kingdom, not surprisingly given the history of program exchange and cross licensing of English-language content, offers Instant Video to its Prime members.

As of this writing it is rumored that Amazon intends to launch Amazon Instant Video in France, Italy, and Spain by the end of 2016.[26] However, these speculations appear to be based on rumors that the company has registered its "Instant Video" brand name in France and also began informal talks with French government officials and there has been no formal announcement from the company nor the French government.

YouTube

YouTube is an internationally accessible website with over a billion users that maintains localized versions in eighty-eight countries.[27] It supports seventy-six different languages in its search feature and claims over 80 percent of its viewers are from outside the United States.[28] It is also the second most used search engine, behind its parent company Google.[29] YouTube operates internationally much the same way it does in the United States and its digital commons function is probably its biggest contribution to an internationalized participatory open archive of video content from across the globe. Because its major focus is video sharing and serving rather than the subscription-based serving of licensed content from behind a paywall, it is not subject to the IP-blocking requirements of Amazon Video and Netflix—as discussed in Chapter 4, it is a platform, not a service. Beyond that, it is enmeshed in the Google/Alphabet international information conglomerate and as such has a completely different revenue model than the other major US-based OVDs.

YouTube makes a variety of interventions in the practices of the international television market. First, YouTube's repository of clips from various professionally produced and distributed shows may serve as promotional paratexts that drive viewers to seek out the original. These may be promotional clips or trailers posted in the channel of the content owner or DIY mashups posted by existing fans. The social media/commentary feature of YouTube can create a space for an international water cooler that provides an additional site for both participatory culture and the mining of fan reactions by the producers.

As discussed in Chapter 4, YouTube also operates as an international distribution platform for broadcasters such as India's Zee Channels—which are available as subscription channels to what is presumably both a local/regional market in India as well as the diasporic Indian community in other countries and regions. Finally, YouTube Red, its foray into content production and subscription paywalls, offers another site of consumption for original programming created by its already established international stars. At present it is only available to US subscribers although there are plans to extend into the European market and to bundle it with Google Play music packages. The rollout of YouTube Red has been less than stellar, however, and of this writing, extensions of its "free trial" periods would seem to indicate that it has either a price point issue, or an exclusivity issue.[30] (One might ask: why would viewers pay to see the performers they have enjoyed for "free" on YouTube Partner Channels?)

Netflix

As with US domestic television, Netflix is a primary disruptor on the international stage as well. "Up until Netflix, television had always been organized on a geographic model. Networks were an association of local affiliates; cable systems, even consolidated ones, were a collection of exclusive license to wire specific communities; cable stations lived or died on their ability to make deals with local cable franchises. And of course, none of this transcended national borders."[31] Of all the SVOD services currently operating in the United States, Netflix has the largest international ambitions as well as the largest international "footprint." As of January 2016, Netflix is either present in or has signed deals to roll out its service in 190 countries representing 130 international television markets.[32] This did not, however, equate to a rise in Netflix's stock price, in fact, just the opposite occurred, a drop of 13 percent.[33] Analysts have identified three major challenges that Netflix now faces: content, pricing, and local competition.[34]

Netflix's content is, of course, its major selling point—it continues to maintain the largest catalog of the major SVODs. However, because global licensing deals are divided by region, and in many cases into countries within that region, its offerings in any one of the 130 markets might be small. The majority of Netflix's offerings are in English which further limits its attractiveness to international audiences. Hong Kong and South Korea have large middle and upper classes for whom an additional monthly subscription would not be a hardship, but they also have a strong preference for local language programming.[35] India, which has the largest English-speaking population in the international market after Australia, already has a robust pay-TV and satellite market with almost universal coverage, whereas its broadband infrastructure is woefully underdeveloped.[36] It also has a thriving film culture which competes directly with any alternative viewing venues.

Due to censorship rules, Netflix's content is unlicensed in Indonesia and according to its regulations "much of its content cannot be shown in cinema and is unsuitable for local audiences."[37] Given that one of the selling points for SVOD in most countries is the availability of content not subject to content regulations or restrictions this creates the need to either strike licensing deals with local producers in the area, or to fund original production specifically for the Indonesian market that may not be attractive to an aftermarket. Like Amazon, Netflix considers the Japanese market lucrative enough to explore the creation of original programming specifically in and for that market, but again those are upfront costs to attract subscribers to the platform.

One of the biggest challenges to Netflix's content strategy is a movement in Europe to enact the same sort of quota system it has used to protect its film industries from the effects of globalization. To that end, the European Commission "wants to impose a quota on on-demand and streaming video services, such as Netflix and Amazon, forcing them to ensure European content makes up at least 20% of the films and television shows in the catalogs."[38] This would not in the immediate moment affect Netflix or its non-regional SVOD competitors in Europe, as a European Audiovisual Observatory survey has already determined that the libraries of foreign SVODs operating in Europe already carry an average of 27 percent European-produced content.[39] However, the European Union is also considering another rule revision that would "allow individual European governments to force online companies to comply with their national quota systems, even if the companies are based outside the country in question."[40] This would, in effect, extend the broadcasting quotas established by the EU's Television without Frontiers directive to OTT television distribution.* This would have a big effect on Netflix's operations in Western Europe and particularly France, which "require[s] national broadcasters and online video companies to contribute directly to the production of European films and TV series, often in the form of a levy on their total revenue. SVOD operators in France have to invest at least 12 percent to 26 percent of their net revenue toward 'the development of European cinematographic and audiovisual works."[41] France further requires that online VOD providers maintain a 60 percent European-produced online catalog and feature European products on their homepages (which may explain why Amazon has been loathe to include streaming video in its French Amazon Prime benefits). While Netflix has thus far avoided EU quota requirements by headquartering its European operations in The Netherlands (which has no quota requirements), the rule revision under consideration would extend these requirements to Netflix.

---

* It should be noted that the Television without Frontiers directive is a product of an environment of channel scarcity since broadcasting, cable, and satellite (the major distribution technologies then and now) are all limited in the number of channels they can provide. One might question if the asynchronous "on demand" delivery systems of OTT television platforms and their only-limited-by-licensing agreements libraries should be subject to restrictions established in response to a scarcity that no longer exists.

For its part, Netflix has invested substantially in European content production, although it has primarily put its money toward English-language programming or genres that will play well to the American market. "Our members around the world love European programming, that's why our investment in European programming, including Netflix original titles created in Europe is growing."[42] Netflix suggests that the proposed rules will "increase demand for inexpensive and library filler programming, not high-quality, original European films and TV series."[43] On its face, this seems odd. If one considers the long tail distribution possibilities of online streaming, it should not necessarily matter to Netflix which programming is being streamed, so long as it is receiving a subscription payment. Therefore, it is curious to see a long tail company make an argument about quality that presupposes a scarcity (the scarcity, in this case, of course, is the funding it has available). The Society of Audiovisual Authors (SAA) (the European equivalent of the Writers Guild of America, or WGA), is supportive of the rule changes and highlights one of the features of the international market: "Regulatory forum shopping, used by some distributors when establishing headquarters in countries with weaker audiovisual regulation, should no longer be a competitive advantage."[44]

A further content challenge is one that Netflix created for itself: by striking licensing deals for its existing competitors in a variety of markets, it has restricted itself from carrying its own content to those markets in the near future. For instance, due to preexisting exclusive deals it has made with regional OVD providers, it will not be able to stream its own shows to the Asian market until 2019.[45] For lack of a better phrase, Netflix may be engaged in an "if we roll it out they will subscribe" action although its ability to offer a unique and substantial content library is substantially compromised by its inability to stream its own shows in these markets.

Netflix's price points can make it an expensive luxury and its price hike in the United States resulted in an unexpected churn as Netflix discovered, perhaps too late, that subscribers were not ready to pay an additional $2.00 a month for its streaming service.[46] In many parts of the world, Netflix is the most expensive SVOD offering and exceeds the cost of existing pay-TV services (such as cable or satellite).[47] Aravind Venugopal, VP of Singapore's Media Partners says that Netflix is aiming at the top 1 percent of Asian markets and unless it introduces variable pricing, it will not be competitive with already established local and regional SVOD and OVD offerings.[48] The churn created by the raise in US subscriber fees is an ominous harbinger and one which works against the availability of capital to invest in more content—which is needed to combat churn and justify subscription increases—"Netflix could find itself in a loop in which higher prices drive higher churn, which drives higher prices and so on."[49]

Internationally, Netflix competes with entrenched and often government-subsidized OTT providers to whom it has already licensed some of its original programming for the short term (which is also, presumably, its roll-out phase). However, it also competes for market share and eyeballs with the same alternative viewing platforms it faces in the US market—existing cable and satellite providers, over-the-air terrestrial broadcasters, and, of course, Amazon Instant Video and YouTube. Here, the availability of vast amounts of DTT (digital terrestrial television—equivalent to US OTA) can create a broadcast channel inventory that rivals larger tiers of cable service in the United States. Additionally due to the PSB roots of so many international television industries, there is a national or supranational stake in the preservation and support of local television systems. In Germany, a market where VOD consumption has doubled since 2014, Amazon Instant Video is now streamed to 34 percent of German homes, twice the number that subscribe to Netflix.[50]

Finally, Netflix may be too unwilling to localize itself—even if it includes more locally originated programming, if it is not willing to accept and work within the technological realities of the markets it seeks to enter, it is not going to attract the subscribers. Netflix is currently available in all fifty-four African nations. However, the number of African viewers who know this, let alone can subscribe to the service is abysmally low. Internet penetration on the entire continent is the lowest in the world—just 20 percent.[51] iRoko, the incumbent "Netflix of Africa" has optimized its delivery system for the way the majority of the 300 million Africans who are connected access the web: mobile phones. While unreliable service and high data costs have worked against the wide adoption of streaming services, iRoko delivers its content through a "mobile-first, Android-first, download-only version."[52]

Marie Lora-Mungai of Kenyan competitor Buni.tv notes that Netflix does not traditionally "modify their platform to adapt to the specificities of local markets."[53] "Netflix is building for the world" says iRoko founder Jason Njoku, "we are building for Africa."[54]

Net neutrality around the world

Because "the net" knows no geographical boundaries, net neutrality is a global issue that, like environmental issues (also global) intersect with the governmental structures and regulatory systems of various nations and regions in overdetermined ways. The Global Net Neutrality Coalition maintains an interactive world map on its website (www.thisisnetneutrality.org) which tracks the status of net neutrality legislation and policy-making throughout the world. As of July, 2016 the major countries and regions that have net neutrality protections are: Canada, the United States, Mexico, the majority of South America, India, Turkey, Norway, Sweden, the Netherlands, Switzerland, Austria, Japan, and South Korea. Other European countries, Australia, South Africa, Nigeria, and Pakistan are "considering protections." Not surprisingly the Russian Federation and China have no protections.[55]

In October 2015, the European Union adopted net neutrality rules that purported to protect net neutrality. Response to the legislation has focused primarily on "loopholes" which allow for "specialized services" to pay to have their content delivered faster (the "paid prioritization" that the FCC rules have outlawed) as well as the legalization of "zero rating" which allows ISPs to favor certain services (such as branded streaming ecosystems) by not charging their customers for data usage by these apps.[56] While the European Union intended for the "specialized services" to be closed systems that require uninterrupted and reliable access bandwidth—such as health and safety monitoring or self-driving cars, the regulations are apparently elastic enough to allow streaming services to enter into prioritization deals with ISPs. It should be noted that these supranational regulations, if adopted, will override the existing net neutrality protections in the Netherlands, Norway, Sweden, Switzerland, and Austria. Therefore the practice and protections of net neutrality around the world can and may be substantially different than they are in the United States and may carry with them additional costs of entry or operation in particular markets.

As present, debates about amendments to these rules are raging at the European Union and the advocates and challengers look pretty much the same there as they did in the United States. The "Save the Internet" contingency argues that these rules will privilege big business and shut the door to innovators and inventors whose work relies on an even online playing field. Industry interests maintain the need to maintain expensive delivery systems that, if truly "neutral" create a situation in which streaming services consume vast amounts of bandwidth and create demands for which the providers are not appropriately compensated. They have gone so far as to threaten to withhold the implementation of high-speed 5G service if the European Union does not allow the regulations allowing discriminatory capping to stand.[57]

The effect of these rules on the streaming market would be what could have happened in the United States—the speed at which streaming services are delivered to the end user will be decided through deals struck between the ISP and the streaming services or their parent companies. This will favor those who are able and willing to pay for the fast lanes and thus could disadvantage those who are unwilling or unable to pay for faster delivery of their content. While this may seem like it will be market driven, it could also be used to create an uneven playing field that privileges local or regional streaming services over international ones since ISPs will be able to choose with whom they enter fast lane or zero rating agreements.

Global market domination: It is not just for American companies anymore

At present, the FCC is reconsidering its policies on the foreign ownership of broadcast licensees. It originally issued a statement in November 2013 to clarify that "alien ownership" of companies that own US broadcast licenses should not exceed 25 percent, a cap enshrined in the Communications Act of

1934.* Broadcasters and their lobbying groups stated that the limitation was not "in the public interest" and that allowing "foreign sources of capital" in excess of the one quarter limit would "increase access to capital and investment financing for the broadcast sector."[58] The Commission found that the 25 percent rule may indeed be restrictive and relaxed in insofar as saying that the Commission "is open to considering proposals for foreign investment in broadband licenses that exceed the 25 percent statutory benchmark."[59] The Commission will review applications on a "case-by-case" basis which "may suggest policy issues or streamlined procedural mechanisms that could be addressed in future Commission proceedings."[60] The underlying presumptions are that foreign ownership will not threaten US sovereignty because the information ecosystem is so abundant with opportunities for the distribution of messages. The openness of the FCC to consider increased amounts of foreign money in local broadcaster (or station group) ownership does indicate, however, that the US broadcast industry—previously protected from the threat (and benefits) of global market exigencies, may now be a new source of investment from international and supranational entities.

The issue of foreign ownership becomes particularly interesting in the realm of MVPDs. Altice, a European telecom company based in the Netherlands, and the fourth largest cable company in Europe, bought Suddenlink, the eighth largest cable MVPD in the United States in 2015.[61] In 2016 it purchased Cablevision, previously the seventh largest cable company in the United States. The new company is now the fourth largest cable company by subscribers in the United States.[62] It is too soon to see exactly what the effect of this internationalization of US cable ownership is going to be, but early news coverage quotes Altice executives as saying: "We have about half of our programming lineup that's up for renewal very soon. There are clearly a lot of channels that

---

* Prohibitions against foreign ownership or investment in American broadcasting go back to the post–World War I period when, fearful of the ways in which American ship-to-shore and radio communications could be negatively affected by foreign interests (such as "American Marconi"), the US Government created the Radio Corporation of America (RCA) a government-sanctioned monopoly/holding company into which it transferred control of patents owned by radio manufacturers such as General Electric and Westinghouse and also arranged for the buyout of the foreign owned Marconi Wireless Telegraph Company. Once radio and television broadcasting were invented foreign ownership was limited to prevent the spread of propaganda to the American people via the scarce spectrum of the airwaves.

we'd like to get rid of" which would seem to indicate new carriage deals will be pursued by negotiators who bring different ideas to the table.⁶³

There are no FCC prohibitions on the ownership of cable companies by non-American citizens so we may be seeing the first steps of what could be an internationalization of US cable ownership (which, of course, includes internet service providers). According to Altice's cost-cutting measures, the result could be a revaluation of carrier contracts if Altice, with its large percentage of market share, leverages lower retransmission and carrier fees from networks and cable networks. This would thrust the domestic US television market into yet another state of liminality by chipping away at a revenue stream which network owners have most recently thought was not only safe, but also a newly guaranteed revenue stream for legacy broadcasters. It might also constrict channel inventory and, if Altice were to take a "nuclear option" and institute a la carte pricing of channels for its Cablevision customers—thrusting the entire US system into a liminal stage for which it is ill-prepared.

7

The Curatorial Future

One of the defining conditions of a liminal stage is the loss of taken-for-granted structures—this loss creates a period of fear and doubt, but also opens a space for generative innovation—where what was does not have to be what will be and new hierarchies can emerge.[1] While all facets of the televisual prism—the international markets, regulation, the production/distribution of content, quantification of viewers, and viewing behavior have experienced rites of passage in the past ten years, some of these facets have emerged from liminality while others remain in flux.

What is clear is that change has and is occurring—we have moved from a gatekept culture in which viewers chose from an industry-selected array of media and entertainment texts to a curatorial culture—the mature period of a world of endless choice. This is the major revolution that will continue, in large and small ways to reorient, reenvision, and revolutionize all media industries that are distributed digitally through the internet. Because of its international presence, mature markets, and entrenched paywalled distribution practices, television may weather these transformations both differently and, from an economic standpoint, better, than journalism and music have. But, of course, the key marker of the liminal is that we remain in a place where much is yet to be determined. In reverse order of their treatment in the book, here is a brief description of the current state of liminality and influence of curatorial culture across the televisual prism.

Global but not globalizing—the international televisual sphere

The title of a *Variety* article from 2015's international content market ("Mipcom: TV Markets Scramble to Make Adjustments as Viewing Habits

Transform") could easily be the sub-sub-title of this entire book. While these transformations began with American viewers as early as 2005, over the past ten years, viewers around the world have begun to "view differently." This has thrust the international production, distribution, and consumption of televisual material into a massive liminal stage from which individual countries and markets will emerge at varying rates.

Key to the eventual form(s) that the global television market will take will be regulatory decisions regarding net neutrality, international licensing deals, global ownership of media producing and distributing companies, and, for the sake of new market growth, the evolution of the technological infrastructure of the countries and regions themselves. What can be clearly seen is that international coproduction is going to rise, driven in no small part by investments in local content production by companies (such as Netflix and Amazon Studios) that wish to be competitive in the largest television markets (namely, Asia). In Netflix's case, this international expansion is probably crucial to its survival since its business model must rely on increasing its subscriber base rather than its advertising offerings.

Internationally, television markets are and will remain a mixture of traditional local and regional channels delivered through broadcast, cable, and satellite and, as broadband or other internet technologies begin to reach a saturation point, OVD. OVD and SVOD services have developed in every market, most often as ancillaries of existing public service broadcasting (PSB) and pay systems so the chance of a predominately American company such as Netflix gaining global dominance is increasingly slim. This is particularly probable if EU net neutrality rulings uphold the rights of ISPs to discriminate between different services and companies in their provision of bandwidth.

The negotiation of international distribution deals will be a particularly interesting space to monitor. At present, Netflix's licensing deals with producers include all 130 of their international markets. This erodes a content owner's chance to sell a popular show in individual overseas markets and to create bidding wars in international regions.[2] It would seem likely that unless Netflix can capture substantial subscriber market share in international markets that it will need to balkanize its licensing agreements, thus re-empowering the content producers to price their shows according to regional demand.

Conglomerates, common carriers, and copyright—regulation in the curatorial age

Another way to conceive of rites of passage is to consider a fourfold division of "breach—crisis—redress—reintegration."[3] In this model the "crisis" and "redress" stages are the liminal part of the transformation. The crisis period is where "sides are taken and power resources calculated."[4] Once these resources have been calculated and the stakeholders have determined the best outcome, they engage in a "cognitive or legal attempt to reinstall order via redressive action."[5] While this redressive action may result in a reversion to crisis if the schisms among the sides is seen as too deep or the redressive action is perceived to favor one over another, it may also appeal "to that which rests on a tradition of coexistence among the predecessors on the current community."[6] That, arguably, is what is and has occurred via certain regulatory actions of the FCC while other decisions have created schisms that create further revolutionary opportunities.

Net neutrality has survived the first legal challenge to its continued implementation. While cases will continue to wend their way through the judicial system (Verizon has vowed to take its fight all the way to the Supreme Court); this will take years and, of course, is subject to political exigencies that, particularly at this moment (July 2016), no one can predict. What will probably occur in this realm is a retrenchment of the ISPs to create alternate ways of increasing revenue through bundling of internet and other services and the offering of tiers of high-speed service (which is a market issue, not a neutrality issue and thus not subject to regulation). Wireless companies may continue to experiment with zero rating deals with streaming apps, which will probably be found to be in violation of neutrality rules unless a compelling market/competition argument can be proffered by the wireless providers.

Ownership of content producers and content distributors as represented by the Comcast/NBCU deal and now the Charter/Time Warner acquisition are nothing new for the entertainment industries. At numerous junctures in the history of the twentieth century the vertical integration of various entertainment industries was legally challenged, intervened upon, and then, through deregulation or market shift, reified. (The Paramount Decrees and Fin-Syn are two of the most obvious and representative examples.) Les Moonves sees this as merely the cost of doing business: "Look, Comcast pays us a lot of money to carry CBS, but they also own NBC, which is our biggest competitor, that's the way of the world today. Our competitors are also our friends."[7]

The common carrier and MVPD/OVD disputes are essentially a conflict over definition and naming because the legal definition of these entities directly impacts their power and place in the power structure. This conflict is firmly in a liminal phase as "in revolutionary moments, one observes a condensed symbolic struggle over the legitimate right to power. The establishment of a new system will be fundamentally shaped by the outcomes of such struggles—struggles over meaning."[8] The struggles over meaning in this case come with fiduciary relationships and requirements—the negotiation of retransmission and carriage fees. The outcome of these disputes will revolutionize the operation of existing OVDs should they be reclassified as MVPDs. As of this writing, the perspectives that underlie the FCC's current debates on the definition of an MVPD may prove to be most influential to the future of the television industry/ies. This decision remains liminal but in its preliminary ruling, the FCC has codified a position on video as technology neutral. This will be key going forward—if one cannot create a taxonomy based on delivery systems then—it is not PBS, CBS, NBC, ABC, or Fox; it is not TBS, TNT, Bravo, or F/X; it is not CBS All Access, CNN.com, or HBO Now; it is not Hulu, Netflix, Amazon Instant Video, or YouTube. It is all simply "television."

The reification of control and integration of new entrants—the American television "industry/ies"

Of all of the televisual facets, "the industry" may be the one that has most completed its liminal phase and emerged into a mature new iteration and completed a rite of incorporation. Thomassen writes: "If moving into liminality can best be captured as a loss of home and a ritualized rupture with the world as we know it, any movement out of liminality must somehow relate to a sort of home-coming, a feeling at home *in* the world and *with* the world, at the levels of both thought and practice."[9] In both its conception of itself and its industrial and cultural practices, the television industry has reincorporated itself into a highly oligopolized entity, in which even the OTT newcomers have vertically integrated themselves and grafted their innovations onto a preexisting structure of manufacturing, wholesaling, and retailing that evolved and matured during the linear age of television. Legacy players have incorporated innovations into their practices so as to capture new economic advantages and replace or subsidize incomes that have become less lucrative for them as a result of the liminality other facets of the televisual have experienced. Thus, "From virtually 100% ad supported, television now gets half of its revenues from non-ad businesses—subscription, licensing, foreign sales."[10] Therefore, the immediate threat of loss of revenue has been successfully grappled with and overcome, which of course creates new challenges.

Production

There has, arguably, never been a better time to be in television production. The fifteen years between 1999 and 2014 saw a 1000 percent increase in scripted series produced for pay and basic cable.[11] While this has reinvigorated a unionized industry that was threatened by runaway productions in the 1990s and 2000s as well as an increase in nonunion reality shows, it has also created fears of overproduction. As F/X Networks' Chief John Landgraf puts it: "there's simply too much TV."[12] The results of this explosion of production cut across all stages of production from development to marketing/promotion:

- "A significant spike in the cost of securing top talent and sought-after source material, from hot scripts to life rights to existing books and movies.
- Rising prices for crews, equipment, stages and locations, among other necessary ingredients for production.
- Higher demand for promotional time coupled with declining ratings for linear channels, making marketing campaigns more costly and less effective.

- Top cable nets cutting back on off-network buys because of increased commitments to original programming.
- Netflix gaining outsized influence due to its growing clout as an off-network buyer."[13]

The fallout will be a course correction in the market which will predictably be governed by the basic economic principles. "'Everybody is enjoying Netflix's (and, presumably the other OTT/VOD companies') emergence as a buyer of all this scripted content, but what we worry about here is supply and demand,' said Michael Nathanson, analyst and partner in Moffett Nathanson. 'The supply of dramas in increasing to the point where in coming years, there are just going to be too many shows.'"[14] As on-demand, curatorial consumption becomes the norm, time and space shifting patterns are going to have "a huge impact on how producers make money on content, from the first exhibition window to long-term library value."[15] Because—the scarce resource now is not the programs, it is the curator-viewer's time and attention.

The explosion of production will necessitate the development of new production schedules. In response to changes in distribution patterns and the competition for high-quality talent, the pilot "season" and traditional schedule the industry has held to as a way of structuring the broadcast year will lessen in influence (and possibly disappear altogether). While this will free top-notch talent for year-round employment, the challenge will be how to organize a "rolling" television schedule for viewers, which will lead to different types of off-the-box promotional activity and strategies. We are already seeing experimentation with these strategies in Netflix and Amazon Instant Videos' all access "drop" of seasons of their original programming.

Paratexts and promotions will grow in importance for content producers and distributors since curatorial culture is driven by discovery and sharing. On-air promotions have already become increasingly irrelevant when the target audience of potential viewers is primarily consuming content elsewhere. Therefore, the inclusion of teasers or trailers on network sites, their release to YouTube and what are perceived to be influential bloggers, use of second screen technologies to pull viewers into an "experience" rather than a "viewing"—all of this will increase, as will the network advertising budgets for online and even more traditional forms of advertising (outdoor, billboard, sporting events) that, much as we may now live online, we cannot avoid. Viewer loyalty and community engagement strategies will be employed across multiple platforms as stand-alone apps, competitions, Easter eggs, games, even producer-created social media networks, second screen experiences, and other as-yet-undeveloped opportunities to reward viewers and enhance fan cultures. These will operate in conjunction with an increased emphasis on brand to create affinity groups around the producing "brand" as well as its shows.

Advertising will remain an important revenue stream, although the economy of advertising will be realigned based on new forms of ad placement, audience quantification, and perhaps consumer choice of advertising experience. More sponsored entertainment will be produced, with one major advertiser footing the production bill for a series or series of episodes. While this is in some ways a throwback to the early days of television, so long as the creative is not interfered with too much by marketers, it may be a lucrative and successful way to solve the problem of program funding and advertising reception and retention. Venue sponsorship has exploded in recent years, so the "naming" rights of shows may not be far behind, although that is probably most likely in what is left of the reality TV cycle: *Monster Energy Drink's Last Ninja Warrior* for instance, rather than *Two and a Half Men*, sponsored by Viagra.

Product placement will increase, particularly in shows that have multiple opportunities for repeated product presence (the beverages *The Big Bang Theory* characters consume during every episode's inevitable meal scene). Again, so long as this is done in conjunction with rather than competition with the dramatic flow of the narrative and the products are natural and expected additions to the program design, it is unlikely this will cause any viewer backlash against the show producer or the advertiser.

The loss of liveness/real time communal experience of broadcast will lead to an increase in the production of "event television" beyond sports and awards shows. While reality television competition shows have successfully attracted and held audiences by harnessing the power of the live "reveal," this genre's popularity is waning and is no longer a consistent mass-attracting performer in prime time. This may lead to additional programming of "spectaculars" (such as NBC's 2013 *The Sound of Music Live*) staged and broadcast live precisely to create a cultural event and drive viewers back to linear viewing.

New televisual genres that are screen-specific or ecosystem-specific will develop and, if they find a revenue-generating audience, have the power to alter larger industry player's practices. YouTube's paid subscription channels are an interesting first foray into this area as the majority of their programming would not find "big-small screen" distribution. The success (or lack of) these channels demonstrate will confirm whether or not a la carte pricing of niche televisual options is a more widely viable practice. This could create a market for highly specialized televisual programming that fulfills the narrowcasting/personcasting prediction that the industry has been unable or unwilling to implement up to this point. While NBC's attempt to migrate web series *Quarterlife* to network in 2008 was both a critical and a ratings disaster, Vice Media's 2016 distribution deal with linear cable network A&E may demonstrate a viable movement of new media to old media platforms.

Distribution

The distribution of television content has traditionally been where the money to continue financing the production of shows has, of course, been made. In a curatorial culture, distribution becomes an even more crucial activity as the availability of content is what drives the curatorial activity. As linear systems have filled up and alternative OTT viewing becomes naturalized, alternatives new challenges develop. The current multiplication of paywalls, subscription, and authentication-based viewing platforms has arguably reached a saturation point. The next iteration of SVOD and the fiduciary health of the pioneers and market leaders will have to grapple with the question of exactly how much viewers are willing to pay for access to programming and how many SVOD systems the market can support. This reveals an interesting conundrum of a matured age of long tail online video distribution in relation to the traditional structure of the television industry—"online trends toward non-exclusive access, and TV licensing in particular is premised on exclusive windows. The much hyped long tail of the internet affords a broader platform for access to library titles than has ever existed before, but the long tail does not prove enhanced monetization of that content."[16]

Netflix, the first in, is, perhaps predictably, the first to begin to experience a decline. When Netflix raised the cost of its basic streaming subscription package $1 in June of 2016, subscribers cancelled in unexpected numbers. This may have been due less to the arguably marginal increase in cost, and more to a reduced library of attractive titles. Netflix's library has shrunk by 40 percent since 2012 and subscriber usage has fallen; "the alert that their Netflix subscription price was going to jump up ever so slightly ... was a reminder to check in on just how much utility the service was providing."[17] This highlights the importance of original programming as well as a library of attractive titles to keep subscribers subscribing. Since Netflix has only subscriber and coproduction income, the maintenance of high-quality original program and competitive bidding on attractive libraries that guarantee long-term viewership (such as Hulu's acquisition of the streaming rights to all of *Seinfeld* for $180 million) are going to be key to its viability. Netflix is experimenting with linear distribution overseas with the airing of its first French coproduction, *Marseille* on French broadcaster TF1.[18] This is seen as not only a way to increase the attractiveness of its SVOD to French subscribers, but also get around the threated quota restrictions discussed in Chapter 6.

Relationships between legacy/linear and SVOD systems have become both intertwined and symbiotic. "As traditional TV networks dive into the SVOD channels business, they're feeling competitive pressure to make their streaming services something more than merely a new way to view their existing linear programming."[19] This is leading to value-added programming or a recreation of exclusivity across the brand—for instance, when CBS launches its new *Star Trek* series in 2017, the first episode will premiere on the linear CBS network. However, fans interested in watching more episodes will have to subscribe to CBS All Access, a $5.99 per month SVOD service to gain access to the series. In this case, CBS is merely following the lead of the OTT entrants that shook up the SVOD world to begin with, but it has learned from their lessons. "Netflix itself, Hulu and Amazon ... learned the hard way that they can't just be catalog content from third parties," says Joel Espelien, senior analyst for

TDG Research. "If an SVOD service doesn't have the exclusive 'wow' show to draw subscribers, they're going to have big problems."[20]

These problems could be exacerbated if this strategy works and if other "untethered" app-based SVOD such as HBO Now take off in the market. Cable relies on bundling for its retail offerings of tiered channels just as less popular "niche" channels rely upon being bundled into these tiers. A la carte pricing of cable channels would both drive the cost of popular cable channels up, and most likely, result in the elimination of cable networks with small viewerships as their subscription base would not be large enough to support their operation. TV Everywhere technologies allowed for time and space-shifted viewing, but kept viewers within the viewing system and economic structure of their cable or satellite subscriptions. CBS All Access and especially HBO Now threaten that closed system—these are SVOD services that are completely untethered from traditional cable or subscriber agreements—these are not TV Everywhere, these are TV a la carte.

Related to this is a new development that demonstrates that the relationship between legacy/linear and online distribution is no longer one-way. Vice Media has launched a 24/7 channel as part of the A&E Networks brand (and with the power of A&E's carriage negotiating position behind them). With youth-oriented programming and international coproduction and partner deals in place, Vice Media already had a vast video library, strong online presence, and perhaps most importantly, high-brand recognition among a desirable but presumably underserved demographic. What it also had was internet advertising revenue. Its movement "back" to a linear distribution service is testimony to the continued economic power of traditional television distribution systems concurrently with rather than ancillary to, OVD. "Vice Media has plenty of eyeballs online, but it hungers for TV's much bigger pool of advertising dollars—which still dwarf digital ad spending in the U.S. by a factor of ten, despite the market's much talked-about challenges."[21]

Live streaming will increase to fill the void for cord cutters, cord shavers, and mobile consumers. The first forays into this technology were centered in DIY apps (Periscope) and social media (Facebook Live), neither of which directly lend themselves to "program distribution." While YouTube has experimented with live streaming since 2011, it recently announced a substantial increase in its live stream offerings, possibly to counter Netflix's movement toward streamed linear programming such as Chelsea Handler's new show.[22] On October 20, 2016, Google announced that it will carry legacy broadcast network CBS on its new YouTube-based web television service "likely to premiere in early 2017."[23] I do not think it is unreasonable to prognosticate that if/when this comes to pass it will legitimize live streaming in an entirely new way and possibly erode legacy network affiliates' and local broadcasters' need for traditional broadcasting licenses to distribute their content. (Which may make it even more likely that broadcast spectrum license holders will sell their allocations back to the FCC in future spectrum auctions of the type discussed in Chapter 5.)

The monetization of content will continue to be the biggest challenge facing the television industry. Additional revenue sources will need to be sought, as well as increased viewership. The industry is stabilized at present, and not, surprisingly in an oligopolistic form that has merely integrated new digital players—"showing them the ropes" after their disruptive appearance. The future of the industry will rely upon the right-sizing of supply and demand (which will be challenging in a world with unlimited "shelf space"), the preservation of existing revenue streams and the innovative exploration of new ones. The new-old model is most probably a converged, conglomerated, transnational one.

The search for common currency—quantifying the curators

For now, the audience quantification industry remains dominated by Nielsen which has successfully kept competitors at bay through market share, service contracts with major networks, media distributors, and advertisers and the purchase of any upstart social media or web-quantification services. Just how long it will be able to maintain this market control is the question that looms as OTT viewing has eluded quantification. Already, we have seen Nielsen and other audience measurement firms change their traditional approaches to on-the-box measurement—today Nielsen and its competitors are dedicated to quantifying and reporting *who* is watching *where* and on *what*. In a curatorial culture, considerably more attention needs to be focused on another "w": the *why*?

Nielsen, for its part, claims to have solved some of these quantification problems with its Total Audience Measurement. However, delays in its full rollout and accessibility raise questions about its value and comprehensiveness, especially since its methodology is carefully guarded. Ratings have always involved a leap of faith on the part of those who rely upon them for setting advertising rates. Due to the power of the industrial players as well as the continued value of the advertising market, it is likely that Nielsen will continue its majority player role in quantification.

This is because the most important aspect of audience quantification is not so much its fundamental accuracy, but that everyone is using the same system—a "common currency." Any interloper into this well established system is going to have to be able to promise not just reliable numbers but a clear and comparable common currency that is more convincingly useful to ad-sellers and ad-buyers as the entrenched Nielsen products.

Social media, in the short term, may become more important—if not in practical demonstration of effect, in theory. The science of influencers has been around since Lippman and it forms the basis of YouTube production studios such as AwesomenessTV. The quantifiable effect of social media mentions will continue to be the holy grail of social scientific market research in television and across the media landscape. This is, of course, complicated by the "opt in" nature of social media usage as well as its duplication of audience across multiple platforms. Content producers may find ways of working directly with social media companies such as Twitter and Facebook to quantify the contributions of these media to viewership or they may even try to build their own. If a reliable common currency of measurement can be decided upon, a "conversion rate" metric expressing the relation of social media mentions to television/content viewership could become a new negotiating point.

Last are the privacy issues associated with being a consumer of networked, digital content. From the earliest days of broadcast, listeners and then viewers agreed to allow commercial television to bring advertising messages into their home. The only way that broadcasters learned about their viewers was through their quantification by a ratings company, which kept the identity of their panel members confidential but not their broad demographic attributes of age, gender, and the like. This was a one-way transmission model and so tacit that it was largely unremarked and unremarkable by the American viewing audience even as the way they received these signals moved from broadcast to cable to interactive cable box and Ethernet.

The online world comes with vast surveillance capabilities on its back end and all current distribution technologies except for antenna-broadcast OTA now have "back channels." Data mining of these back channels, whether DVR or web, is both the threat and the opportunity—the use of cookies by websites, their ability to track you and, perhaps most dangerously, the search histories that Google and other search engines keep and can cross reference with ISPs and account holders of those networked technologies—we are all enmeshed in big data now. Freud was right: there are no coincidences, especially in the serving of ads related to your recent (or more distant searches). The privacy issues regarding how this information can be quantified, used, and sold have not yet been fully identified, adjudicated, legislated, nor regulated, and it will be interesting to see how they play out in various nations and supranational regulatory bodies. Additionally, even if regulations are passed, they may require audiences to "opt out" of the granting of private data mining rights hidden in obscure language within lengthy user agreements. (Be honest, when was the last time you read the EULA that popped up prior to your download of the latest iTunes update?)

While many viewers have been similarly accustomed to zapping and zipping commercials and found ways to avoid them on linearly delivered content, the online space is creating its own norms and practices, which take different forms and yield different quantifiable metrics. They also encourage new types of advertising and viewer behavior. Anyone who has automatically placed their cursor in the right hand corner of a YouTube video in anticipation of the "Skip Ad in" seconds countdown has already acclimated to this new advertising ecosystem. You can skip the commercial, but first you need to pay sufficient attention to the first five seconds to be ready to skip it. In that time you will, at minimum, be exposed to the name of the company and product the advertisement is selling. While watching the video you may be served "snipes" or "overlays" which again, being used to the web environment and pop-ups, become as much a part of the landscape as the "bug" in the corner of your television screen that shows you what network you are watching or as the crawl that brings weather and other pertinent information to your local newscast.

The key point is—today's viewer has come to accept the interference of advertising messaging with their online viewing experience on certain platforms as well as the mining of their personal data and search activity. It is part of the experiential cost of gaining access to the content. We will probably see these innovations continue to evolve which will create new norms and expectations: "the choose your own advertisement" system of Hulu for instance—you have to watch (or be served) an ad—that is non-negotiable. How relevant you want your ad experience to be depends on how much data you want to release about yourself—since you can "curate" your ad experience along with your programming.

Power to the people—curators triumph

Victor Turner, writing on pilgrimage, observed how "a liminal state may become 'fixed,' referring to a situation in which the suspended character of social life takes on a more permanent character."[24] This is, I believe, the current and future state of the curator-viewer—a fixed liminality. The multiplicity of viewing options and the increasing number of viewing sites and types of consumption activities ensure that the activity of cultural text consumption will remain contested, generative, revolutionary, and liminal.

All types of viewing will remain in place—the continued viability of linear television alongside new on demand forms will support both ritualistic and intentional viewing. As the viewer is the economic fuel of the industrial engines that drive television production and distribution, much will depend upon the willingness of viewers to invest in subscription services or a la carte purchases. This will drive new genre cycles and innovations in the production field, and require producers and distributors to work harder to attract curators.

The encouragement of new content discovery will become the major money-suck for producers—transmedia ad campaigns that bridge the analog and digital will become standard operating practice (poster ads on bus shelters with QR codes that take viewers to a mobile website from which they can tweet or post their interest/discovery to their social networks for instance). The subindustry of social media promoters and "marketers" will expand along with bridge content and second screen app producers. Search engine optimization (SEO) will become crucial to producing/distributing brands. Refined search terms and SEO of sites that carry television content will be key to helping curators locate shows going forward—the type of tagging and describing that YouTube's amateur archivists have engaged in for the past twelve years can help one find clips from among hours of existing televisual content loaded to the site. Search optimization that helps curators find what they are looking for within and across television environments is going to be the key to the new environment of programming discovery and rediscovery.

This will make the development of curatorial helpers a new growth area developing— curating apps rather than aggregational ones will be the new goal of tech and information companies. Netflix's Cinematch system was a step in this direction, bringing together search-related objective criteria such as genre, actor, director, subject matter with more ephemeral aspects that could not be quantified nor utilized by an aggregator to suggest viewing options. However, it still relies upon a profile of "the user" as a referent rather than the existence of the viewer as an individual person.

The New York Times has already announced an effort in this area, advertising in January 2016 for new staff to work on "a film and TV recommendation tool which will help users make sense of the ever more complex streaming video landscape."[25] This is a very interesting convergence of old and new media in the interest of informed cultural intermediation. *The Times* calls this "service journalism" and because it intends to charge for this service, which will integrate its criticism and cultural reporting, it will serve the informed choice mandate of the curator while harnessing the computational/sorting power of the aggregator. This initiative is based on its NYT Cooking feature, a free website and app which was launched in 2014 and presumably attracts five million monthly users.[26] The streaming TV web tool has yet to launch and mention of it appears to have gone dormant as of this writing. While there are many possible explanations for the delay, one could be that while food metaphors may have worked their way into our conception of viewing (television diet, bingeing); the planning of a menu and the commitment of one's time and attention to the television series vary in ways that are not interchangeable.

And it is that individualization of interest and attention that is precisely what is so freeing and revolutionary about curatorial culture. Interests are driven not only by some standardized demographic-based inclinations, but also by the individual quirks that are part of everyone's makeup. Viewing interests can vary with mood, company, location, weather, and often by convenience of use. Curatorial viewers are the true disruptive forces and they remain elusive tricksters—first daring the industry to follow and find them and now challenging them to remain relevant and popular in the long tail.

The curatorial viewer does not, however, escape responsibility for the viewing transaction, customizable as it has become. Curation exists and operates on two levels—the personal and the public (or social) and each of these has its own responsibilities and complicating factors.

On the personal level, curatorial citizens need to be willing and interested in doing the work that brings them what they want. Their responsibility is to themselves and how deeply they care about their television consumption. "As we've moved from edited, curated media into search and social media, we have increasing choice over the picture of the world we assemble for ourselves. We also have increased responsibility for building a picture of the world that's accurate and comprehensive enough that we can navigate threats and seize opportunities."[27] Curating is labor and cultural production.

The stakes of choosing a television program are not that personally high. If you begin watching a show you do not like, you can turn it off, and if you think you've been watching the "wrong" thing, it is easy enough to catch up with the "right" show. However, individual show choice scales to larger industrial activity that has a cultural effect. Newton Minow's vast wasteland was driven by complacency on all sides—the industry had a captive audience, the cost of entry into the oligopolized system was too expensive for upstarts to create alternative networks, and viewers were reasonably content with the system they inherited from radio and to which they knew no alternative. Now, more than ever, the choices we make about our viewing result in revenue streams to various companies who create the majority of our viewing choices. Therefore, the most active and engaged curators may have a responsibility to share their choices and publicly advocate or contextualize for the legitimacy of their viewing expertise. This is social curating which occurs when viewers share their televisual viewing choices in the networked public sphere created by Web 2.0.

Socially curated television provides the opportunity for crowdsourcing and public reification of the popularity of shows, which may not be reflected in industry metrics such as the Nielsen ratings—*Arrested Development's* critical success and ostensible "quality" as entertainment was clear prior to its cancellation. (Upon winning his second consecutive Emmy for "Best Writing—Comedy," showrunner Mitchell Hurwitz quipped: "We'd be remiss if we didn't point out the fact that the Academy has twice rewarded us for something that you people won't watch."[28]) The fan base of the show kept it alive on social media which led to new episodes produced by and distributed on Netflix whose alternative (and confidential) means of tracking viewer engagement demonstrated its continued popularity and viability as a television show—most recently *Full House* and *Gillmore Girls* have been picked up for either a sequel production or new iterations as new OTT producers look at the current curated viewing statistics of long-cancelled properties.

At the same time, social curation may result in conclusions that represent aspirational curation rather than actual viewing. TV apps and profiles/likes on social networking science are an inexact way of quantifying a show's popularity or influence—one needs to account for the ineffable—these likes may be "aspirational"—("I wish I was the sort of person who watches *Boardwalk Empire* and I want you to think I am—so I am going to "like" them on Facebook while I am watching *The Real Housewives of Who Cares Where* and playing Halo.") Socially networked curated television needs to be assessed through the same perspective that other expressions of self on the anonymous internet are—with the assumption that we are portraying our "best digital selves." Social curating or socially networked curating is about seeking, finding, and arranging a set of art works or television shows that you are willing to let others know you watch. It intersects with theories about social media usage and the construction of self in the digital age—we put our idealized best foot forward when we are creating online profiles or participating in non-anonymous message board discussions.

The creation of reward and additional value for the viewers to go out of their way to find their programming, celebrate it on websites and blogs, and "like" it on social media is the challenge for content programmers and distributors today. This will encourage and activate the curators of culture who take their responsibility to cut through the dross seriously.

Curatorial culture has transformed the practices, experiences, and relationships among content producers and distributors, audience quantifiers, advertisers, and, of course, viewers in myriad ways. All stakeholders in the televisual transaction have seen their understandings of and interactions with industrial norms and televisual forms change. Curatorial culture is thus a contested space where industry and audience symbiotically and symbolically pursue often conflicting goals. Curatorial culture empowers viewer/users to confront, contextualize, and cohere the long tail of undifferentiated everything created by the digital revolution and Web2.0. It enables truly curatorial citizens to refuse passivity and actively seek and achieve fulfillment in an on-demand world.

Glossary

Active audience—A term developed by television studies academics in the 1980s to discuss certain fan communities or viewers who were more engaged with the shows that they liked than the average viewer. Current examples may be audiences who tweet or use a branded second screen app to engage with a social media community about the show or who edit tribute or mashup videos and post them on YouTube.

AdSense—A Google service which YouTube uses to serve ads against YouTube videos.

AdWords—A Google service which allows advertisers to "bid" on certain words so as to have their links prioritized in the results.

Affiliate—A locally licensed broadcast television station that has an agreement with a network. The network provides programming and "netcomp" to the affiliate in return for the advertising revenue generated by national sales of the programming provided to the affiliate.

Aftermarket—Any subsequent distribution venue or arrangement with the original content producer of a series beyond its original/premiere distributor. See also "Syndication" and "Backend."

Aggregation—A collection of disparate items. In our context, the process whereby a computer uses algorithms to create collections of viewing options.

A la carte pricing—A cable pricing system in which viewers would be free to choose only the networks they wish to pay for—in effect to create their own "bundles." See also "bundling."

Algorithms—Formulas or procedures that solve problems. In our context the set of rules and processes used by computers to determine what shows may be liked by a particular viewer based on his or her viewing or search history as well as any other data the program running the algorithm has access to and can examine via its formula.

Appointment television—A television show that is so popular as to encourage a substantial viewership of new episodes at a scheduled time on a scheduled day. See also "Destination programming" and "FOMO."

Asynchronous audience—An audience that watches televisual content according to its own schedule and not in relationship with or response to the "scheduled" time of the show's premiere or availability.

AVOD—Advertiser-supported video on demand—VOD systems that include advertising in their feeds.

Backend—A way of designating the economic potential of a series after its "first-run" or "premiere." Predominantly linked to how "repeatable" it is or how much audiences would be interested in "reruns." Certain genres (such as reality TV shows that rely upon contests or competitions) are said to have "no" backend.) See also "Aftermarket" and "Legs."

Bandwidth—Used in several senses:
  Cable television—The amount of electromagnetic signal space on a hard-wired system required for the transmission of a usable signal.
  Internet communications—The speed at which a network can move data across it—the higher the bandwidth the faster the transmission.
  Radio/Television/traditional broadcasting—The range of frequencies on the electromagnetic spectrum required for the transmission of a usable signal.
In all senses and situations, analog transmission requires more bandwidth than digital.

Banner advertisement—A rectangular ad that appears above or below a video player on a website. (Term and practice borrowed from traditional web-based advertising.)

Barter time—Advertising time given to a network or local station by a content owner or distributor in place of or for a reduction in a syndication licensing fee. Often a way of creating a revenue stream from a less popular or monetizeable property.

Beyond the box (viewing)—What OTT and mobile viewing is called in Europe.

Binge watching—A consumption pattern in which four or more episodes of a television series are viewed at one sitting.

Block booking—A linear programming strategy in which shows expected to attract the same type of audience are scheduled in a "block" which can then be promoted to that demographic as a group.

Blocking—The restriction of access to legal content on the web by an internet service provider. (Made illegal in the United States by the FCC's 2015 Open Internet ruling.)

Bookend—The first or last ad slot in a commercial pod. Due to DVR technology's back up feature the "bookend" slots are often the most valuable as they are most likely to be consciously seen, at least in part, by the viewer.

Brand community—A group formed around shared appreciation of a particular product or, for our purposes, television franchise, network, or series. Fealty to the community will vary among members but could manifest itself in social media mentions as well as watching.

Branded entertainment—Original content built around and specifically designed to promote a specific product or brand. BMW short films are an example of branded entertainment.

Broadcast—The traditional (and historically first) way of distributing a radio or television signal—by sending a signal out on a particular frequency via the electromagnetic spectrum. The signal is received via antenna and reassembled into a viewable form by the television set. See also "Digital Conversion."

Broadcast network—A television-distributing entity whose affiliates are comprised of local broadcasters that operate under FCC licenses and are owned independently, by station groups, or by the network itself. While these stations are also available to local cable subscribers in the areas they serve, they also broadcast their signal digitally and can be received by non-cable or satellite subscribed viewers who have antennas. See also "OTA."

Bug—An overlaid image, usually in the bottom right hand corner of a screen. Bugs are usually used to display network branding or logos.

Bumper—A promotional spot for the network or one of its shows that precedes or follows a commercial pod.

Bundling—Cable pricing protocol in which multiple services (telephone, television, internet) are combined into levels of service priced for the consumer in an "all or nothing" or "all or more expensive" structure. Also used to refer to the arrangement of cable networks into tiers of service where consumers receive all channels within a particular tier regardless of their interest or viewing of individual networks. See also "a la carte" and "channel inventory."

Burn off—A linear programming strategy that moves the remaining episodes of a cancelled show to a less popular time frame in order to "just air them and be done with it." (Alternative—leaving the shows, against which advertising may have already been sold "in the can" and providing the advertisers with make-goods or other compensation.)

Cable—A hard-wired method of distributing a television signal whereby the content is sent out via coaxial or fiber optic cables into the home. See also "MSO."

Cable network—A branded channel of television content that prior to the growth of internet distribution was only available via a cable or satellite system subscription.

Cancel/cancellation—The termination of a network's agreement to carry a particular show on its network or in its scheduled programming.

Cancellation threshold—The quantifiable ratings point at which the production/acquisition costs of a series exceed its revenue-generating potential.

Carriage contract—An agreement signed between a cable network and a cable or satellite MSO specifying the per-subscriber/per-month fee the MSO will compensate the network for carrying its signal on its system.

Carriage fees—Per-subscriber fees paid by a cable or satellite provider to a cable network or its owner in exchange for carrying that network on the cable or satellite provider's service.

Channel—Per the FCC: "a portion of the electromagnetic frequency spectrum which is used in a cable system and which is capable of delivering a television channel (as television channel is defined by the Commission by regulation)" (47 US Code § 522(4)).

Channel inventory—The number of channels available to a viewer through his or her primary television reception system or subscription. For example, a viewer relying on OTA signals in the New York City area may have a channel inventory of about twelve (2, 4, 5, 7, 9, 11, 13, 21, 25, 31, 47, 55). A viewer who subscribes to Time Warner basic cable in New York City may have a channel inventory in the hundreds.

Channel repertoire—The number of channels regularly or most commonly watched by a particular viewer. Research has discovered that despite an average channel inventory numbering in the hundreds (on most cable and satellite systems), the average number of channels in the average subscribers repertoire is about fifteen.

Churn—The bane of a subscription service—when subscribers drop their subscriptions following the end of a popular series (or their completion of their viewing of a series that drops all on one day).

Collaborative filtering—A computer-generated way to create personalized recommendations via the use of algorithms that make predictions about a user's likes, dislikes and interests based on the processing of previous activity and preferences expressed by other users the algorithm determines are similar. CF may use user-provider ratings, employ models based on data it has mined or, most often some combination of the two in its creation of "suggestions for you."

Commercial ratings—Collective term for the Nielsen C3 and C7 ratings which measure the viewership of individual commercials within a particular show.

Commodity audiences—The most prized demographics for advertisers—presumably because they are the ones most likely to purchase goods that are advertised due to their spending power.

Common carrier—Per the 1934 Communications Act: "The term 'common carrier' or 'carrier' means any person engaged as a common carrier for hire, in interstate or foreign communication by wire or radio or in interstate or foreign radio transmission of energy, except where reference is made to common carriers not subject to this Act" (47 US Code § 153(10)).

Common ownership—In general: a form of vertical integration in which production companies, broadcast, and cable networks are all owned by the same corporate entity. In practice this means that the broadcast and/or cable network has part- or total- ownership of the series it is distributing which results in multiple revenue streams for the conglomerate parent corporation—advertising money during the series' first-run as well as syndication income on the backend. This funding model became possible only after the expiration of the Fin-Syn rules.

Companion apps—Second screen apps that sync with a viewer's mobile device to provide information that connects to the episode being watched. TBS's *The Big Bang Theory* app and IntoNow are examples.

Conglomerate—A corporation that owns or owns controlling interest in a number of smaller companies that engage in a variety of disparate activities across different economic sectors.

Connected viewing—Viewing done while interacting with the content online (e.g., via a second screen app), or while interacting with an online community via social media.

Content bubble—A search-based phenomenon where a viewer only sees a particular type of content or is only served a particular type of content based on his or her past viewing choices being so targeted or narrow.

Convergence—The integration and intersection of media industries, media technologies, and media usages into singular interfaces or "appliances." (e.g., the television and the computer "technologically converge" to yield the smart TV and the tablet.)

Cord cutters—Viewers who have cancelled their cable or satellite service in favor of alternative viewing options.

Cord nevers—Viewers who have never subscribed to a cable or satellite system or who have never been the account holder/responsible party on a cable or satellite subscription.

Cord shavers—Viewers who have downsized their cable subscription to a lower tier of service than they previously had in favor of alternative viewing options.

CPM—Cost per thousand (M is the Roman numeral for 1000). Metric used to calculate advertising rates—advertisers buy advertising based upon the "cost per thousand" views of their ad.

Cultural intermediary—Per Pierre Bourdieu, any producer of a symbolic good or service who encourages or aids in the reception and consumption of a media or entertainment text. Per a Bourdieuain—a professional television reviewer or critic, a blogger, a social media influencer who interprets and assesses cultural texts (such as television) for a larger audience so as to aid the audience members in making viewing choices.

Cume—(ratings)—Cumulative audience—the measurement of the total number of unique audience members over a specified period of time.

Curation—Per Hans Ulrich Obrist—The activity of making junctions between objects, quasi-objects, non-objects, and hyper-objects. For our purposes—the act of human assessment, discernment, interest and taste-making that affects the purposeful choice of cultural texts to consume and the arrangement of these texts into a consumable pattern.

Curatorial culture—A media consumption environment in which an excess of accessible cultural texts and a scarcity of viewer/user time shifts the power from the content creator or distributor to the consumer of the content. Consumers then bear the responsibility of finding, selecting and organizing their media consumption and may also use social media or other web-based interactive platforms to publicly exhibit or engage with the content they or others have selected to consume.

Data caps—A limit on the amount of data subscribers can transfer across a wireless network as imposed by the wireless carrier.

Daypart—The organizing unit of the linear programming schedule. Linear programmers use the daypart to determine what programming will be shown at which times.

Deficit financing—The traditional way network shows have been funded in which the production company covers the entire cost of the original production of episodes, recouping 60–70 percent of that cost in a per-episode licensing fee paid to it by the network the show airs on. This fiduciary model relies upon the syndication market or "backend" of the show for the production company to fully recoup its investment and for the show to begin to turn a profit.

Demographic—Descriptors of age, gender, class, income, race, ethnicity, and delivery system/consumption site of the program which are used by ratings companies to provide additional specifics to advertisers, networks, and other ratings product consumers.

Designated market area (DMA)—A geographical area determined originally by broadcast footprints and used to determine local broadcasting spectrum allocation by the FCC as well as local markets for Nielsen ratings. There are 210 DMAs in the United States, the largest of which is New York City.

Destination programming—A linear television programming strategy in which a popular show is broadcast or cablecast at a particular time. See also "appointment television."

Destination viewing—What Europeans call "destination programming." Interesting distinction—"destination programming" is about where the linear television executive decides to place a particular show, "destination viewing" is the same concept, but from the perspective of the viewer of the program.

Digital conversion—The FCC mandated conversion of all television broadcasting in the United States from analog to digital transmission. This conversion, originally scheduled for 2006 was substantially delayed, but the analog signal was finally "turned off" on June, 2009 at which point any viewers without digital tuners ceased to receive broadcast signals.

Digital Millennium Copyright Act of 1998—Legislation which stated that websites are not liable for content that others upload to them. Ergo YouTube is not financially responsible for any damages incurred by copyright holders whose work has been uploaded to YouTube without the copyright owners' permission. YouTube must, however, act in good faith and with speed to remove any illegally posted copyrighted material once it receives a "takedown notice" from the content owner.

Digital rights management—See DRM.

Digital subchannel—Additional OTA broadcast channels created by the digital conversion of 2009. Local broadcasters use these subchannels to provide additional content streams. PBS has used digital subchannels to create additional branded content streams nationwide—such as PBS World, PBS Kids, PBS Food. Digital subchannels are tuned in by adding a decimal to the original channel designation, such as WNET 13.1; WNET 13.2, and so on.

Digital terrestrial television—See DTT.

Digital watermark—A type of DRM—machine-readable code inserted into a digital media file to identify it as copyrighted material.

Discriminatory capping—When an internet service provider or cell phone company limits the amount of data that can be used by certain "types" of activity by one of its subscribers. For example, a provider might allow unlimited use of data for talk and text, but place a cap on the amount of data one can "stream" during a particular month.

Disintermediation—A distribution model in which content producers and programmers offer particular content (series) direct to viewers and separate from traditional delivery systems such as broadcast or cable networks.

Download—A digital distribution technology that is the opposite of streaming, often used for electronic sell-through of episodes. The content is delivered to the viewer via the web as a digital file which is then stored on the viewer's hard drive.

DRM—Digital rights management—Machine readable code that prevents (or attempts to prevent) piracy and duplication of copyrighted material.

DTT—Digital terrestrial television—Term used primarily in Europe to indicate an over-the-air broadcaster whose signal is delivered in a digital format—following the digital conversion of 2009, this term could also apply to US OTA broadcasters, although it is not in common use in the American context.

Dynamic advertising insertion—The ability of a VOD distribution platform to customize the ads served to a particular viewer based on geographical location of the viewer or other data mined from his or her previous viewing/search choices.

Electromagnetic spectrum—A naturally occurring geophysical phenomenon that encompasses the range of frequencies over which electromagnetic radiation extends in the earth's atmosphere. These frequencies (spectra) can be used for the broadcast of signals as well as wireless communication and also include such phenomena as visible light and x-ray. In the United States, the use of the frequencies of the electromagnetic spectrum is regulated by the Federal Communications Commission.

Electronic sell through (EST)—A type of digital per-episode or per-series purchase that delivers the content to the viewer via the internet and is usually stored on the viewer's hard drive. The viewer can then move the episode or series to other devices for mobile viewing.

Engagement—An audience quantification metric that attempts to quantify the level of attention that an audience has for a particular series in a way that may justify higher advertising prices for that series.

Federal Communications Commission (FCC)—The regulatory body of communications technologies and industries in the United States. Established by the Communications Act of 1934, the FCC is composed of five commissioners appointed by the president.

Fin-Syn (financial interest and syndication rules)—A set of restrictions enacted by the FCC in the 1970s to break up the monopoly the three legacy networks had on the primetime television schedule. The rules were allowed to expire in the 1990s when the explosion of cable networks coupled with the deregulation of the 1980s made arguments for their irrelevancy legitimate.

First run syndication—Shows that are produced specifically to be sold to locally licensed broadcasters or station groups who program them into dayparts besides primetime. Game shows, daytime talk shows, and court shows are examples of first-run syndicated shows.

Flightings—Particular weeks during a particular season for which an advertiser wants its spot to run—these are negotiated during media buys during "upfronts."

FOMO—Fear of missing out. See also "Water Cooler Moment."

Franchise apps—Second screen apps that are mobile versions of the series' website. These often offer short videos and bonus content (paratexts), message boards, games, and even full episodes for viewing via the franchise branded application.

Frankenmetrics—An unreliable quantification of viewership or usership created by the comparison or usage of incompatible/incomplete data.

Frictionless sharing—A Facebook innovation where anything you are listening to, reading, or watching via Facebook is automatically added to your Facebook Timeline where it can be seen by others.

Gatekeeper—Any person or thing that controls access to a resource, experience, or service.

Genre—Traditionally, a way of "typing" series according to narrative features, content, and style (drama, comedy, serial, reality.) In recent years new "genres" have developed that use less more ephemeral criteria or the industrial means of production or distribution ("Quality TV" "HBO" "streaming original") to help define the genre.

Genre cycle—A period of time during which a large number of shows with similar narrative elements may dominate television production. Cycles generally begin with an innovation upon an existing type of television show. If the innovated show becomes popular it will be followed by a great deal of imitation as competing producers make their "own" versions of it. When the market is saturated with these shows, the popularity of the genre will begin to decline and new innovations will occur.

Genre silo—A set of similar programs offered under the umbrella of a particular distribution site or environment. Contributes to the establishment of a distributor-based brand identity.

Give backs—Advertising money returned to advertisers by networks when a particular upfront ad buy underperforms particularly badly and the advertiser is unsatisfied with the "make goods."

Gross rating point—A Nielsen metric used to express a rating and representative of 1 percent of the total number of television homes in the United States. As of 2016 one GRP = 1.16 million viewers. During upfronts, a certain number of GRPs of exposure are negotiated by the advertiser for each ad buy.

Homes using television (HUT)—The number of homes whose televisions are turned on at any given moment (used in the calculation of ratings share (see "share")

Hybrid genre—A "typing" term used to denote a series that has elements of more than one genre—arguably the first series to use a hybrid nomenclature was *The Days and Nights of Molly Dodd* (NBC, 1987–1988; Lifetime, 1988–1991) which established the "dramedy" genre.

Incidental viewing—Viewing that occurs because the television has been turned on for company or out of habit, not out of a particular interest in what is showing on the television at that moment.

Influencers—A produser (producer-user) of social media who has attracted a large number of followers or viewers and thus accumulated cultural capital that can be harnessed to promote goods or services, or encourage particular types of viewing or media consumption activities.

Information services—Per the FCC: "the offering of a capability for generating, acquiring, storing, transforming, processing, retrieving, utilizing, or making available information via telecommunications, and includes electronic publishing, but does not include any use of any such capability for the management, control, or operation of a telecommunications system or the management of a telecommunications service" (47 US Code § 153(20)). For our purposes: internet access.

Instrumental viewing—A type of television viewing that is intentional and directly predicated upon the watching of a particular show at a particular time. See also "appointment television."

Intellectual property rights—The general term for the legal assigning of ownership over a creation of the mind through patents, copyrights, and trademarks. Ownership ensures that the creator retains and can protect his or her right to profit from his or her creation and preserve its original contributions to culture.

Interactive program guide (IPG)—A service provided by a cable, satellite, or independent DVR company (such as TiVo), which provides a listing of scheduled programming that the viewer can actively scroll through by use of the remote. Viewers may advance the program guide to see future offerings, use the remote keypad to go directly to a particular channel, set "favorite" channels, and also plan recordings of shows or entire series. IPGs are currently the most popular and used curatorial interface.

IPTV—Internet Protocol Television—Systems that use the internet and packet-switching technology to delivery television content and signals to viewers as opposed to broadcast, cable, or satellite technologies.

"Last mile"—The connection that allows a subscriber/consumer to connect to the internet or cable system via their internet service provider.

Legacy network—NBC, CBS, ABC—The broadcast television networks that were originally established as radio networks in the 1920s.

Legs—A particular series' potential for longer term revenue streams, such as international distribution or syndication. See also "Backend."

Licensing fee—(traditional) A per-episode fee paid by the network to the production company for the "premiere" airing of the episode plus a "rerun." In the deficit financing model the licensing fee is 60–70 percent of the total cost of production of the episode.

Licensing fee—(OTT) A per-episode or per-season fee paid by the OTT entity to the production company for the right to make the series available on their platform (usually exclusively) for a particular amount of time.

License (station)—The FCC-granted right to operate on a particular broadcast frequency in a particular market for a particular period of time.

Lifecycle management—The scaffolding of exclusive access to a particular season of a series so as to maximize the backend profit. See also "Windowing."

Liminality—A term originated by the structural anthropologist Arnold Van Gennep to denote the period of "becoming" or "in-betweeness" that occurs during a "rite of passage." In this period the normal structures of authority can be suspended as the neophyte undergoes a destruction of his or her previous identity and the new transformed identity is created.

Linear television—A traditional way of producing, distributing, and watching television that is tied to a specific schedule and synchronous viewing (antonym: "on demand.")

Local broadcaster—A television station that is licensed by the FCC and granted exclusive use of a particular range of frequencies on the broadcast spectrum for a particular amount of time in a specified geographic location.

Local PeopleMeter—The same as a PeopleMeter, only these are installed in the homes of Nielsen families in the largest 56 local markets to measure their viewership. Data from these PeopleMeters are combined with national data four times during the year. See also "Sweeps."

Make goods—Additional runs of an advertisement that a network provides to an advertiser for free when the original time the advertiser bought to run its ad in does not deliver the agreed-upon audience.

Mass audience—A large, passive viewership which homogenizes in its consumption of culture.

Mass medium—Any technologically mediated form of communication intended to attract and reach a large undifferentiated public.

Master service agreement—A multi-year contract a stakeholder requiring viewership metrics signs with a ratings provider (most probably Nielsen) to provide ratings products to said stakeholder for the period of the agreement. One of the ways Nielsen has been able to ensure fealty to its ratings products and processes is by staggering the expiration dates of these agreements so that all stakeholders are not simultaneously in the market for a new audience measurement provider.

Media buying/buyers—A specialized activity within advertising that involves the assessment of advertising venues and options and determines the best yield for the clients' dollar. In the television industry, media buyers attend upfronts and scrutinize ratings products to determine the best advertising purchases for their clients.

Meta business—A business whose economic model is based on the aggregation of content or information developed by others (and for whose creation it does not need to pay.) The meta business relies on the real or implied "value added" that it provides to the content and information which purportedly/ultimately benefits the original creators of the information. YouTube and Vimeo are meta businesses.

Multichannel environment—Any televisual ecosystem in which there are more than merely the VHF/UHF spectrum's OTA channels. Cable was the first innovation to create a multichannel environment.

Multi-system operator (MSO)—A company that owns many different cable systems in many disparate municipalities.

Must-carry Laws—Regulations established in the mid-1960s which required cable and satellite operators to carry all locally broadcast television channels that were present in a particular service area or DMA. Originally designed to protect local broadcasters, the increased popularity of subscription services proved to place local broadcast station owners at a financial disadvantage since their stations did not receive retransmission fees. See also "retransmission fees."

MVPD—Multichannel video programming distributor—Any company that provides video programming to the home via cable or satellite for a fee. As of this writing, the FCC has sought commentary on the definition of "channel" as freed from the constraints of the electromagnetic spectrum or cable delivery (i.e., to include video delivered via the internet in this definition); however, it has not yet come to a definitive decision. Therefore YouTube, Hulu, and other internet-based video delivery platforms are not legally defined as MVPDs.

Narrowcaster—A television distributing entity (traditionally a UHF broadcaster or cable channel) that targets a particularly small audience with specialized programming. See also "niche programming."

Natural monopoly industry—Per Crawford, any industry in which start-up or initial costs of establishment are high while the cost of serving additional customers once the start-up has been completed are low. Therefore, each additional customer brings not only additional revenue, but also lowers the per customer average cost for the company. Because the cost of market entry is so high, these industries favor the incumbents and pioneers and create "natural" monopolies because it is economically illogical or unfeasible for competitors to enter the market.

Net neutrality—The belief that ISPs (internet service providers) should allow equally fast and unfettered access to all legal websites and/or applications that their subscribers seek to access without discrimination.

Netcomp—The compensation networks pay to their local affiliates in return for the affiliation and the revenue from national ad sales in the programming that the network provides to the affiliate.

Network—In broadcasting—a large program production and distribution company that distributes television content nationally through agreements with locally licensed broadcast stations owned independently or by station groups. In cable—a television production and distribution company whose content is only available via cable or satellite systems that it is carried on. In computing—a group of computers that are connected via the internet and which transmit information and share resources across their connections. See also "broadcast network," "cable network," and "legacy network."

Network era—The period in US broadcast history when the three legacy networks were the predominant, if not only source for nationally distributed television programming. Generally periodized as the 1950s to mid-1980s. See also "post network era."

Newfronts—"Upfronts" for internet-native video distributors. See also "upfronts."

Niche media—Content produced and designed to appeal to the interests of a narrow segment of an audience. See also "narrowcasting."

Nielsen family—A home using television randomly selected to be part of the panel from which Nielsen generates its ratings products. At present, each Nielsen family represents approximately 1.12 million American viewers.

Nielsen rating—A metric of viewership generated by the Nielsen company and expressed as "rating/share" where "rating" indicates the number of television homes tuned to a particular show out of all the television homes in the United States and "share" indicates the percentage of television homes tuned to a particular show out of all of the homes using television (HUT) in the United States during a particular time slot. Note that Nielsen now produces multiple ratings "products" that quantify rating and share by sampling different data points and sets. See also "rating (generic)," "rating (specific)," "share," and "ratings product."

Nielsen Television Index (NTI) (see also "overnights")—A preliminary quantification of viewership produced by Nielsen based on data from the PeopleMeters in the homes of Nielsen families. These ratings are released the day after the original premiere of the episode and revised as additional data becomes available to produce the C3, C7, and Total Audience Measurement ratings products.

Notice and takedown provision—The part of the Digital Media Copyright Act of 1998 that releases websites such as YouTube from responsibility for users posting copyrighted work so long as YouTube acts to immediately remove said content upon being notified that it has been posted to their site.

O&O—owned and operated—A locally licensed broadcast television station that is owned and operated by a broadcast network.

Off-network syndication—An aftermarket revenue stream created when older series of a television show are licensed to cable networks or independent local broadcasters or station groups for programming within the non-primetime dayparts of those entities schedules. See also "Backend."

Oligopoly—An industrial structure in which the control of all activities within a particular industry are controlled by a small number of very powerful conglomerates or companies who often make fiduciary arrangements with each other so as to shore up their control over the industry. The media industries of the United States are all oligopolistic in their structure.

On-the-box (OTB)—A way to denote viewing that occurs via a fixed television set regardless of the mode of content delivery (broadcast, cable, satellite, internet connection) that brings the content to the set.

Online video distributor (OVD)—Any video distributor that exclusively uses the internet to deliver its content (as opposed to broadcasting, cablecasting, or sending the signal via satellite.) Netflix, Hulu, and YouTube are representative examples. See also "MVPD."

Overlay—An advertisement that appears over the video content that is being played, usually in the lower thirds position, popular on YouTube.

Overnights—See Nielsen Television Index.

Over-the-air (OTA)—In the United States—the distribution of a television signal via broadcast—the electromagnetic spectrum. See also "broadcast" and "terrestrial television."

Over-the-top (OTT)—Television viewing that is distributed via the internet or directly to the television set without cable or satellite operator interface or technology. Not an exclusive term—although cord cutters of needs view OTT content exclusively, the majority of OTT viewers currently also have cable or satellite subscriptions.

Paid prioritization—The speeding up or optimizing of traffic from a particular website by an internet service provider in return for a payment or other consideration. (Made illegal in the United States by the FCC's 2015 Open Internet ruling.)

Paratext—Per Jonathan Gray. Term originally borrowed from literary theory to refer to additional content or "special features" created to accompany a DVD release of a television season. Now applicable to any "extratextual" content pertaining to a television show and designed to promote, engage, or reward viewers or viewsers—apps, second-screen experiences, Twitter feeds, Facebook page, and the like (Note—these may or may not encourage or allow for interaction with viewers.)

PeopleMeter—A proprietary audience measurement device that the Nielsen company installs on the televisions of its Nielsen families. This device monitors whether the set is on or off and what channel it is tuned to at 15 minute intervals, automatically sending the information back to Nielsen. Nielsen families are each assigned a button on the PeopleMeters' remote and are prompted to "check in" to indicate their presence in the room where the television is on in order to calculate the viewership of the program.

Platform—Any distinct technology that distributes media content in a way that it can be consumed by the end user. A very elastic term—that is, Facebook, Instagram, and Twitter are all considered "social media platforms" even though all are also social media.

Platform agnosticism—A digital media product that can be consumed across more than one delivery technology or an attribute of a person who consumes that content without favoring one consumption technology over another. For instance, television may be becoming "platform agnostic" in that be consumed "on the box" but also via computer, mobile phone, tablet, and the like.

Platform mobility—The ability to begin watching a show on one digital consumption technology (a living room set for instance), and to continue the viewing experience on another device (such as a tablet or mobile phone) without having to find one's place in the show or to start over.

Pods—Advertising breaks in programming that are comprised of several advertisements ("spots") for different companies and products.

Pop ups—A type of advertising originally only on the web, but now integrated into on the box viewing experiences wherein a graphic or advertising message suddenly appears on the screen to promote series or reinforce network brand identity.

Portal—An online site that provides a precurated ecosystem to the user among other services or functions. (Facebook, Yahoo, and AOL are "portals.")

Post network era—Per Amanda Lotz—the period of US television history (early 2000s forward, but particularly post-2005) that saw the decline of the legacy network's power as cable reached a saturation point of subscribers and the power and audience share of the legacy networks declined, causing ruptures in traditional industry practices.

Post-roll—An advertisement that autoplays after a video on an internet-delivery platform. Most cannot be fast-forwarded through.

Pre-roll—An advertisement that autoplays before a video on an internet-delivery platform. Most can either not be fast-forwarded through or must be watched for a certain number of seconds before the viewer can "skip ad."

Product integration—An advertising form in which a product or service is made part of the narrative of a particular show and referenced (positively) by name by the characters. A character specifically asking for a type of soft drink or the episode engaging in a subplot about the character's search for that particular type of soft drink and refusal to drink any other is an example.

Product placement—An advertising form in which an identifiable product is used as a prop in a television show but not integrated into the storyline nor referred to by name.

Produser—Neologism used to describe a producer-user of a particular media technology. One who makes as well as consumes the media in question.

Pull media—A media distribution system in which active users locate and consume media texts on their own time and at their convenience. They may find this media on sites that are both sanctioned and unsanctioned by the content creator.

Push media—A media distribution system in which media texts are delivered to a passive consumer via a schedule and through very clear gatekept channels owned and controlled by content producers.

Rating (generic)—An umbrella term given to a quantification of viewership of a particular show. See also "Nielsen rating."

Rating (specific)—The number of television homes tuned to a particular show out of all the television homes in the United States at any given time.

Ratings floor—The minimum rating a series must receive in order to avoid cancellation. See also "cancellation threshold."

Ratings product—A generic term for a "type" of quantification of viewership developed through proprietary processes and sold to advertisers, media buyers, broadcasters, and networks by ratings company.

Reallocation—The movement of first-run episodes of an underperforming show developed for and premiered on a broadcast network to a sibling cable network within the conglomerate family.

Repurposing—A distribution agreement in which the network is allowed to run new episodes more than once on the same network after their premiere and/or allowed to air it on a sibling cable network shortly after its premiere on its first-run network. This increases the revenue the network and production company can generate from the content prior to its formally going into the syndication market.

Rerun—A replay of a television episode that has already been broadcast or cablecast.

Retransmission fees—The "wholesale" per-subscriber/per month fee a cable or satellite provider pays to a network to carry that networks' programming on its system. The owners of local broadcasting stations were previously exempt from receiving "retrans" fees due to "must-carry" laws, but increasingly the owners of all channels carried on a cable or satellite system are requiring retransmission compensation in return for their signals and programming.

Ritualistic viewing—A type of ambient use of television in which the set is on for company, background noise, or out of habit—the actual show that is "on" not of primary relevance to this type of viewing

ROI—Return on investment—Shorthand used by advertisers to name their expectation of particular ratings or positive results of their ad placements and media buys.

Satellite—Television distribution technology that sends content via the Ku band directly to subscribers homes. Subscribers to satellite technology must have their own dish in order to receive the signal which is unscrambled via their set-top box.

Scatter market—The ad market during the season itself when unsold ad time (spots) is sold to advertisers. The scatter market still relies upon ratings and projected GRPs for its CPMs but does not offer "make goods" or viewership guarantees.

Season—Traditionally the period from September through May when first-run television episodes of broadcast and cablecast series would premiere. New patterns of programming and distribution have made the temporal aspect of the season irrelevant although the term continues to be used to denote a number of episodes (traditionally 22–26, now, for some off-network shows as few as 6–12) that are shot in the same production time period and meant to be distributed together or watched sequentially.

Second screen experiences—Apps or websites designed to engage viewers on their mobile device or computer while they watch a particular show.

Seriality—A narrative feature that extends storylines over multiple episodes and seasons within a series. Seriality rewards loyal watching and also requires that the episodes be consumed in a particular order for the narrative to make sense.

Share—A ratings "metric"—the percentage of viewers using television watching a particular show during a particular time slot. Used to compare the popularity of shows in relationship to other viewing options being watched in the same time period.

Shared exclusivity—An aftermarket situation where a series may be in off-net syndication and cable network syndication simultaneously and thus play across both platforms in the same market.

Single-source measurement—A consumer tracking technology or system that would aggregate all behavior by that consumer (credit and loyalty card transactions and media consumption) to reveal a comprehensive assessment of exposure to advertising and subsequent purchasing behavior.

Skyscraper (advertisement)—A rectangular ad that appears to the left or right of a video player on a website. (Term borrowed from traditional web-based advertising.)

Smart TV—A television capable of receiving high-speed internet via an ethernet port or a Wi-Fi receiver. These televisions also have their own operating systems and run apps such as Netflix, Vudu, YouTube, Amazon Video, as well as proprietary software from their manufacturers (Panasonic, Samsung, Sony). Navigation from cable or broadcast viewing to app viewing is achieved through the use of a simple stick remote making the internet viewing experience seamless and indistinguishable from the traditional experience of shifting a set to a VCR or DVD input.

Snipe (advertisement)—A graphic that appears on the television screen to promote an upcoming series, event, or a product. These can be served by the cable or satellite company, an ISP, or in the case of SMART televisions, the operating system of the television itself. (Ergo an ad for Tide can appear in the lower thirds when you first turn on (or really, "boot up") your television.)

Social media—Internet-based websites and/or applications that encourage and facilitate the creation and sharing of content as well as interactivity among the users.

Social networking app—Proprietary and branded second screen experience apps that engage viewers in social media conversations around particular shows and series produced by the company that has branded and designed the app. (HBO Connect, Peel's "Idol Interactive Experience.")

Spectrum auction—A sale of broadcast spectrum access in the United States. FCC spectrum auctions may take the form of reverse auctions (when broadcast spectrum license holders sell spectrum "back" to the FCC) or forward auctions (when the FCC offers spectrum that it controls or has bought back in a reverse auction to the highest bidders for exclusive use of these frequencies.)

Spoiler alert—A development of the asynchronous age—announcement it is polite to make when discussing the most recent plot development on a series so as to give those who are not current with their viewing the opportunity to "opt out" of hearing what the plot development is.

Spot market—The chronologically last advertising market (after upfronts and scatter) during which specific timeslots on specific shows and days are sold to advertisers. These spots are "leftovers" from the other two markets and thus almost always on low performing or unpopular shows or at unusual times or opposite counterprogramming (such as live sporting events) that guarantee low audience.

Streaming—An internet-based distribution technology that sends content as a continuous flow such that it is received by the viewer as an uninterrupted and immediate experience of the content.

Strip—A programming strategy in which the same show is aired in the same time slot five days a week. While traditionally this has most often been used to schedule off-net syndicated content or daytime content, the success of competition shows such as *American Idol* and *Who Wants to Be a Millionaire* expanded this strategy to prime time.

Subscription video on demand (SVOD)—Any system that serves content asynchronously to viewers but is behind a paywall.

Sweeps—Weeks in February, May, July, and November during which local diary and PeopleMeter data is combined with the National Television Index so as to create a more comprehensive metric of viewership. Advertising rates are based on the performance of shows during these weeks.

Synchronous audience—Viewers who consume a television show during its linearly scheduled premiere time.

Syndication—The licensing of either first-run or rerun programming for distribution via a broadcast station or cable network. See "aftermarket."

Synergy—The collaboration of two or more companies in such a way as to achieve a goal that neither one could achieve as well on its own.

Target marketing—The crafting of advertising/promotional messages that are aimed at a clearly defined group of prospective consumers based on an understanding of that groups preferences, likes, and dislikes.

Telco—Shorthand for a telecommunications company. See also "telecommunication services."

Telecommunications/telecommunications services—Per the FCC, "The term 'telecommunications' means the transmission, between or among points specified by the user, of information of the user's choosing, without change in the form or content of the information as sent and received.

Telecommunications Carrier—The term 'telecommunications carrier' means any provider of telecommunications services, except that such term does not include aggregators of telecommunications services" (47 US Code § 153(43–44)).

Television—If you don't have your own working definition after reading this book, I'm not giving you one here.

Television home—A fixed domestic space (home, apartment, condo) that has a television set and a way in which the television set can receive content (broadcast antenna, cable, satellite subscription).

Terrestrial broadcasting/terrestrial television—See OTA, DTT.

Throttling—The purposeful and discriminatory slowing of particular internet traffic by an internet service provider. (Made illegal in the United States by the FCC's 2015 Open Internet ruling.)

Transactional financing—An episode-by-episode or "series pass" payment model for televisual content. The most obvious and first of these models was pioneered by iTunes, but this form of content pricing is now found on YouTube and Amazon Instant Video. In addition to making subscription-only content available to a wider audience, this is also a viable way to fund niche content.

Transindustrial integration—When conglomerates integrate companies that control the production, distribution, and exhibition within a particular media industry with the activities of companies that are equally as controlling of these three media operations within another media industry. The result is an increased concentration of ownership that is vertically and horizontally integrated within and across multiple media industries—it's the oligopolization of oligopolies.

Transmedia—A digital storytelling technique that extends a particular narrative across multiple platforms—an example would be a television show that airs on NBC but has additional storylines that are explored via webisodes on NBC.com and also maintains Twitter accounts in the identities of the fictional characters which are referenced and used in the narrative development of the television show and webisodes.

Tribe of affinity—Per Chris Anderson—Online and social media communities of viewers who publicly express engagement with particular series or viewing experiences via those platforms.

Upfronts—Industry screenings of the "new" television season for advertisers, sponsors, and media buyers and during which ad time may be purchased at a discount. These closed screenings are usually held in New York in May and are responsible for about 70 percent of all advertising sales for the fall "season." Advertising time not sold during upfronts is sold during the season in the "scatter market," used to provide "make goods" to ads in underperforming timeslots or, if unsold, used for network promotion of upcoming episodes.

Video on demand (VOD)—Any system that serves video content asynchronously and in response to a viewer request. See also "AVOD," and "SVOD."

Video programming—Per the FCC: "programming provided by, or generally considered comparable to programming provided by, a television broadcast station." (47 US Code § 522 (20)).

Viewser—Per Dan Harris. Portmanteau neologism combining "viewer" and "user" to indicate an audience subject position that is constructed as both a passive "viewer" of televisual content and an active "user" of that content, primarily through the apps or websites through which the audience member accesses the content.

Virality—An attribute of a piece of media that encourages its sharing via social media.

Virtual MSO or MVPD—Any Internet distributor that delivers programming via wired or wireless broadband rather than traditional coaxial or satellite signal.

Water cooler moment—Term used to describe a televisual event or plot development during the linear age of television that was of such popular interest and import that viewers would go out of their way to make sure they saw it when broadcast so as to ensure they would not be left out of the conversation "around the water cooler" the next day at work. See also "FOMO."

Web 2.0—Internet sites that invite or encourage participation in and interaction with as well as consumption of information.

Windowing—A distribution structure in which a media text is made available to viewers via particular platforms or consumption sites. Windowing is a form of aftermarket which relies upon exclusive license and time-based availability.

Word of mouth—In the days before social media, people used to speak to each other informally about what television shows they were watching. If you're under 30, ask your parents.

Zapping—Using a remote control to change a channel so as to avoid watching an advertisement or to mute the volume so as to avoid hearing the audio of the advertisement.

Zero rating—When a wireless provider does not charge data usage fees for its customers to use a particular app or family of apps to stream content.

Zero-TV household—A fixed domestic space that uses a broadband or wireless connection to access video distributed over the Internet

Zipping—Using a remote control to fast-forward past an advertisement on a prerecorded show so as to avoid viewing the advertisement in real time and also to avoid hearing the audio of the advertisement.

Notes

Chapter 1

1 Horace Newcomb, *Television: The Critical View*, 7th ed. (London: Oxford University Press, 2006).
2 Qtd. in Susan Murray, "'I Think We Need a New Name for It': The Meeting of Documentary and Reality TV," in *Reality TV: Remaking Television Culture*, ed. Susan and Laurie Ouellette Murray (New York: New York University Press, 2009), p. 66.
3 George Lakoff and Mark Johnson, *Metaphors We Live By* (Chicago: University of Chicago Press, 1980), p. ix.
4 Ibid., p. 3.
5 Ibid., p. 10.
6 Ibid., p. 3.
7 Chris Baldick, "Synecdoche," in *The Oxford Dictionary of Literary Terms* (London: Oxford University Press, 2008).
8 Lakoff and Johnson, *Metaphors We Live By*, p. 36.
9 Ibid.
10 Bjorn Thomassen, *Liminality and the Modern: Living through the In-Between* (Surrey, England: Ashgate, 2014), p. 3.
11 Arnold Van Gennep, *The Rites of Passage* (Chicago: University of Chicago Press, 1960), p. 11.
12 Ibid.
13 Thomassen, *Liminality and the Modern*, p. 92.
14 Ibid., p. 75.
15 Ibid., p. 80.
16 Ibid., p. 89.
17 Ibid., p. 116.
18 Ibid., p. 117.
19 Ibid., p. 134.
20 Amanda Lotz, *The Television Will Be Revolutionized*, 2nd ed. (New York: New York University Press, 2014), p. 276.
21 Thomassen, *Liminality and the Modern*, p. 118.
22 Ibid., p. 210.
23 Ibid.

24 Ibid., p. 86.
25 Ibid.
26 Ibid., p. 118.

Chapter 2

1 Amanda Lotz, *The Television Will Be Revolutionized*, 2nd ed. (New York: New York University Press, 2014), p. 8.
2 Ibid., p. 3.
3 Dan Harries, "Watching the Internet," in *The New Media Book*, ed. Dan Harries (London: British Film Institute, 2002).
4 Amanda Lotz, *The Television Will Be Revolutionized* (New York: New York University Press, 2007), p. 141.
5 Ibid., p. 145.
6 John Palfrey and Urs Gasser, *Born Digital: Understanding the First Generation of Digital Natives* (New York: Basic Books, 2010), p. 6.
7 "Curate," in *New Shorter OED on Historical Principles*, ed. Lesley Brown (Oxford: Clarendon, 1993), p. 136.
8 Ibid.
9 "Curate," in *Oxford English Dictionary*, ed. J. A. and E. S. C. Weiner Simpson (Oxford: Clarendon Press, 1989).
10 Kate Fowle, "ICI Perspectives in Curating," in *Thinking Contemporary Curating*, ed. Terry Smith (New York: Independent Curators International, 2012), p. 20.
11 Ibid., p. 18.
12 Ibid., pp. 17–18.
13 "Curate—Draft Additions, July 2011," in *Oxford English Dictionary—Online* (Oxford: Oxford University Press, 2014).
14 Ibid.
15 Tadas Viskanta to Abnormal Returns: A Wide-Ranging, Forecast-Free Investment Blog, February 12, 2010, http://abnormalreturns.com/content-vs-aggregation-vs-curation.
16 Steven Rosenbaum, *Curation Nation: Why the Future of Content Is Context* (New York: McGraw Hill, 2011), p. 21.
17 Henry Jenkins, *Convergence Culture: Where Old and New Media Collide*, revised ed. (New York: New York University Press, 2008).
18 Ibid.

19 Lotz, *The Television Will Be Revolutionized*, 2nd ed., p. 5.
20 Lakoff and Johnson, *Metaphors We Live By*, p. 14.
21 Ibid., p. 61.
22 Ibid., p. 68.
23 Ien Ang, *Desperately Seeking the Audience* (New York: Routledge, 1991), p. ix.
24 James Webster, Patricia Phalen, and Lawrency Lichty, *Ratings Analysis: The Theory and Practice of Audience Research*, 3rd ed. (New York: Routledge, 2006(2009)), p. 180.
25 Ibid.
26 Ibid.
27 Ibid., p. 181.
28 A. M. Rubin, "Ritualized and Instrumental Television Viewing," *Journal of Communication* 34, no. 3 (1984), p. 68.
29 Webster, Phalen, and Lichty, *Ratings Analysis*, p. 181.
30 Lotz, *The Television Will Be Revolutionized*, 2nd ed., p. 14.
31 Rubin, "Ritualized and Instrumental Television Viewing," p. 68.
32 Lotz, *The Television Will Be Revolutionized*, 2nd ed., p. 3.
33 Tom Vanderbilt, *You May Also Like: Taste in an Age of Endless Choice* (New York: Knopf, 2016), p. 92.
34 William Uricchio, "Television's Next Generation: Technology/Interface Culture/Flow," in *Television after TV: Essays on a Medium in Transition*, ed. Lynn Spigel and Jan Olsson (Durham, NC: Duke University Press, 2004), p. 169.
35 Robert V. Bellamy and James R. Walker, *Television and the Remote Control: Grazing on a Vast Wasteland* (New York: Guilord Press, 1996), p. 32.
36 Ibid., pp. 44–45.
37 Douglas Ferguson, "Channel Repertoire in the Presence of Remote Control Devices, VCRs, and Cable Television," *Journal of Broadcasting & Electronic Media* 36, no. 1 (1992), p. 89.
38 Jason Mittell, "Tivoing Childhood: Time-Shifting a Generation's Concept of Television," in *Flow TV: Television in the Age of Media Convergence*, ed. Kackman et al. (New York: Routledge, 2011), p. 47.
39 Ibid., p. 50.
40 Ibid.
41 Ibid., p. 51.
42 M. Von Rimscha, "How the DVR Is Changing the TV Industry—a Supply Side Perspective," *JMM: The International Journal on Media Management* 8, no. 3 (2006), p. 117.

43 D. Chamberlain, "Television Interfaces," *Journal of Popular Film & Television* 38, no. 2 (2010), p. 86.
44 Derek Kompare, "Publishing Flow: DVD Box Sets and the Reconception of Television," *Television and New Media* 7, no. 4 (2006), p. 338.
45 Ibid., p. 349.
46 Ibid., p. 338.
47 Don Thompson, *The Supermodel and the Brillo Box: Back Stories and Peculiar Economics from the World of Contemporary Art* (New York: Palgrave Macmillan, 2014), p. 134.
48 Michael Curtin and Jane Shattuc, *The American Television Industry* (London: Palgrave Macmillan, 2009), p. 85.
49 Kompare, "Publishing Flow," p. 339.
50 Ibid., p. 340.
51 Raymond Williams, *Television: Technology and Cultural Form*, Routledge Classics (London: Routledge, 1990), p. 97.
52 Leslie Goldberg, "ABC Cancels 'Last Resort,' '666 Park Avenue,'" *The Hollywood Reporter*, November 16, 2012.
53 Karen Buzzard, *Tracking the Audience: The Ratings Industry from Analog to Digital* (New York: Routledge, 2012), p. 126.
54 "Field of Streams: Netflix, Youtube Cue up Original Content," *Variety*, May 4, 2011.
55 Rider Research, "Requiem for the Television: Tablets, OTT, Faster Broadband to Make Today's TV Unrecognizeable" (Rider Research, 2013).
56 Mike Proulx and Stacey Shepatin, *Social TV: How Marketers Can Reach and Engage Audiences by Connecting Television to the Web, Social Media and Mobile* (Hoboken, NJ: John Wiley, 2012), p. 210.
57 Ibid., pp. 213–16.
58 Todd Spangler, "Netflix Grabs for the Remote," *Multichannel News*, January 10, 2011.
59 Ibid.
60 Proulx and Shepatin, *Social TV*, p. 214.
61 Ibid., p. 219.
62 Ibid., p. 220.
63 Janko Roettgers, Writer at GigaOM/NewTeeVee, qtd. in Proulx and Shepatin, *Social TV*, p. 220.
64 Ibid., p. 189.
65 Lotz, *The Television Will Be Revolutionized*, 2nd ed, p. 31.
66 Andrew Jezierski, *Television Everywhere: How Hollywood Can Take Back the Internet and Turn Digital Dimes into Dollars* (Bloomington, IN: Universe, 2010), p. 42.

67 Ibid., p. 43.
68 Thompson, *The Supermodel and the Brillo Box*, p. 29.
69 Ibid., p. 30.
70 Paul Bloom, *How Pleasure Works: The New Science of Why We Like What We Like* (New York: W. W. Norton, 2010), p. 155.
71 Ibid., pp. 2–6.
72 Ibid., p. 7.
73 Ibid.
74 Ibid., p. 22.
75 Qtd in Vanderbilt, *You May Also Like*, p. 45.
76 Bloom, *How Pleasure Works*, p. 70.
77 Ibid., p. 171.
78 Thompson, *The Supermodel and the Brillo Box*, p. 32.
79 Ibid., p. 22.
80 Lotz, *The Television Will Be Revolutionized*, 2nd ed., p. 272.
81 Vanderbilt, *You May Also Like*, p. 167.
82 Ibid.
83 Bloom, *How Pleasure Works*, p. 127.
84 Rosenbaum, *Curation Nation*, p. 91.
85 Laurie Ouellette, *Viewers Like You? How Public TV Failed the People* (New York: Columbia University Press, 2002), p. 2.
86 Pierre Bourdieu, *The Field of Cultural Production: Essays on Art and Literature* (New York: Columbia University Press, 1993), p. 36.
87 Ibid., p. 75.
88 Henry Jenkins, Sam Ford, and Joshua Green, *Spreadable Media: Creating Value and Meaning in a Networked Culture* (New York: New York University Press, 2013), p. 142.
89 Ethan Zuckerman, *Rewire: Digital Cosmopolitans in the Age of Connection* (New York: W. W. Norton, 2013), p. 27.
90 "Top Sites In: All Categories>Arts," Alexa, http://www.alexa.com/topsites/category/Top/Arts.
91 Andrew Keen, *The Cult of the Amateur* (New York: Doubleday, 2007), p. 46.
92 Clay Shirky, *Here Comes Everybody: The Power of Organizing without Organizations* (New York: Penguin, 2008), p. 67.
93 Ibid.
94 Jenkins, Ford, and Green, *Spreadable Media*, p. 80.
95 Ibid., p. 81.
96 Ben Mc Connell and Jackie Huba, *Citizen Marketers: When People Are the Message* (Chicago, IL: Kaplan, 2007), p. 5.
97 Ibid.

98   Ibid., p. 17.
99   Ibid., p. 10.
100 Ibid., p. 19.
101 Ibid., p. 20.
102 Qtd in Zuckerman, *Rewire*, p. 111.
103 Mc Connell and Huba, *Citizen Marketers*, p. 29.
104 Ibid.
105 James Surowiecki, *The Wisdom of Crowds: Why the Many Are Smarter than the Few* (London: Abacus, 2005), p. 43.
106 Zuckerman, *Rewire*, p. 26.
107 Surowiecki, *The Wisdom of Crowds*, p. 43.
108 Jenkins, Ford, and Green, *Spreadable Media*, p. 85.
109 Ibid.
110 Zuckerman, *Rewire*, p. 19.
111 Ibid., p. 6.
112 Ibid., p. 10.
113 Ibid., p. 224.
114 Ibid., p. 229.

Chapter 3

1   Jason Lynch, "A First Look at Nielsen's Total Audience Measurement and How It Will Change the Industry," *AdWeek*, October 20, 2015.
2   Eileen Meehan, "The Ratings System and Its Effects," in *The Television History Book*, ed. Michele Hilmes (London: British Film Institute, 2003), p. 129.
3   Webster, Phalen, and Lichty, *Ratings Analysis*, p. 108.
4   Lotz, *The Television Will Be Revolutionized*, 2nd ed., p. 208.
5   Jenkins, Ford, and Green, *Spreadable Media*, p. 118
6   Webster, Phalen, and Lichty, *Ratings Analysis*, p. 171.
7   Ibid.
8   Proulx and Shepatin, *Social TV*, p. 113.
9   Christopher Sterling and John Kittross, *Stay Tuned: A History of American Broadcasting*, 3rd ed. (Mahwah, NJ: Lawrence Erlbaum Associates, 2002), pp. 800–1.
10 Buzzard, *Tracking the Audience*, p. 17.
11 Meehan, "The Ratings System and Its Effects," p. 131.
12 Buzzard, *Tracking the Audience*, p. 1.
13 Meehan, "The Ratings System and Its Effects," p. 131.

14 Webster, Phalen, and Lichty, *Ratings Analysis*, p. 161.
15 Ibid., p. 144.
16 Ibid., p. 152.
17 Ibid., p. 153.
18 Lynch, "A First Look at Nielsen's Total Audience Measurement."
19 Nielsen, "Nielsen Estimates 116.4 Million TV Homes in the U.S. for the 2015–16 TV Season," (www.nielsen.com: Nielsen 2015). Webster, *Ratings Analysis*, p. 161.
20 Ibid., p. 61.
21 Ibid.
22 Eileen Meehan, "Why We Don't Count: The Commodity Audience," in *Logics of Television*, ed. Patricia Mellencamp (Bloomington: Indiana University Press, 1990), p. 132.
23 Jenkins, Ford, and Green, *Spreadable Media*, p. 129.
24 Buzzard, *Tracking the Audience*, p. 5.
25 Ibid., p. 62.
26 Lotz, *The Television Will Be Revolutionized*, 2nd ed., p. 219.
27 Buzzard, *Tracking the Audience*, p. 62.
28 Proulx and Shepatin, *Social TV*, p. 114.
29 Lotz, *The Television Will Be Revolutionized*, 2nd ed., p. 219.
30 Buzzard, *Tracking the Audience*, p. 130.
31 Ibid.
32 Ibid., p. 76.
33 Ibid.
34 Lynch, "A First Look at Nielsen's Total Audience Measurement."
35 Ibid.
36 Ibid.
37 Ibid.
38 Ibid.
39 Ibid.
40 Ibid.
41 Ibid.
42 Jenkins, Ford, and Green, *Spreadable Media*, p. 116.
43 Coffey, qtd. in Buzzard, 2001, *Tracking the Audience*, p. 122.
44 Oppelaar, 2000, qtd. in Buzzard, *Tracking the Audience*, p. 106.
45 Ibid.
46 Ibid., p. 108.
47 Ibid.

48. Ibid., p. 109.
49. Ibid., p. 110.
50. Ibid., p. 127.
51. Ibid.
52. Ibid.
53. A. J. Marechal, "TCA: Netflix Looks to Join TV Big Leagues," *Variety*, January 9, 2013.
54. Ibid.
55. Ibid.
56. Paul Bond, "Analyst: Netflix Might Be Most-Watched 'Cable Network' in the U.S. Today," *The Hollywood Reporter*, April 11, 2013.
57. Ibid.
58. David Kirkpatrick, *The Facebook Effect: The Inside Story of the Company That Is Connecting the World* (New York: Simon & Schuster, 2010), p. 215.
59. Buzzard, *Tracking the Audience*, p. 119.
60. Ibid., p. 120.
61. Taylor, 2001, qtd. in Buzzard, *Tracking the Audience*, p. 121.
62. Ibid., p. 121.
63. Proulx and Shepatin, *Social TV*, p. 118.
64. Jenkins, Ford, and Green, *Spreadable Media*, p. 75.
65. Proulx and Shepatin, *Social TV*, p. 116.
66. Lotz, *The Television Will Be Revolutionized*, 2nd ed., p. 221.
67. Proulx and Shepatin, *Social TV*, p. ix.
68. Ibid., p. 4.
69. Ibid., p. 24.
70. Mike Isaac, "Twitter Acquires Social TV Tracker Trendrr," *AllThingsDigital*, August 28, 2013.
71. Peter Kafka, "Why Twitter Is Buying Bluefin—and Why Bluefin Is Selling," *AllThingsDigital*, February 4, 2013.
72. Proulx and Shepatin, *Social TV*, p. 127.
73. Qtd. in Jenkins, Ford, and Green, *Spreadable Media*, p. 125.
74. Ibid., p. 125.
75. Lotz, *The Television Will Be Revolutionized*, 2nd ed., p. 231.

Chapter 4

1. Susan Crawford, *Captive Audience: The Telecom Industry and Monopoly Power in the New Gilded Age* (New Haven, CT: Yale University Press, 2013), p. 111.

2. Joe and Suzanne Vranica Flint, "Television-Ad Spending Shows Signs of Revival," *The Wall Street Journal*, April 17, 2016.
3. Jeffrey Ulin, *The Business of Media Distribution: Monetizing Film, TV and Video Content in an Online World* (Burlington, MA: Focus Press, 2010), pp. 33–4.
4. Lotz, *The Television Will Be Revolutionized*, p. 146.
5. Ibid., p. 147.
6. Howard Blumenthal and Oliver Goodenough, *This Business of Television: The Standard Guide to the Television Industry*, 3rd ed. (New York: Billboard Books, 2006), p. 4.
7. Ibid., p. 5.
8. Ibid., p. 9.
9. Ibid., pp. 10–12.
10. Flynn, 2014, qtd. in "The Economics of Allowing Aereo Television on Internet," http://www.graphic-design.com/Allowing_Aereo.
11. Lotz, *The Television Will Be Revolutionized*, p. 89.
12. Ibid., p. 91.
13. Ibid.
14. Ibid., p. 95.
15. Chad Gervich, *Small Screen, Big Picture: A Writer's Guide to the TV Business* (New York: Three Rivers Press, 2008), p. 29.
16. Ibid., pp. 34–6.
17. Ibid., pp. 36–7.
18. Blumenthal and Goodenough, *This Business of Television*, p. 123.
19. Gervich, *Small Screen, Big Picture*, p. 97.
20. Ibid., pp. 80–92.
21. Ibid., pp. 80–2.
22. Ibid., p. 82.
23. Ibid., p. 81.
24. Ibid., pp. 84–5.
25. "1963: First Consumer-Only Video Tape Recorder," http://www.cedmagic.com/history/ampex-signature-v.html.
26. Gervich, *Small Screen, Big Picture*, p. 87.
27. Ibid.
28. Ibid., p. 88.
29. Blumenthal and Goodenough, *This Business of Television*, p. 73.
30. Gervich, *Small Screen, Big Picture*, p. 181.
31. Blumenthal and Goodenough, *This Business of Television*, p. 74.
32. Stuart Elliott, "'Upfront' Market for TV Ad Sales Begins to Move," *The New York Times*, June 6, 2014.

33 Nielsen Media, "Glossary–Gross Rating Point," http://www.nielsenmedia.com/glossary/terms/G/G.html.
34 Curtin and Shattuc, *The American Television Industry*, p. 51.
35 Blumenthal and Goodenough, *This Business of Television*, p. 74.
36 Gervich, *Small Screen, Big Picture*, p. 183.
37 Ibid., p. 75.
38 Ibid., pp. 177–84.
39 Blumenthal and Goodenough, *This Business of Television*, p. 76.
40 Gervich, *Small Screen, Big Picture*, p. 184.
41 Ulin, *The Business of Media Distribution*, p. 44.
42 Derek Kompare, "The Benefits of Banality: Domestic Syndication in the Post-Network Era," in *Beyond Primetime: Television Programming in the Post-Network Era*, ed. Amanda Lotz (New York: Routledge, 2009), p. 58.
43 Ibid., p. 61.
44 Ibid., pp. 62–3.
45 Ulin, *The Business of Media Distribution*, p. 103.
46 Williams, *Television*, p. 86.
47 Gervich, *Small Screen, Big Picture*, pp. 31–2.
48 Robert J. Thompson, *Television's Second Golden Age: From Hill Street Blues to ER* (New York: Continuum, 1996), pp. 13–15.
49 Ibid., p. 34.
50 Ibid.
51 Ibid., p. 35.
52 Ibid.
53 Cynthia Littleton, "Windfall for CBS' 'Wife': SVOD Digital Deals on Amazon Prime, Hulu Plus Will Hike Syndie Haul to $2 Million Per Episode," *Variety*, March 14, 2013.
54 Ibid.
55 Ibid.
56 Moonves, 2013, qtd. in Marisa Guthrie, "'Good Wife' Syndication Deal Includes Amazon, Hulu Plus and Hallmark Channel," *The Hollywood Reporter*, March 13, 2013.
57 Kompare, "The Benefits of Banality," p. 56.
58 Thomassen, *Liminality and the Modern*, p. 104
59 Lewis Hyde, *Trickster Makes This World: Mischief, Myth and Art* (New York: Farrar, Straus and Giroux, 1998), p. 7.
60 Ibid., p. 7.
61 Ibid., p. 283.
62 Ibid., p. 290.

63 Ibid., p. 9.
64 Ibid.
65 Ibid., p. 14.
66 Lotz, *The Television Will Be Revolutionized*, 2nd ed., p. 71.
67 Cecilia Kang, "Netflix Thrives, but Can It Survive?" *The Washington Post*, July 11, 2014.
68 Alex Ben Block, "Netflix's Ted Sarandos Explains Original Content Strategy," *The Hollywood Reporter*, April 7, 2012.
69 Ben Fritz and Joe Flint, "Netflix Is Bulking up on TV Offerings for Subscribers through Its on-Demand Internet Streaming Service, Including Reruns and Its First Original Series," *Los Angeles Times*, February 5, 2012.
70 Block, "Netflix's Ted Sarandos Explains Original Content Strategy."
71 Fritz, "Netflix Is Bulking up on TV Offerings for Subscribers."
72 Ibid.
73 Marechal, "TCA: Netflix Looks to Join TV Big Leagues."
74 Ibid.
75 Joe Flint, "Chelsea Lately Prefers Netflix: Late Night TV Host Handler Will Move Her Party from E! To the Streaming Service," *The Los Angeles Times*, June 20, 2014.
76 Ibid.
77 Ibid.
78 Bill Carter, "After Her Show on E! Ends, Chelsea Handler Will Host a Late-Night Talk Show on Netflix," *The New York Times*, June 20, 2014.
79 Andrew Wallenstein, "Amazon Studios Opens Door to TV," *Variety*, May 2, 2012.
80 Ibid.
81 Natalie Jarvey, "YouTube to Launch Subscription Service with Original Series from Fine Brothers, Pewdiepie," *The Hollywood Reporter*, October 21, 2015.
82 Jean Burgess and Joshua Green, *YouTube: Online Video and Participatory Culture* (Cambridge: Polity, 2009), p. 4.
83 Jenkins, Ford, and Green, *Spreadable Media: Creating Value and Meaning in a Networked Culture*, p. 3.
84 Burgess and Green, *YouTube: Online Video and Participatory Culture*, p. 88.
85 Ibid.
86 "Viacom International, Inc. et al. v. YouTube, Inc. et al.," in *1:07-cv-02103, No. 364* (New York: S.D.N.Y., 2010).
87 YouTube, "Terms of Service," https://www.youtube.com/static?template=terms.
88 Jenkins, Ford, and Green, *Spreadable Media*, p. 95.

89. Gray and Prelinger, 2009, both qtd. in Burgess, *YouTube: Online Video and Participatory Culture*, 89.
90. Ibid., p. 91.
91. YouTube, "Creator Benefits," https://www.youtube.com/yt/creators/creator-benefits.html.
92. "How Ads Are Chosen," https://support.google.com/youtube/answer/94523?hl=en&ref_topic=1115890.
93. Ibid.
94. "YouTube Advertising Formats," https://support.google.com/youtube/answer/2467968?hl=en&ref_topic=1115890.
95. Ibid.
96. Google Ads, "Adsense: How It Works," http://www.google.com/adsense/start/how-it-works.html.
97. SocialBlade, "How Are Estimated Earnings Calculated?" http://socialblade.com/youtube/help.
98. Harrison Jacobs, "We Ranked YouTube's Biggest Stars by How Much Money They Make," Business Insider, http://www.businessinsider.com/richest-youtube-stars-2014-3?op=1.
99. Madeline Berg, "The World's Highest-Paid YouTube Stars 2015," *Forbes*, November 2, 2015.
100. Ibid.
101. Jacobs, "We Ranked YouTube's Biggest Stars by How Much Money They Make."
102. Alex Pham, "YouTube Confirms Investment in Vevo," *The Hollywood Reporter*, July 3, 2013.
103. Ibid.
104. Ibid.
105. Natalie Jarvey, "Awesomeness TV's Brian Robbins on Billion-Dollar Deals, Vine's Value and the Future of Content Delivery," *Variety*, May 16, 2014.
106. Ibid.
107. Ibid.
108. Paul Bond, "YouTube Space La Chief on Hosting Matt Damon and Charging to Watch Videos," *The Hollywood Reporter*, May 15, 2013.
109. Ibid.
110. YouTube, "Paid Channels," https://www.youtube.com/channels/paid_channels.
111. HereTV, "Homepage," http://www.heretv.com/.
112. Essel Group, "Our Companies--Zee Media Corporation Limited," http://www.esselgroup.com/zee-media-corporation-limited.html.
113. Megan Mullen, *The Rise of Cable Programming in the United States: Revolution or Evolution?* (Austin: University of Texas Press, 2003), p. 94.

114 Federal Communications Commission, "Annual Assessment of the Status of Competition in the Market for the Delivery of Video Programming," (Washington, DC: FCC, 2013).
115 Burgess, *YouTube: Online Video and Participatory Culture*, p. 104.
116 Ibid. p. 106.
117 Bond, "YouTube Space LA Chief on Hosting Matt Damon and Charging to Watch Videos."
118 Qtd. in Brian Stelter, "Serving up Television without the TV Set," *The New York Times*, March 10, 2008.
119 Jezierski, *Television Everywhere*, p. 27.
120 Proulx and Shepatin, *Social TV*, p. 199.
121 Debra Birnbaum, "'Star Trek: Discovery' Delayed on CBS All Access until May, 'Good Wife' Spinoff Moved Up," *Variety*, September 14, 2016.
122 CBS, "CBS All Access," https://www.cbs.com/all-access/.
123 Thompson, *The Supermodel and the Brillo Box*, p. 33.
124 Ibid., p. 77.
125 Proulx and Shepatin, *Social TV*, p. 146.
126 Ibid., pp. 149–50.
127 Ibid., p. 154.
128 Ibid., p. 138.
129 Andrew Wallenstein, "Without Its Architect, Hulu Needs New Grounding," *Variety*, January 4, 2013.
130 Chuck Tryon, *Reinventing Cinema: Movies in the Age of Media Convergence* (New Brunswick, NY: Rutgers University Press, 2009), p. 112.
131 Proulx and Shepatin, *Social TV*, p. 199.
132 Ibid., p. 200.
133 Ibid.
134 Ibid., p. 186.
135 Buzzard, *Tracking the Audience*, p. 85.
136 Will Richmond, editor and publisher of Videonuz, 2012, qtd. in Proulx and Shepatin, *Social TV*, p. 187.
137 Buzzard, *Tracking the Audience*, p. 85.
138 Proulx and Shepatin, *Social TV*, p. 194.
139 Crawford, *Captive Audience*, p. 117.
140 Alex Ben Block, "Cable TV's Bold Play to Buy Loyalty," *The Hollywood Reporter*, June 13, 2013.
141 Ibid.
142 Ibid.
143 Proulx and Shepatin, *Social TV*, p. 85.

144 Ibid., pp. 95–6.
145 Ibid., p. 98.
146 Ibid., p. 99.
147 Ibid., p. 101.
148 Ibid., p. 100.
149 Ibid., p. 102.
150 Ibid., pp. 103–4.
151 Ibid., p. 104.
152 Ibid., p. 13.
153 Ibid., p. 17.
154 Ibid., p. 14.
155 Ibid., p. 6.
156 Ibid., p. 14.
157 Ibid., p. 196.
158 Ibid., p. 197.
159 Thomassen, *Liminality and the Modern*, p. 1.
160 Mikhail Bakhtin, *Rabelais and His World* (Bloomington: Indiana University Press, 2009).
161 Thomassen, *Liminality and the Modern*, p. 2.
162 Jezierski, *Television Everywhere*, p. 27.
163 Michael Wolff, *Television Is the New Television: The Unexpected Triumph of Old Media in the Digital Age* (New York: Portfolio/Penguin, 2015), p. 94.
164 Ibid.

Chapter 5

1 Jennifer Holt, "Regulating Connected Viewing: Media Pipelines and Cloud Policy," in *Connected Viewing: Selling, Streaming & Sharing Media in the Digital Age*, ed. Jennifer Holt and Kevin Samson (New York: Routledge, 2014), p. 30.
2 Federal Communications Commission, "Tom Wheeler FCC Chairman," www.fcc.gov/about/leadership/tom-wheeler.
3 Edward Wyatt, "F.C.C. Commissioner Leaving to Join Comcast," *The New York Times*, May 11, 2011.
4 CTIA—The Wireless Association, "About Us," http://ctia.org/about-us.
5 Thomas Streeter, *Selling the Air: A Critique of the Policy of Commercial Broadcasting in the United States* (Chicago: University of Chicago Press, 1996), p. 315.

6. Federal Communications Commission, "About the FCC: Leadership," www.fcc.gov/about/leadership.
7. 47 U.S.C. § 214.
8. Sterling and Kittross, *Stay Tuned*, p. 574.
9. Patrick Parsons, *Blue Skies: A History of Cable Television* (Philadelphia, PA: Temple University Press, 2008), p. 495.
10. Crawford, *Captive Audience*, pp. 133–4.
11. Federal Communications Commission, "Telecommunications Act of 1996," https://apps.fcc.gov/edocs_public/attachmatch/DOC-339798A1.pdf.
12. Ibid.
13. Jennifer Holt, *Empires of Entertainment: Media Industries and the Politics of Deregulation, 1980–1996* (New Jersey: Rutgers University Press, 2011), p. 140.
14. Buzzard, *Tracking the Audience*, p. 5.
15. Holt, *Empires of Entertainment*, p. 165.
16. Tim Wu, "Network Neutrality, Broadband Discrimination," *Journal of Telecommunications and High Technology Law* 2 (2003), p. 146.
17. Ibid.
18. Federal Communications Commission, "In the Matter of Protecting and Promoting the Open Internet," ed. Federal Communications Commision (Washington, DC, 2015).
19. Ibid.
20. United States Congress, "Communications Act of 1934: As Amended by Telecom Act of 1996," ed. US Congress (Washington, DC, 1934). Sec. 202. [47 U.S.C. 202].
21. Federal Communications Commission, "In the Matter of Protecting and Promoting the Open Internet."
22. Telecommunications Act of 1996, 47 U.S.C. 51 et. Seq. § 706 (a).
23. Ibid.
24. Federal Communications Commission. In the Matter of Protecting and Promoting the Open Internet. GN Docket No. 14–28. February, 26 2015 § II D.51.
25. Ibid.
26. *United States Telecom Association, et al. v. Federal Communications Commission* (2016).
27. Tom Wheeler, "Statement of FCC Chairman Tom Wheeler Regarding DC Circuit Decision to Uphold FCC's Open Internet Rules," news release, June 14, 2016, https://apps.fcc.gov/edocs_public/attachmatch/DOC-339798A1.pdf.
28. Holt, *Empires of Entertainment*, p. 2.

29 Eileen Meehan, *Why TV Is Not Our Fault: Television Programming, Viewers and Who's Really in Control* (Lanham, MD: Rowman & Littlefield, 2005), p. 48.
30 Ibid., p. 48.
31 Jason (Frugal Dad) to FrugalDad.Com: Common Sense for College by FrugalDad, July 5, 2016, 2011, www.frugaldad.com/media-consolidation-infographic.
32 Crawford, *Captive Audience*, p. 5.
33 Ibid., p. 5.
34 Ibid.
35 Ibid.
36 Ibid., p. 9.
37 Ibid., p. 65.
38 Ibid., p. 117.
39 Federal Communications Commission, "DTV: Digital Television: What Every Consumer Should Know," ed. Media Bureau and Consumer & Governmental Affairs Bureau (Washington, DC: FCC, 2008).
40 "Auction 73–700mhz Band," FCC, http://wireless.fcc.gov/auctions/default.htm?job=auction_summary&id=73.
41 Tom Wheeler, "Statement Re: Expanding the Economic and Innovation Opportunities of Spectrum through Incentive Auctions" (www.apps.fcc.gov: Federal Communications Commission, 2016).
42 Colin Gibbs, "600mhz Incentive Auction Primer: Who Will Bid, When Will It Happen, How Will It Work, and How Much Money It Will Raise," *FierceWireless*, March 22, 2016.
43 Wheeler, "Statement Re: Expanding the Economic and Innovation Opportunities of Spectrum through Incentive Auctions."
44 Crawford, *Captive Audience*, p. 157.
45 Ibid., p. 5.
46 Ibid., p. 157.
47 Ibid., p. 234.
48 Ibid., p. 17.
49 Ibid.
50 Ibid.
51 Brian Fung, "Here's Why Big Cities Aren't Getting Google Fiber Anytime Soon," *The Washington Post*, February 20, 2014.
52 47 U.S.C. § 522 (13).
53 Mike Farrell, "Eat or Be Eaten: Consolidation Creates a Top-Heavy List of 25 Largest MVPDS," *Multichannel News*, August 17, 2015.

54 Federal Communications Commission, "In the Matter of Promoting Innovation and Competition in the Provision of Multichannel Video Programming Distribution Services," ed. Federal Communications Commission (Washington, DC, 2014). p. 15996.
55 Tom Wheeler, "Statement of Chairman Tom Wheeler Re: Promoting Innovation and Competition in the Provision of Multichannel Video Programming Distribution Services, MB Docket No. 14–261," (www.fcc.gov: Federal Communications Commission, 2014).
56 Katherine Boehret, "Aereo Shines with Live TV on the Go," *Wall Street Journal*, July 18, 2012.
57 Ted Johnson, "Supreme Court Ruling on Aereo Will Be Significant, No Matter Who Wins?" *Variety*, 2014.
58 Larry Downes to Harvard Business Review Blog Network, March 7, 2013, http://blogs.hbr.org/2013/03/aereo-tv-barely-legal-by-desig/.
59 Ibid.
60 Ibid.
61 Ibid.
62 Johnson, "Supreme Court Ruling on Aereo Will Be Significant, No Matter Who Wins?"
63 Ibid.
64 Ibid.
65 Downes Title of Weblog. Larry Downes, "Aereo TV: Barely Legal by Design." In *Harvard Business Review Blog Network*, March 7, 2013.
66 Adam Liptak and Emily Steel, "Aereo Loses at Supreme Court, in Victory for TV Broadcasters," *The New York Times*, June 25, 2014.
67 Ibid.
68 Ibid.
69 "Barry Diller on Aereo Ruling: 'We Did Try, but It's over Now,'" *The Hollywood Reporter*, June 25, 2014.
70 Ibid.
71 Dwight Silverman to Seattle Post Intelligencer, July 24, 2014, http://blog.seattlepi.com/techblog/2014/07/22/aereo-reveals-some-subscriber-numbers-and-theyre-tiny/#22153101=0.
72 Peter Kafka to Recode, July 24, 2014, http://recode.net/2014/07/21/heres-how-many-subscribers-aereo-had-last-year/.
73 Kate Cox, "Tivo Invokes Aereo's Corporate Corpse to Market an 'Exclusive' Deal That Costs $70 More Than No Deal at All," *Consumerist*, July 6, 2015.
74 Todd Spangler, "Comcast to Stream Netflix on Cable Set-Tops," *Variety*, July 5, 2016.

Chapter 6

1. "British Netflix Users Are Getting a Raw Deal—Here's How to Watch American Netflix in the UK," *The Mirror*, March 19, 2016.
2. Brants and Siune, 1997, qtd. in Chris Barker, *Global Television: An Introduction* (Oxford: Blackwell, 1997), p. 32.
3. Blumenthal and Goodenough, *This Business of Television*, p. 484.
4. IDATE Consulting and Research, "Global TV 2010 Markets & Trends Facts & Figures—2008–2013," (France: IDATE, 2013), p. 9.
5. Ibid., p. 9.
6. Ibid., p. 10.
7. International Telecommunication Union, "Internet Live Stats," http://www.internetlivestats.com/internet-users/.
8. Ibid.
9. Ibid.
10. Timothy Havens, *Global Television Marketplace* (London: British Film Institute, 2006), p. 66.
11. Randee Dawn, "Mipcom: TV Markets Scramble to Make Adjustments as Viewing Habits Transform," *Variety*, September 30, 2015.
12. Ibid.
13. Ibid.
14. Ibid.
15. Ibid.
16. Alyssa Rosenberg, "How the International Market Will Change Television," *The Washington Post*, September 28, 2015.
17. "Priyanka Chopra" (imbb.com, 2016).
18. Dwayne Johnson, "Time Magazine's 100 Most Influential People: Priyanka Chopra," *Time*, April 21, 2016.
19. Rosenberg, "How the International Market Will Change Television."
20. Alexa, "The Top 500 Sites on the Web," http://www.alexa.com/topsites.
21. Neal Ungerleider, "What Amazon Prime Is Like around the World," *Fast Company*, January 5, 2016.
22. Ibid.
23. Ibid.
24. To France: Ending the Cultural Exception, November 3, 2014, http://www.worldpolicy.org/blog/2014/11/03/france-ending-cultural-exception.
25. Ungerleider, "What Amazon Prime Is Like around the World."

26 Robert Briel to Broadband TV News, July 18, 2016, http://www.broadbandtvnews.com/2016/07/18/amazon-prime-video-to-launch-in-france-italy-and-spain/.
27 YouTube, "Statistics," https://www.youtube.com/yt/press/statistics.html.
28 Ibid.
29 Ian Henderson, "Lights, Camera, Global! How to Create an International YouTube Strategy," http://www.business2community.com/youtube/lights-camera-global-create-international-youtube-strategy-01133086#YHPz2kpYLpirJ5Gs.97.
30 Don Crothers, "Google Is Now Giving Away Four Free Months of YouTube Red and Google Play Music Unlimited," *Inquisitr.com*, July 3, 2016.
31 Wolff, *Television Is the New Television*, p. 92.
32 Voice of America, "Netflix Expands to 190 Countries," *VOA Learning English* (January 13, 2016), http://learningenglish.voanews.com/a/netflix-expands-to-190-countries/3144530.html.
33 Lior Ronen, "Netflix Likely to Face Growth Headwinds Globally," *AmigoBulls.com*, July 25, 2016.
34 Scott Roxborough and Georg Szalai, "Why Is Netflix Struggling Overseas?," *The Hollywood Reporter*, July 22, 2016.
35 Patrick Frater, "In Asia, Netflix Opts for Trial by Fire," *Variety*, February, 2016, p. 111.
36 Ibid.
37 Ibid.
38 Scott Roxborough, "Europe Calls for Netflix, Amazon Content Quotas," *The Hollywood Reporter*, May 25, 2016.
39 Ibid.
40 Ibid.
41 Ibid.
42 Ibid.
43 Ibid.
44 Ibid.
45 Frater, "In Asia, Netflix Opts for Trial by Fire," p. 111.
46 Joseph Lovinger and Ben Popper, "Netflix Stock Price Tanks as Customers Quit over Higher Prices," *The Verge*, July 18, 2016.
47 Roxborough and Szalai, "Why Is Netflix Struggling Overseas?"
48 Roxborough, "Europe Calls for Netflix, Amazon Content Quotas."
49 Ronen, "Netflix Likely to Face Growth Headwinds Globally."
50 Roxborough, "Europe Calls for Netflix, Amazon Content Quotas."

51 Christopher Vourlias, "Africa's No Dream for Streaming: Infrastructure Biggest Concern for Netflix," *Variety*, February, 2016. p. 111.
52 Ibid.
53 Ibid.
54 Ibid.
55 Global Net Neutrality Coalition, "Net Neutrality around the World," https://www.thisisnetneutrality.org/.
56 Amar Toor, "Sir Tim Berners-Lee Makes a Last-Minute Plea to Save Net Neutrality in Europe," *The Verge*, July 15, 2016.
57 Harrison Kaminsky, "European Telecom Companies Deliver '5G Manifesto' to Recommend against Net Neutrality Regulation," *Digital Trends*, 2016.
58 Federal Communications Commission, "In the Matter of Commission Policies and Procedures under Section 310(B)(4) of the Communications Act, Foreign Investment in Broadcast Licensees," ed. Federal Communications Commission (Washington, DC, November 14, 2013), p. 1.
59 Ibid., p. 9.
60 Ibid.
61 Farrell, "Eat or Be Eaten: Consolidation Creates a Top-Heavy List of 25 Largest MVPDs."
62 Nick Kostov and Shalini Ramachandran, "Altice's Big U.S. Cable Ambitions Begin with Austerity," *The Wall Street Journal*, June 28, 2016.
63 Ibid.

Chapter 7

1 Thomassen, *Liminality and the Modern*, p. 205.
2 Cynthia Littleton, "Shelf Shock," *Variety*, September 14, 2014, p. 30.
3 Thomassen, *Liminality and the Modern*, p. 202.
4 Ibid.
5 Ibid.
6 Ibid., p. 203.
7 Alex Ben Block, "Leslie Moonves: CBS Is Open to Licensing Content to Aereo," *The Hollywood Reporter*, July 15, 2014.
8 Thomassen, *Liminality and the Modern*, p. 208.
9 Ibid., p. 17.
10 Wolff, *Television Is the New Television*, p. 85.
11 Littleton, "Shelf Shock," p. 28.

12 "FX Networks Chief John Landgraf: 'There Is Simply Too Much Television,'" *Variety*, August 7, 2015.
13 Littleton, "Shelf Shock," p. 28.
14 Ibid.
15 Ibid.
16 Ulin, *The Business of Media Distribution*, p. 299.
17 Rob Toledo to The Extreamist, July 21, 2016, http://exstreamist.com/people-arent-cancelling-netflix-because-of-price-increases-theyre-cancelling-because-the-library-is-shrinking/.
18 Nelson Granados, "Netflix Is Putting Its Head in the Sand over Rising Competition," *Forbes*, July 19, 2016.
19 Cynthia Littleton, "Networks Boldly Go into Digital Universe," *Variety*, November 10, 2015, p. 9.
20 Ibid.
21 Ibid., p. 10.
22 Rae Votta to The Daily Dot, June 24, 2016, http://www.dailydot.com/upstream/youtube-keynote-vidcon-2016/.
23 Joe Flint and Shalini Ramachandran, "Google Signs up CBS for Planned Web TV Service," *The Wall Street Journal*, October 20, 2016.
24 Thomassen, *Liminality and the Modern*, p. 82.
25 Shan Wang, "The New York Times Wants to Tell You Which TV Shows Are Worth Binging on with a New Product," *Nieman Lab*, January 29, 2016.
26 Ibid.
27 Zuckerman, *Rewire*, p. 75.
28 "Arrested Development Emmy Win (Season 1)," (2005).

Bibliography

"1963: First Consumer-Only Video Tape Recorder." http://www.cedmagic.com/history/ampex-signature-v.html.

Alexa. "The Top 500 Sites on the Web." http://www.alexa.com/topsites.

Alexa. "Top Sites In: All Categories>Arts." http://www.alexa.com/topsites/category/Top/Arts.

Anderson, Chris. *The Long Tail: Why the Future of Business is Selling Less of More*. NY: Hachette, 2008.

Ang, Ien. *Desperately Seeking the Audience*. New York: Routledge, 1991.

"Arrested Development Emmy Win (Season 1)," 2005. https://www.youtube.com/watch?v=ebcrLHst2Ns&t=6s.

Bakhtin, Mikhail. *Rabelais and His World*. Bloomington: Indiana University Press, 2009.

Barker, Chris. *Global Television: An Introduction*. Oxford: Blackwell, 1997.

"Barry Diller on Aereo Ruling: 'We Did Try, but It's over Now.'" *The Hollywood Reporter*, June 25, 2014.

Bellamy, Robert V., and James R. Walker. *Television and the Remote Control: Grazing on a Vast Wasteland*. New York: Guilord Press, 1996.

Berg, Madeline. "The World's Highest-Paid YouTube Stars 2015." *Forbes*, November 2, 2015.

Birnbaum, Debra. "'Star Trek: Discovery' Delayed on CBS All Access until May, 'Good Wife' Spinoff Moved Up." *Variety*, September 14, 2016.

Block, Alex Ben. "Netflix's Ted Sarandos Explains Original Content Strategy." *The Hollywood Reporter*, April 7, 2012.

Block, Alex Ben. "Cable TV's Bold Play to Buy Loyalty." *The Hollywood Reporter*, June 13, 2013.

Block, Alex Ben. "Leslie Moonves: CBS Is Open to Licensing Content to Aereo." *The Hollywood Reporter*, July 15, 2014.

Bloom, Paul. *How Pleasure Works: The New Science of Why We Like What We Like*. New York: W. W. Norton, 2010.

Blumenthal, Howard, and Oliver Goodenough. *This Business of Television: The Standard Guide to the Television Industry*. 3rd ed. New York: Billboard Books, 2006.

Boehret, Katherine. "Aereo Shines with Live TV on the Go." *Wall Street Journal*, July 18, 2012.

Bond, Paul. "Analyst: Netflix Might Be Most-Watched 'Cable Network' in the U.S. Today." *The Hollywood Reporter*, April 11, 2013.

Bond, Paul. "YouTube Space LA Chief on Hosting Matt Damon and Charging to Watch Videos." *The Hollywood Reporter*, May 15, 2013.

Bourdieu, Pierre. *The Field of Cultural Production: Essays on Art and Literature*. New York: Columbia University Press, 1993.

Briel, Robert. "Amazon Prime Video to Launch in France, Italy and Spain." In *Broadband TV News*, July 18, 2016.

"British Netflix Users Are Getting a Raw Deal—Here's How to Watch American Netflix in the UK." *The Mirror*, March 19, 2016.

Burgess, Jean, and Joshua Green. *YouTube: Online Video and Participatory Culture*. Cambridge: Polity, 2009.

Buzzard, Karen. *Tracking the Audience: The Ratings Industry from Analog to Digital*. New York: Routledge, 2012.

Carter, Bill. "After Her Show on E! Ends, Chelsea Handler Will Host a Late-Night Talk Show on Netflix." *The New York Times*, June 20, 2014.

CBS. "CBS All Access." https://www.cbs.com/all-access/.

Chamberlain, D. "Television Interfaces." *Journal of Popular Film & Television* 38, no. 2 (2010): pp. 84–88.

Cox, Kate. "Tivo Invokes Aereo's Corporate Corpse to Market an 'Exclusive' Deal That Costs $70 More Than No Deal at All." *Consumerist*, July 6, 2015.

Crawford, Susan. *Captive Audience: The Telecom Industry and Monopoly Power in the New Gilded Age*. New Haven, CT: Yale University Press, 2013.

Crothers, Don. "Google Is Now Giving Away Four Free Months of YouTube Red and Google Play Music Unlimited." *Inquisitr.com*, July 3, 2016.

CTIA—The Wireless Association. "About Us." http://ctia.org/about-us.

"Curate—Draft Additions, July 2011." In *Oxford English Dictionary—Online*. Oxford: Oxford University Press, 2014.

Curtin, Michael, and Jane Shattuc. *The American Television Industry*. London: Palgrave Macmillan, 2009.

Dawn, Randee. "Mipcom: TV Markets Scramble to Make Adjustments as Viewing Habits Transform." *Variety*, September 30, 2015.

Downes, Larry. "Aereo TV: Barely Legal by Design." In *Harvard Business Review Blog Network*, March 7, 2013.

"The Economics of Allowing Aereo Television on Internet." http://www.graphic-design.com/Allowing_Aereo.

Elliott, Stuart. "'Upfront' Market for TV Ad Sales Begins to Move." *The New York Times*, June 6, 2014.

Essel Group. "Our Companies—Zee Media Corporation Limited." http://www.esselgroup.com/zee-media-corporation-limited.html.

Farrell, Mike. "Eat or Be Eaten: Consolidation Creates a Top-Heavy List of 25 Largest MVPDs." *Multichannel News*, August 17, 2015.

Federal Communications Commission. "About the FCC: Leadership." http://www.fcc.gov/about/leadership.

Federal Communications Commission. "Annual Assessment of the Status of Competition in the Market for the Delivery of Video Programming." Washington, DC: FCC, 2013.

Federal Communications Commission. "Auction 73–700MHz Band." FCC, http://wireless.fcc.gov/auctions/default.htm?job=auction_summary&id=73.

Federal Communications Commission. "DTV: Digital Television: What Every Consumer Should Know." Edited by Media Bureau and Consumer & Governmental Affairs Bureau. Washington, DC: FCC, 2008.

Federal Communications Commission. "In the Matter of Commission Policies and Procedures under Section 310(B)(4) of the Communications Act, Foreign Investment in Broadcast Licensees." Edited by Federal Communications Commission. Washington, DC: FCC, November 14, 2013.

Federal Communications Commission. "In the Matter of Promoting Innovation and Competition in the Provision of Multichannel Video Programming Distribution Services." Edited by Federal Communications Commission, 15995–6051. Washington, DC: FCC, 2014.

Federal Communications Commission. "In the Matter of Protecting and Promoting the Open Internet." Edited by Federal Communications Commision, 5601–6001. Washington, DC: FCC, 2015.

Federal Communications Commission. "Telecommunications Act of 1996." https://apps.fcc.gov/edocs_public/attachmatch/DOC-339798A1.pdf.

Federal Communications Commission. "Tom Wheeler FCC Chairman." http://www.fcc.gov/about/leadership/tom-wheeler.

Ferguson, Douglas. "Channel Repertoire in the Presence of Remote Control Devices, VCRs, and Cable Television." *Journal of Broadcasting & Electronic Media* 36, no. 1 (Winter 1992): pp. 83–92.

"Field of Streams: Netflix, YouTube Cue up Original Content." *Variety*, May 4, 2011.

Flint, Joe. "Chelsea Lately Prefers Netflix: Late Night TV Host Handler Will Move Her Party from E! To the Streaming Service." *The Los Angeles Times*, June 20, 2014.

Flint, Joe, and Shalini Ramachandran. "Google Signs up CBS for Planned Web TV Service." *The Wall Street Journal*, October 20, 2016.

Flint, Joe, and Suzanne Vranica. "Television-Ad Spending Shows Signs of Revival." *The Wall Street Journal*, April 17, 2016.

Fowle, Kate. "ICI Perspectives in Curating." In *Thinking Contemporary Curating*, edited by Terry Smith, pp. 1–27. New York: Independent Curators International, 2012.

"France: Ending the Cultural Exception." In *World Policy Blog*, 2014.

Frater, Patrick. "In Asia, Netflix Opts for Trial by Fire." *Variety*, February, 2016, pp. 110–12.

Fritz, Ben, and Joe Flint. "Netflix Is Bulking up on TV Offerings for Subscribers through Its On-Demand Internet Streaming Service, Including Reruns and Its First Original Series." *Los Angeles Times*, February 5, 2012.

Fung, Brian. "Here's Why Big Cities Aren't Getting Google Fiber Anytime Soon." *The Washington Post*, February 20, 2014.

Gervich, Chad. *Small Screen, Big Picture: A Writer's Guide to the TV Business*. New York: Three Rivers Press, 2008.

Gibbs, Colin. "600MHz Incentive Auction Primer: Who Will Bid, When Will It Happen, How Will It Work, and How Much Money It Will Raise." *FierceWireless*, March 22, 2016.

Global Net Neutrality Coalition. "Net Neutrality around the World." https://www.thisisnetneutrality.org/.

Goldberg, Leslie. "ABC Cancels 'Last Resort,' '666 Park Avenue.'" *The Hollywood Reporter*, November 16, 2012.

Google Ads. "Adsense: How It Works." http://www.google.com/adsense/start/how-it-works.html.

Granados, Nelson. "Netflix Is Putting Its Head in the Sand over Rising Competition." *Forbes*, July 19, 2016.

Guthrie, Marisa. "'Good Wife' Syndication Deal Includes Amazon, Hulu Plus and Hallmark Channel." *The Hollywood Reporter*, March 13, 2013.

Harries, Dan. "Watching the Internet." In *The New Media Book*, edited by Dan Harries, pp. 172–82. London: British Film Institute, 2002.

Havens, Timothy. *Global Television Marketplace*. London: British Film Institute, 2006.

Henderson, Ian. "Lights, Camera, Global! How to Create an International YouTube Strategy." http://www.business2community.com/youtube/lights-camera-global-create-international-youtube-strategy-01133086 – YHPz2kpYLpirJ5Gs.97.

HereTV. "Homepage." http://www.heretv.com/.

Holt, Jennifer. *Empires of Entertainment: Media Industries and the Politics of Deregulation, 1980–1996*. New Jersey: Rutgers University Press, 2011.

Holt, Jennifer. "Regulating Connected Viewing: Media Pipelines and Cloud Policy." In *Connected Viewing: Selling, Streaming & Sharing Media in the Digital Age*, edited by Jennifer and Kevin Samson Holt, pp. 19–39. New York: Routledge, 2014.

Hyde, Lewis. *Trickster Makes This World: Mischief, Myth and Art*. New York: Farrar, Straus and Giroux, 1998.

IDATE Consulting and Research. "Global TV 2010 Markets & Trends Facts & Figures—2008–2013." France: IDATE, 2013.

International Telecommunication Union. "Internet Live Stats." http://www.internetlivestats.com/internet-users/.

Isaac, Mike. "Twitter Acquires Social TV Tracker Trendrr." *AllThingsDigital*, August 28, 2013.

Jacobs, Harrison. "We Ranked YouTube's Biggest Stars by How Much Money They Make." Business Insider, http://www.businessinsider.com/richest-youtube-stars-2014-3?op=1.

Jarvey, Natalie. "Awesomeness TV's Brian Robbins on Billion-Dollar Deals, Vine's Value and the Future of Content Delivery." *Variety*, May 16, 2014.

Jarvey, Natalie. "YouTube to Launch Subscription Service with Original Series from Fine Brothers, Pewdiepie." *The Hollywood Reporter*, October 21, 2015.

Jason (Frugal Dad). "Media Consolidation: The Illusion of Choice (Infographic)." In FrugalDad.Com: Common Sense for College by FrugalDad. http://www.frugaldad.com, 2011.

Jenkins, Henry. *Convergence Culture: Where Old and New Media Collide*. Revised ed. New York: New York University Press, 2008.

Jenkins, Henry, Sam Ford, and Joshua Green. *Spreadable Media: Creating Value and Meaning in a Networked Culture*. New York: New York University Press, 2013.

Jezierski, Andrew. *Television Everywhere: How Hollywood Can Take Back the Internet and Turn Digital Dimes into Dollars*. Bloomington, IN: Universe, 2010.

Johnson, Dwayne. "Time Magazine's 100 Most Influential People: Priyanka Chopra." *Time*, April 21, 2016.

Johnson, Ted. "Supreme Court Ruling on Aereo Will Be Significant, No Matter Who Wins?" *Variety*, April 16, 2014.

Kafka, Peter. "Why Twitter Is Buying Bluefin—and Why Bluefin Is Selling." *AllThingsDigital*, February 4, 2013.

Kafka, Peter. "Here's How Many Subscribers Aereo Had Last Year." In *Recode*, July 21, 2014.

Kaminsky, Harrison. "European Telecom Companies Deliver '5G Manifesto' to Recommend against Net Neutrality Regulation." *Digital Trends*, July 10, 2016.

Kang, Cecilia. "Netflix Thrives, but Can It Survive?" *The Washington Post*, July 11, 2014.

Keen, Andrew. *The Cult of the Amateur*. New York: Doubleday, 2007.

Kirkpatrick, David. *The Facebook Effect: The inside Story of the Company That Is Connecting the World*. New York: Simon & Schuster, 2010.

Kompare, Derek. "Publishing Flow: DVD Box Sets and the Reconception of Television." *Television and New Media* 7, no. 4 (November 2006): pp. 335–60.

Kompare, Derek. "The Benefits of Banality: Domestic Syndication in the Post-Network Era." In *Beyond Primetime: Television Programming in the Post-Network Era*, edited by Amanda Lotz, pp. 55–74. New York: Routledge, 2009.

Kostov, Nick, and Shalini Ramachandran. "Altice's Big U.S. Cable Ambitions Begin with Austerity." *The Wall Street Journal*, June 28, 2016.

Lakoff, George, and Mark Johnson. *Metaphors We Live By*. Chicago: University of Chicago Press, 1980.

Liptak, Adam, and Emily Steel. "Aereo Loses at Supreme Court, in Victory for TV Broadcasters." *The New York Times*, June 25, 2014.

Littleton, Cynthia. "Windfall for CBS' 'Wife': SVOD Digital Deals on Amazon Prime, Hulu Plus Will Hike Syndie Haul to $2 Million Per Episode." *Variety*, March 14, 2013.

Littleton, Cynthia. "Shelf Shock." *Variety*, September 14, 2014, pp. 27–31.

Littleton, Cynthia. "FX Networks Chief John Landgraf: 'There Is Simply Too Much Television.'" *Variety*, August 7, 2015.

Littleton, Cynthia. "Networks Boldly Go into Digital Universe." *Variety*, November 10, 2015, pp. 9–10.

Lotz, Amanda. *The Television Will Be Revolutionized*. New York: New York University Press, 2007.

Lotz, Amanda. *The Television Will Be Revolutionized*. 2nd ed. New York: New York University Press, 2014.

Lovinger, Joseph, and Ben Popper. "Netflix Stock Price Tanks as Customers Quit over Higher Prices." *The Verge*, July 18, 2016.

Lynch, Jason. "A First Look at Nielsen's Total Audience Measurement and How It Will Change the Industry." *AdWeek*, October 20, 2015.

Marechal, A. J. "TCA: Netflix Looks to Join TV Big Leagues." *Variety*, January 9, 2013.

McConnell, Ben, and Jackie Huba. *Citizen Marketers: When People Are the Message*. Chicago, IL: Kaplan, 2007.

Meehan, Eileen. "Why We Don't Count: The Commodity Audience." In *Logics of Television*, edited by Patricia Mellencamp, pp. 117–37. Bloomington: Indiana University Press, 1990.

Meehan, Eileen. "The Ratings System and Its Effects." In *The Television History Book*, edited by Michele Hilmes, pp. 129–32. London: British Film Institute, 2003.

Meehan, Eileen. *Why TV Is Not Our Fault: Television Programming, Viewers and Who's Really in Control*. Lanham, MD: Rowman & Littlefield Publishers, 2005.

Mittell, Jason. "Tivoing Childhood: Time-Shifting a Generation's Concept of Television." In *Flow TV: Television in the Age of Media Convergence*, edited by Michael Kackman et al., pp. 46–54. New York: Routledge, 2011.

Mullen, Megan. *The Rise of Cable Programming in the United States: Revolution or Evolution?* Austin: University of Texas Press, 2003.

Murray, Susan. "'I Think We Need a New Name for It': The Meeting of Documentary and Reality TV." In *Reality TV: Remaking Television Culture*, edited by Susan and Laurie Ouellette Murray. New York: New York University Press, 2009.

New Shorter OED on Historical Principles. 2 vols. Oxford: Clarendon, 1993.

Newcomb, Horace. *Television: The Critical View*. 7th ed. London: Oxford University Press, 2006.

Nielsen. "Nielsen Estimates 116.4 Million TV Homes in the U.S. for the 2015–16 TV Season." http://www.nielsen.com: Nielsen 2015.

Nielsen Media. "Glossary—Gross Rating Point." http://www.nielsenmedia.com/glossary/terms/G/G.html.

Ouellette, Laurie. *Viewers Like You? How Public TV Failed the People*. New York: Columbia University Press, 2002.

Oxford English Dictionary. 2nd ed. Oxford: Clarendon Press, 1989.

The Oxford Dictionary of Literary Terms. London: Oxford University Press, 2008.

Palfrey, John, and Urs Gasser. *Born Digital: Understanding the First Generation of Digital Natives*. New York: Basic Books, 2010.

Parsons, Patrick. *Blue Skies: A History of Cable Television*. Philadelphia, PA: Temple University Press, 2008.

Pham, Alex. "YouTube Confirms Investment in Vevo." *The Hollywood Reporter*, July 3, 2013.

"Priyanka Chopra." imbb.com, 2016.

Proulx, Mike, and Stacey Shepatin. *Social TV: How Marketers Can Reach and Engage Audiences by Connecting Television to the Web, Social Media and Mobile*. Hoboken, NJ: John Wiley, 2012.

Rider Research. "Requiem for the Television: Tablets, OTT, Faster Broadband to Make Today's TV Unrecognizeable." Rider Research, 2013.

Ronen, Lior. "Netflix Likely to Face Growth Headwinds Globally." *AmigoBulls.com*, July 25, 2016.

Rosenbaum, Steven. *Curation Nation: Why the Future of Content Is Context.* New York: McGraw Hill, 2011.

Rosenberg, Alyssa. "How the International Market Will Change Television." *The Washington Post*, September 28, 2015.

Roxborough, Scott. "Europe Calls for Netflix, Amazon Content Quotas." *The Hollywood Reporter*, May 25, 2016.

Roxborough, Scott, and Georg Szalai. "Why Is Netflix Struggling Overseas?" *The Hollywood Reporter*, July 22, 2016.

Rubin, A. M. "Ritualized and Instrumental Television Viewing." *Journal of Communication* 34, no. 3 (1984): pp. 67–77.

Shirky, Clay. *Here Comes Everybody: The Power of Organizing without Organizations.* New York: Penguin, 2008.

Silverman, Dwight. "Aereo Reveals Some Subscriber Numbers, and They're Tiny." In *Seattle Post Intelligencer*, 2014.

SocialBlade. "How Are Estimated Earnings Calculated?" http://socialblade.com/youtube/help.

Spangler, Todd. "Netflix Grabs for the Remote." *Multichannel News*, January 10, 2011.

Spangler, Todd. "Comcast to Stream Netflix on Cable Set-Tops." *Variety*, July 5, 2016.

Stelter, Brian. "Serving up Television without the TV Set." *The New York Times*, March 10, 2008.

Sterling, Christopher, and John Kittross. *Stay Tuned: A History of American Broadcasting.* 3rd ed. Mahwah, NJ: Lawrence Erlbaum Associates, 2002.

Streeter, Thomas. *Selling the Air: A Critique of the Policy of Commercial Broadcasting in the United States.* Chicago: University of Chicago Press, 1996.

Surowiecki, James. *The Wisdom of Crowds: Why the Many Are Smarter Than the Few.* London: Abacus, 2005.

Thomassen, Bjorn. *Liminality and the Modern: Living through the In-Between.* Surrey, England: Ashgate, 2014.

Thompson, Don. *The Supermodel and the Brillo Box: Back Stories and Peculiar Economics from the World of Contemporary Art.* New York: Palgrave Macmillan, 2014.

Thompson, Robert J. *Television's Second Golden Age: From Hill Street Blues to ER.* New York: Continuum, 1996.

Toledo, Rob. "People Aren't Cancelling Netflix Because of Price Increases, They're Cancelling Because the Library Is Shrinking." In *The Extremist*, July 21, 2016.

Toor, Amar. "Sir Tim Berners-Lee Makes a Last-Minute Plea to Save Net Neutrality in Europe." *The Verge*, July 15, 2016.

Tryon, Chuck. *Reinventing Cinema: Movies in the Age of Media Convergence*. New Brunswick, NY: Rutgers University Press, 2009.

Ulin, Jeffrey. *The Business of Media Distribution: Monetizing Film, TV and Video Content in an Online World*. Burlington, MA: Focus Press, 2010.

Ungerleider, Neal. "What Amazon Prime Is Like around the World." *Fast Company*, January 5, 2016.

United States Congress. "Communications Act of 1934: As Amended by Telecom Act of 1996." Edited by the US Congress. Washington, DC, 1934.

United States Telecom Association et al. vs Federal Communications Commission, (2016).

Uricchio, William. "Television's Next Generation: Technology/Interface Culture/Flow." In *Television after TV: Essays on a Medium in Transition*, edited by Lynn and Jan Olsson Spigel, pp. 168–72. Durham, NC: Duke University Press, 2004.

Van Gennep, Arnold. *The Rites of Passage*. Chicago: University of Chicago Press, 1960.

Vanderbilt, Tom. *You May Also Like: Taste in an Age of Endless Choice*. New York: Knopf, 2016.

"Viacom International, Inc. et al. vs YouTube, Inc. et al." In *1:07-cv-02103, No. 364*, New York: S.D.N.Y., 2010.

Viskanta, Tadas. "Content vs. Aggregation vs. Curation." In *Abnormal Returns: A Wide-Ranging, Forecast-Free Investment Blog*, 2010.

Voice of America. "Netflix Expands to 190 Countries." *VOA Learning English* (January 13, 2016). http://learningenglish.voanews.com/a/netflix-expands-to-190-countries/3144530.html.

Von Rimscha, M. "How the DVR Is Changing the TV Industry—a Supply Side Perspective." *JMM: The International Journal on Media Management* 8, no. 3 (2006): pp. 116–24.

Votta, Rae. "YouTube Announces Plenty of New Shows Along with Changes in Comments, Livestreaming." In *The Daily Dot*, 2016.

Vourlias, Christopher. "Africa's No Dream for Streaming: Infrastructure Biggest Concern for Netflix." *Variety*, February, 2016, p. 111.

Wallenstein, Andrew. "Amazon Studios Opens Door to TV." *Variety*, May 2, 2012.

Wallenstein, Andrew. "Without Its Architect, Hulu Needs New Grounding." *Variety*, January 4, 2013.

Wang, Shan. "The New York Times Wants to Tell You Which TV Shows Are Worth Binging on with a New Product." *Nieman Lab*, January 29, 2016.

Webster, James, Patricia Phalen, and Lawrency Lichty. *Ratings Analysis: The Theory and Practice of Audience Research*. 3rd ed. New York: Routledge, 2006(2009).

Wheeler, Tom. "Statement of Chairman Tom Wheeler Re: Promoting Innovation and Competition in the Provision of Multichannel Video Programming Distribution Services, MB Docket No. 14–261." http://www.fcc.gov: Federal Communications Commission, 2014.

Wheeler, Tom. "Statement of FCC Chairman Tom Wheeler Regarding DC Circuit Decision to Uphold FCC's Open Internet Rules," news release, June 14, 2016, https://apps.fcc.gov/edocs_public/attachmatch/DOC-339798A1.pdf.

Wheeler, Tom. "Statement Re: Expanding the Economic and Innovation Opportunities of Spectrum through Incentive Auctions." http://www.apps.fcc.gov: Federal Communications Commission, 2016.

Williams, Raymond. *Television: Technology and Cultural Form*. Routledge Classics. London: Routledge, 1990. 1974.

Wolff, Michael. *Television Is the New Television: The Unexpected Triumph of Old Media in the Digital Age*. New York: Portfolio/Penguin, 2015.

Wu, Tim. "Network Neutrality, Broadband Discrimination." *Journal of Telecommunications and High Technology Law* 2 (2003): pp. 141–80.

Wyatt, Edward. "F.C.C. Commissioner Leaving to Join Comcast." *The New York Times*, May 11, 2011.

YouTube. "Creator Benefits." https://www.youtube.com/yt/creators/creator-benefits.html.

YouTube. "How Ads Are Chosen." https://support.google.com/youtube/answer/94523?hl=en&ref_topic=1115890.

YouTube. "Paid Channels." https://www.youtube.com/channels/paid_channels.

YouTube. "Statistics." https://www.youtube.com/yt/press/statistics.html.

YouTube. "Terms of Service." https://www.youtube.com/static?template=terms.

YouTube. "YouTube Advertising Formats." https://support.google.com/youtube/answer/2467968?hl=en&ref_topic=1115890.

Zuckerman, Ethan. *Rewire: Digital Cosmopolitans in the Age of Connection*. New York: W. W. Norton, 2013.

Index

a la carte pricing 82, 114, 115, 116, 168, 176, 178, 182
advertising 3, 13, 14, 17, 25, 31, 57–9, 65, 67, 72, 73, 75, 78, 80–4, 87–9, 100, 105, 111, 118–19, 134, 141, 170, 174–5, 180–3
   interactivity 126–7
Aereo 146–8
aftermarket 84, 99–100 (*see also* backend)
aggregators/aggregation 19, 21–4, 65, 70, 124, 183
algorithms 12, 19, 22–4, 28, 75, 102, 106
Altice 140–1, 144, 167, 168
Amazing Race, The 38
Amazon 48, 50, 72, 98, 112, 113, 125, 158–9, 161, 162, 170, 177
   Instant Video 2, 3, 14, 15, 36, 37, 57, 71, 83, 84, 96, 97, 103–4, 112–15, 144, 156, 157, 158, 160, 164, 172, 174
   Kindle Fire 39
   Studios 9, 14, 18, 36, 37, 39, 78, 83–5, 95, 103–4
American Crime Story 95
American Idol 38
Anderson, Chris 44
Android (operating system) 38, 39, 112, 125, 164
AOL 70, 72, 119, 121
Apple 125
   AppleTV 14, 19, 37, 38, 68, 72, 78
   iPad/iPhone 39, 126
   iTunes 39, 112, 181
Atwell-Baker, Meredith 132
Arrested Development 35, 71, 100, 185
AT&T 135, 139, 142, 143, 144
Audience 12, 14, 19, 22, 24, 28, 30, 35, 36, 41, 50, 53, 60–5, 80–91, 96, 99, 101, 149, 157, 179–81
   active 18, 29
   international 159–61

mass 126
measurement/quantification (*see also* Nielsen) 10, 13, 25, 28, 48, 57–60, 175
niche 24, 43, 114, 116
AwesomenessTv 80, 98, 112–13

backchannel 33, 72, 74, 75, 76, 127–8, 181
backend 78, 84, 93, 101, 157 (*see also* aftermarket)
barter time 84, 89, 134
Bateson, Gregory 97
Bergman, Cory 127
Bewkes, Jeff 123
Bezos, Jeff 9, 98
Big Bang Theory, The 2, 79, 84, 92, 175
Big Brother 95
Big Data 42, 181
binge viewing/watching 6, 25, 33, 35, 84, 96, 97, 101, 102, 139, 184
blogging/bloggers 20, 24, 49, 50, 51, 52, 53, 174, 186
Bloom, Paul 42
BlueFin Labs 74–5
Bochco, Steven 95
Bourdieu, Pierre 49
Boxee 37–8
bridge content 120–1, 183 (*see also* paratext)
British Broadcasting Corporation (BBC) 152, 153, 154
broadcast networks 3, 9, 12, 13, 14, 15, 61, 62, 66, 67, 79, 81, 118–19
   station types
      local affiliates 80, 81, 84, 89, 149
      owned and operated (O&O) 79
broadcasting 2, 17, 26, 28, 30, 32, 34, 35, 37, 38, 39, 53, 57, 58, 66, 71, 78, 79, 82, 85, 90–4, 110, 115, 116, 122, 124–9, 134, 135, 140–1, 145, 151, 156, 162, 170, 175, 179–80

liveness 175–6
regulation (*see* Federal Communications Commission)
spectrum auction of 142–4
Buzzard, Karen 65

cable 1, 9, 15, 17, 24, 26, 28, 31, 33, 35, 37, 57, 60–1, 62, 71, 77, 78, 80, 81–4, 90, 94, 99, 113–14, 115, 116, 123–5, 132, 133–4, 140–1, 144–5, 148, 154, 162, 167–8, 178
Cablevision 124, 140, 144, 146–7, 168
cancellation threshold 64, 156
carriage contract/carriage fees 80–1, 116, 134, 145, 154, 168, 172, 178
CBS 59, 64, 79, 83, 96, 106, 119, 178, 179
CBS All Access 2, 40, 119, 172, 177–8
Cellular Telecommunications and Internet Association (CTIA) 132
channel inventory 31, 154, 164, 168
channel repertoire 30–1
Charter/Time Warner 80–1, 140, 144, 171
China 154–5
churn 83, 102, 119, 163–4
citizen marketers 52–3
CNN 45, 124, 172
CNNgo 45
Comcast/NBC 15, 80–1, 121–3, 132, 136, 140–1, 144, 149, 171, 172
common carrier 12, 132, 137–9, 149, 171–2
ComScore 69, 70, 112
conglomerate 59, 70, 72, 78, 80, 81–4, 90, 128, 134, 140, 141, 160, 171–9, 183
context 23, 47–9
convergence 17, 18, 24, 37, 38, 48, 74, 105, 128, 135, 149, 155, 183
convergent culture 24–5
copyright 2, 105–6, 107, 109, 115, 132, 147, 171–2
Copyright Act of 1976 146–7
cord cutters 39, 141
cord shavers 39, 141
Crawford, Susan 78, 141, 143, 144
cultural exception (France) 159, 162
cultural intermediary 13, 27, 49
curation 6, 13, 19–24, 44, 45, 46–7, 49, 51, 54, 74, 81, 105, 110, 113, 184

curatorial culture 11–12, 13, 16, 17, 21, 23, 24–7, 43, 44, 46, 48, 51, 55, 151–2, 169, 174, 176, 178, 180, 182–4, 186
preconditions of 25–7
curatorial studies 20–1
curatorial viewers 117, 121, 126, 129, 156, 174, 183
aspirational curating 185
social curating 185

data caps 138
daypart 91–3, 99
deficit financing 83, 86, 156
DeGeneres, Ellen 117
demographic (ratings) 2, 8, 40, 60, 61, 64, 65, 68–9, 73, 76, 82, 94, 108, 118, 126, 178, 181, 184
Designated Market Area (DMA) 15, 59, 62, 79
digital citizenship 49–50
digital conversion of 2009 (US) 10, 142
Digital Millennium Copyright Act of 1998 106
digital subchannels 81
digital video disc (DVD) 32–6, 90, 101, 123
digital video recorder (DVR) 25, 32–3, 64–6, 67, 68, 106, 122, 125, 146, 147, 148, 149, 181
discriminatory capping 166
Downton Abbey 96–7, 153
Duchamp, Marcel 46–7
dynamic advertising insertion 118

E! 70
electromagnetic spectrum 133
electronic program guide (EPG) 31–3, 124
electronic sell through (EST) 39, 112
Emmy Awards 4, 102–3, 185
engagement 1, 5, 13–15, 18, 19, 24, 27, 53, 69, 70, 73–4, 85, 102, 120, 126, 175, 185
European Union (EU) 154, 162, 165–6, 170
event television 175
exhibition 34, 43, 44, 46–9, 54, 55

Facebook 26, 40, 46, 54, 72–3, 74, 75, 120–1, 127–8, 178, 180, 185
Family Guy 35
fans 24, 25, 51, 52, 75, 82, 106, 119, 160, 177
Federal Communications Commission (FCC) 4, 9, 15, 62, 79, 82, 117, 121, 131–2, 139, 143, 165, 166–8, 171–2, 179
   1934 Communications Act 133, 137, 138, 140, 166
   1965 First Report and Order on Cable 133
   1992 Cable Television Consumer Protection and Competition Act 134, 147
   1996 Telecommunications Act 80, 134–5, 137, 142
   2015 Open Internet Ruling 137
flow 18, 30, 34–5, 40, 91–2
Fowle, Kate 21

gatekeeper/gatekeeping 15, 19, 24, 107, 169–70
General Agreement on Tariffs and Trade 156, 159
genre 5, 24, 28, 38, 43, 84, 91, 92–7, 110, 111–12, 114, 163, 175, 176, 183
genre cycle 14, 15, 28, 43, 44, 86, 97, 108, 181, 182
genre silo 86, 97, 157
GetGlue 74
Global Net Neutrality Coalition 165
global television markets 169–70
globalization 169–70
Good Wife, The 95, 96
Google 21–2, 38, 48, 54, 72, 105, 106, 109, 111, 113, 115, 158, 159, 160, 179, 181
   AdSense 110–11
   AdWords 111
   Chromecast 38
   GoogleFiber 125, 144
   GooglePlay 38, 112, 160
   GoogleTV 37–8
Gray, Jonathan 34

Grey's Anatomy 25, 95
gross rating point 68, 87, 88

Handler, Chelsea 103, 179
Hastings, Reed 9
HBO 71, 82, 102, 125, 129
   HBO Go 40
   HBO Now 125, 172, 178
HereTV 114–15
Hill Street Blues 95
Holt, Jennifer 135
House of Cards 35, 43, 71, 72, 100, 101, 103, 157
Hulu 2, 3, 4, 14, 25, 36, 37, 78, 84, 96, 97, 100, 118, 121–3, 128, 129, 136, 141, 144, 145, 156, 158, 172, 176, 177, 182
Hulu Plus 83, 95, 121–3
Hyde, Lewis 98

instrumental viewing 29, 181
interactive television 125, 127, 181
International Curators International 21
internet 9, 15, 16, 17, 19, 25, 26, 36, 37, 38, 49, 69, 72, 84, 93, 107, 110, 121, 124, 125, 131, 135, 136, 139, 143, 145, 152, 155, 164, 166, 185
internet protocol television (IPTV) 16, 38, 116, 141, 143, 149, 151, 152, 154, 155
internet ratings 58, 69–70, 125
internet service provider (ISP) 15, 78, 117, 136, 137, 140–1, 165, 166, 168, 170, 171, 180
iRoko (Africa) 164
IT Crowd, The 99, 153

Jenkins, Henry 24, 51, 53, 107, 119
   Convergence Culture 24
   Fans, Bloggers & Gamers 24
   Spreadable Media 53, 98, 107, 109
Johnson, Mark 5
journalism 12, 16, 18, 22, 50, 169, 183

Keen, Andrew 51
Kimmel, Jimmy 117

Klein, Paul 28, 41, 48
Kompare, Derek 34, 90, 97

Lakoff, George 5
Landgraf, John 173
Law & Order 35, 90
Law & Order SVU 35, 84
Lazarfeld, Paul 53
least objectionable programming (LOP) 28–9
liking 41–2
Lillehammer 101
liminality 7–10, 44, 77, 78, 79, 98, 128–30, 131, 148, 158, 168, 169, 171, 172–3, 182
liminoid 8
linear television 13, 14, 16, 18, 26, 29, 30, 35, 45–6, 68, 73, 79–81, 85, 90, 91–2, 101, 108, 121, 122, 128, 145, 157, 173, 176–9, 181, 182
Littleton, Cynthia 96
liveness 26, 39, 175
long tail 12, 18, 27, 31, 51, 86, 97, 99, 102, 130–1, 151, 152, 156, 163, 176, 177, 184, 186
Lorre, Chuck 108
Lotz, Amanda 9, 17–18, 19, 29, 58

Malcom in the Middle 61
Man in the High Castle, The 158
mass medium 3, 4, 10, 11, 13, 16, 17, 26, 64, 131
McConnell, Ben 52
Mead, Margaret 5
mere exposure effect 43, 85
meta business 105
metaphor 5–7, 27, 29, 36, 41, 183
metonymy 6, 77
millennials 40, 108
Minow, Newton 184
MISO 74
Mittell, Jason 32
Moonves, Leslie 96, 148, 172
Mozart in the Jungle 104
MTV 28, 154
multichannel environment 40, 61, 65, 77, 134, 154
multichannel transition 17

multichannel video programming distributor (MVPD) 117, 135, 136, 144–9, 167, 172
music industry 12, 16, 18, 36, 140, 169
Must Carry 81, 133–4

narrowcasting 28, 116, 176
National Cable Television Association (NCTA) 132
NBC 8, 9, 15, 31, 59, 64, 79, 92, 100, 132, 136, 145, 172, 176
NBCUniversal 50, 59, 80, 81, 100, 121, 132, 140, 141
net neutrality 4, 15, 131, 132, 136–9, 141, 143, 165–6, 170, 171
Netflix 2, 3, 9, 14, 15, 18, 35, 36, 37, 38, 39, 48, 55, 57, 71, 72, 78, 83–5, 95, 96, 97, 98, 99–103, 118, 123, 124, 128, 129, 136, 139, 144, 145, 149, 151, 153, 160–5, 170, 172, 174, 177, 179, 183, 185
    international expansion of 156–8
Netflix Surge 78
network era 40, 58, 93, 97
New York Times, The 183
Newcomb, Horace 3
Newfronts 119
niche audience 24, 76, 100, 157
niche content/media 4, 4, 11, 17–18, 44, 76, 93, 100, 105, 108, 114, 115–16, 133, 134, 176, 178
niche viewing 76, 115–16
nichification 12–13
Nielsen Ratings Company 3, 13, 48, 51, 58–64, 65, 66, 122, 125, 179–80
    Nielsen family 60–2
    Nielsen Net Ratings 69–70
    Nielsen Television Index (NTI) 61
    PeopleMeter 61, 62
    ratings products
        Anytime Anywhere Media Measurement (A2/M2) 71
        C3 62, 66–7, 68
        C7 35, 66–7, 68, 71, 87, 89
        Total Audience Measurement 67, 75, 178
    sweeps 63

oligopoly 12, 14, 173, 179
online video distributor (OVD) 117,
    144–9, 152, 155, 156, 158, 159, 160,
    163, 170, 172
Orange is the New Black 35, 101, 102, 157
Ouellette, Laurie 5, 48
over-the-top (OTT) 26, 36–8, 55, 71–2,
    78, 82, 84, 86, 89, 90, 96, 97, 98, 99,
    130, 131, 141, 149–52, 156, 157,
    173, 174, 176, 185
ownership 15, 80, 107, 135, 136, 149, 156,
    166–8, 170, 171
ownership caps 135, 136, 138, 139–41

paid prioritization 137–8, 165
Pan Am 35
paratext 34, 98, 106, 109, 120–1, 160, 174
Parisier, Eli 54
participatory culture 24, 25, 49, 119, 160
paywall 57, 101, 115, 120, 124–5, 160,
    169, 176
Perry, Grayson 47
PewDiePie 25, 105, 111
pilot season 14, 85–6, 91, 98, 102–4, 174
platform agnosticism 38, 40, 112, 129
portal 22, 54, 70, 72–3, 98
post network era 17, 81, 119
Powell, Michael 132
primetime 68, 80, 87, 92, 95
privacy 14, 57, 76, 78, 108, 180
product placement 14, 57, 78, 108, 175
public interest 132, 133, 137, 142, 143,
    153, 167
Public Service Broadcasting (PSB) 152–4,
    164, 170
pull media 12, 17, 18, 29, 33, 38, 47, 100
push media 12, 17, 18, 29, 53

Quality TV 94–7
Quantico 157
Quarterlife 176

Radiohead conundrum 109
ratings 60–5, 180 (*see also* Nielsen Ratings
    Company)
ratings product 3, 14, 58, 59, 66,
    68, 74, 76

reality television 95–6
recommendation engines 101, 102, 109,
    124–5, 183
remote controls 1, 26, 30–1, 37, 38, 65
retransmission fees 14, 81, 133–4, 145, 147,
    148, 149, 168, 172
Return on Investment (ROI) 67, 70
Rimes, Shonda 108
rites of passage 7, 8, 10, 11, 16, 169, 171–2
Robbins, Brian 98, 112–13
Roku 37, 38, 68, 125
Roseanne 48
Rosenbaum, Steven 21, 45

Saltz, Jerry 44
Sarandos, Ted 71, 72, 98, 101, 102, 103
satellite 3, 13, 26, 31, 33, 37, 38, 39, 40, 57,
    60, 62, 77, 81, 105, 115–16, 123–5,
    134, 143, 144, 152, 154, 155, 161,
    164, 170, 178
second screen apps/experiences 32, 125–8,
    174, 175, 183
seriality 94–7, 101
Sesame Street 114–15
Shirky, Clay 51
showrunner 14, 95–6, 108, 120, 185
Showtime 71, 82, 102
soap opera 93–7, 101
social media 10, 13, 14, 15, 16, 19, 26, 27,
    37, 42, 44, 48–9, 51, 52, 54, 57, 70,
    73–6, 96, 98, 105, 110, 120, 121,
    125, 126, 127–8, 175, 178–80, 183,
    184, 185, 186
social proof 49, 53
social television 40, 74, 75
SocialGuide 75
Soloway, Jill 104
Sony Corp. of America v. Universal
    City Studios Inc. (Sony Betamax
    Case) 146
space shifting 36, 40, 65, 123–4
spectrum (*see also* Federal
    Communications Commission)
    allocations 136
    auction 142–4
Star Trek: Discovery 119, 120, 177
Streeter, Thomas 132

Surowiecki, James 53
syndication 83, 84, 89–91, 122, 130
   first-run 89–90
   off network 90–1
synecdoche 6, 10

telecommunications/telecommunications services 124, 135, 137
television critics 13, 27, 49–52
Television Critics Association 49, 71, 103
Television Everywhere 39, 70, 122–3, 124, 178
Television Without Frontiers (EU) 154, 162
televisionwithoutpity.com 26, 50
This is Us 25
Thomassen, Bjorn 8, 11, 173
Thompson, Robert 94–6
throttling 137, 138
time shifting 13, 32–3, 34, 40, 65, 66, 67, 87, 146, 147, 174
TiVO 32, 148
transmedia 98, 120, 182
Transparent 2, 43, 83, 103, 104, 184
tribe of affinity 44, 121
trickster 78, 97–9, 130
Turner, Victor 8, 97, 182
Twitter 74, 75, 120–1, 127–8, 180

UHF 17, 133
upfronts 85, 87–9, 117, 119

Van Gennep, Arnold 7, 8, 97, 101
Verizon 125, 135, 137, 139, 142, 143, 144, 171
Verizon v. FCC 137
Vevo 109, 112
VHF 17, 133
VHS 65, 105
viewser 3, 15, 18, 45
Viacom Intl. v. YouTube 106
Video on Demand (VOD) 1, 67, 68, 98, 99, 141, 164, 174, 179
   subscriber (SVOD) 57, 68, 83, 155, 161, 162, 163, 164, 170, 176–8
Vimeo 15, 47, 98

Walking Dead, The 25
Wasko, Janet 3

water cooler moment 13, 51, 74, 160
Weinberger, David 105
Wheeler, Tom 9, 132, 139, 142, 145
Williams, Raymond 36, 91
windows/windowing 3, 14, 39, 41, 69, 79, 89, 97, 120, 128, 129, 156, 174, 176
wireless information service (cellular telephone) 15, 37, 131, 132, 133, 135, 137–9, 142–3, 146, 149, 171
Wolff, Michael 129
word of mouth 52, 120
Wu, Tim 136

X Files, The 33–4

Yahoo 14, 70, 72, 78, 119, 121
YouTube 2, 3, 10, 18, 25, 36, 37, 46, 47, 55, 72, 78, 95, 98, 104–18, 123, 139, 158, 159–60, 164, 172, 174, 180, 181, 183
   as broadcast platform 108–13
   as cable system 113–18
   as democratized archive 105–8
   as social media/social network 26, 48, 180
   channels 110
   Creator Class 113
   genres 110, 111–12
   Maker Studios 112
   stars 14, 18, 85
   Pansino, Rosanna 111
   subscription channels 114, 176
   YouTube partners program 110–13
   YouTube Red 105, 160
   YouTube Space LA 113

Zajonc, Robert 43
zapping 30, 65, 127, 181
Zee Channels 115–16, 160
zero rating 139, 165–6, 171
zipping 30, 65, 181
Zucker, Jeff 9, 118
Zuckerberg, Mark 72
Zuckerman, Ethan 49–50, 53–4

www.ingramcontent.com/pod-product-compliance
Lightning Source LLC
Chambersburg PA
CBHW062134300426
44115CB00012BA/1918